I0759485

Insightful and inspiring! This devotional, *365 Hebrew Words Every Christian Should Know*, will stretch your faith, increase your understanding, and give you a deeper perspective into the Word of God and the layered truth in Scripture. Ed Grifenhagen does a masterful job of weaving biblical truth and meaning with application and humor. I found myself challenged and inspired by learning Hebrew words and how they were spoken. But this book is not just about learning a new language. The Lord spoke these words as he taught and walked with the disciples and preached to the masses. I encourage every believer to read through this devotional over the next year, and I have no doubt that you, too, will find treasure as you deepen your love of God's Word.

**Alex Kendrick**, writer and director

Truly Holy Spirit inspired, Ed's words really bring these beautiful biblical truths to life in ways that are so tangible and applicable to my life. Your heart, too, will be greatly impacted as you meditate on these devotions. Thank you, Ed, for writing such a palatable and simple—yet rich and deep—take on these Hebrew words that will help all of us see Jesus like we never have before.

**Franni Cash Cain**, original member of We the Kingdom

This devotional is a daily invitation to discover the riches of God's Word—more valuable than gold and sweeter than honey. Each entry draws you deeper into the heart of Scripture, reminding you that the Bible is not just a book but God's personal revelation of his love, purpose, and grace. It was a gift each day to learn a new Hebrew word, which helped me connect more personally to the Lord. In a world full of noise and distraction, this devotional gently redirects your focus to what truly satisfies—the presence of God and the truth of his Word. It's a well of wisdom and encouragement that refreshes the soul one day at a time.

**Shari Rigby**, filmmaker, author, and speaker

I had the absolute joy of meeting Ed and his beautiful wife, Susan, on a movie set, and from the very beginning, I knew they were something special. They are the kind of people who radiate the love of Jesus without ever needing to say a word. Their kindness, humility, and servant hearts are living testimonies to the one whom they follow. Ed is not only a gifted storyteller, but he also carries the heart of a shepherd and a deep well of biblical wisdom. His book, *365 Hebrew Words Every Christian Should Know*, is more than a devotional. It's an invitation to go deeper in your walk with Jesus. Every page is rich with insight, encouragement, and truth that will strengthen your faith and stir your heart. I promise that you won't just read this book; you'll experience it.

**Shannen Fields-Braswell**, award-winning actress, producer, speaker, and cofounder of Uncover Marriage

I have often said within my teaching of God's Word that to truly understand, one must hear what the original hearer heard and understand what the original speaker spoke. Within these pages, Ed Grifenhagen explores what readers may have only understood on the surface. Take the dive. It's well worth it.

**Cameron "Camy" Arnett**, founder of Christ over Career (COC), filmmaker, and speaker

# 365 HEBREW WORDS Every Christian Should Know

A DAILY DEVOTIONAL

ED GRIFENHAGEN

BroadStreet
PUBLISHING

BroadStreet Publishing® Group, LLC
Savage, Minnesota, USA
BroadStreetPublishing.com

*365 Hebrew Words Every Christian Should Know: A Daily Devotional*


9781424570478 (faux leather)
9781424570485 (ebook)



Cover and interior by Garborg Design Works | garborgdesign.com

Printed in China

26 27 28 29 30 5 4 3 2 1

To Susan Grifenhagen, my best friend and loyal, loving wife. I have loved you since the first moment I saw you. Had God not providentially crossed our paths in high school, I would not know Jesus as my Lord and Savior.

Minyan Mishnah Mitzvah Paroche
Rav Rosh Hashanah Seder Shabb
uot Shekinah Shema Shofar Simch
Talmud Tefillin Tzitzit Yahwe
KippurAbba Chuppah
him Galil Hashem Hespe
riah Kiddush pah Hanukka
Omer Lev Minyan Mishna
ochet Pesach Purim Rav Ros
eder Shalom Shavu
ema Shofar Simcha Sukkot Ta
in Tzitzit Yahweh Yeshua Yo
a Chametz Chuppah El Shadd
Goel Hashem Hesped Kashr
ish Kippah Hanukkah Hesed L
Mikvah Minyan Mishnah Mitzv

# Foreword

I love Ed Grifenhagen. He is a brilliant writer, a bold proclaimer of the gospel of Jesus, and a tenderhearted servant to the greatest and the least among us. Ed's writing is fun to read because he communicates with a joyful pastor's heart and balances rich truth with sincere love. He is a friend to leaders and has, through this book, given a great gift not only to pastors but to the body of Christ.

Ed's story is unique. He grew up in Columbus, Georgia, in a passionate and devout Jewish family. After he left school each day when he was a young boy, he would then study Hebrew and Jewish traditions in the local synagogue where his father served as president. As Ed memorized the history and meanings of Hebrew words, it never entered his yarmulke-covered head that one day, as a successful businessman, he would have a radical encounter with the living Messiah of the New Testament. And just like Jesus does to anyone who comes to him by faith, Ed's world was turned upside down, and he has never been the same.

Now as a passionate evangelist, ministry leader, and disciple maker, Ed has been faithfully pouring out his life into others and teaching believers across his street and around the world. My wife and I know Ed and his wife, Susan, personally. I've served alongside them on film sets and at ministry events on multiple occasions. We've laughed, cried, and prayed together. They have modeled Christian hospitality and a willingness to go wherever God leads. I've found them to be humble, genuine, loving, and sincere believers.

In the pages of this book, Ed has strategically leveraged his background as a Jew, his heart as a pastor, and his studies as a researcher to create a powerful 365-day devotional for us to enjoy. It's a beautiful and delicious salad of truth, wit, kindness, and grace. Each day sheds light on the rich meaning behind one of the most important Hebrew words. This devotional is captivating to read and will be inspiring for anyone who loves God's Word and would like to study it through a fresh lens. I invite you to approach these pages with an open heart and prayerfully ask God to speak to you through his Word. May you taste and see that the Lord is good, be blessed with the fresh bread and savory meat of the Bible, and enjoy sitting down at the feet of our great Messiah.

Blessings,

Stephen Kendrick

Writer, speaker, and film producer

# Introduction

The devotional you're holding has been a labor of love, inspired by the Jesus I met in 2001. He was born a Jew, walked the dusty roads of Israel as a Jew, was crucified as a Jewish rebel, and ran out of the tomb as the Jewish Messiah. I'm thrilled to share this journey with you, one deeply woven in my Jesus story—a journey from a Jewish upbringing to a life transformed through the Word of God by the risen Christ.

Over the next year, you will embark on a journey to uncover the rich tapestry of Jewish culture alongside the profound depths of Christian faith. In this devotional, I'll walk you through 365 Hebrew words Christians should know, showing how they connect to our faith in Christ. You'll learn how these ancient practices point to the Savior and how they enrich our understanding of Scripture and the Holy Spirit's work in our lives.

The Bible Jesus metaphorically "had in his back pocket" was the Old Testament, written in Hebrew and Aramaic—the language he spoke. I can't wait for you to dive in and explore the richness of his language and its ties to the gospel.

I pray *365 Hebrew Words Every Christian Should Know* deepens your relationship with Jesus, enriches your daily walk with him, and leaves you better equipped to share the gospel with a world that desperately needs him.

## How to Speak Like Yeshua (Sort of)

One of my desires is that you learn, at least a little, how to pronounce many of the words Yeshua (Jesus) spoke. Each devotion includes the Hebrew word(s), a transliteration, and the English translation. The transliterations are nontraditional and may look a little funny to you because they are spelled phonetically. Hebrew words often have a variety of English spellings, but these transliterations should help you see more clearly how these words should sound. Below is a key that should help. If I missed anything, do the best you can! There won't be a test at the end. In addition to the phonetic transliteration at the start of each devotion, for words that have a common English spelling, I have included it in parentheses in the devotion.

It may also be helpful to note that unlike English, Hebrew is read right to left.

| **Transliteration** | **Pronunciation** | **Sounds Like** |
|---|---|---|
| *ah* | short *a* sound | stick out your tongue and say "ah" |
| *ay* | long *a* sound | pale |
| *eh* | short *e* sound | let |
| *ee* | long *e* sound | she |
| *ai* | long *i* sound | I |
| *o* + consonant + *e* | long *o* sound | old |
| *oo* | long *oo* sound | loot |
| *tz* | just like it looks | blitz |
| *kh* | a guttural, throaty sound | |

In addition, the original biblical Hebrew did not have vowels. Pronunciation was based on oral tradition and context. For example, *dg* becomes *dog* or *dig* based on context. Between the sixth and tenth centuries AD, the Masoretes added vowels below the consonants (with one exception) to preserve the oral tradition and pronunciation. They also added a system of cantillation marks (sometimes called *tropes*) that are musical and syntactical symbols used in the Hebrew Bible for chanting, reading, and interpreting the text. You will notice several of these in the pages of this devotional.

Most of the Hebrew words appearing in *365 Hebrew Words Every Christian Should Know* were taken from the *Biblia Hebraica Stuttgartensia*[1] version of the Hebrew Old Testament, which is based upon the Leningrad Codex, the oldest dated manuscript of the Hebrew Bible. Below is a simple chart of the vowels and cantillation marks most frequently used.

| **Vowels** | ָ | ַ | ֶ | ֵ | ִ | ֹ | ֻ | וּ | ְ | ֲ | ֱ | ֳ |
|---|---|---|---|---|---|---|---|---|---|---|---|---|
| **Cantillation Marks** | ֑ | ֣ | ֥ | ֦ | ֗ | ֒ | ֞ | ֜ | ֮ | ֙ | ֤ | ֽ |

1 Karl Elliger, Wilhelm Rudolph, and Gérard E. Weil, *Biblia Hebraica Stuttgartensia* (German Bible Society, 2003).

Minyan Mishnah Mitzvah Paroche
Rav Rosh Hashanah Seder Shabba
uot Shekinah Shema Shofar Simch
Talmud Tefillin Tzitzit Yahwe
KippurAbba Chuppah
him Galil Hashem Hespe
iah Kiddush Hanukka
Omer Lev Minyan Mishna
ochet Pesach Purim Rav Ros
eder Shabbat Shalom Shavuo
ema Shofar Simcha Sukkot Tal
in Tzitzit Yahweh Yeshua Yo
a Chametz Chuppah El Shado
Goel Hashem Hesped Kashr
sh Kippah Hanukkah Hesed La
Mikvah Minyan Mishnah Mitzvah

# צִיצִת—*Tzeetzeet*

## "Fringe; Tassel"

"If I touch even his garments, I will be made well."
Mark 5:28 ESV

There is a stunning seventeen-foot-wide mural on one of the basement walls in the Encounter Chapel of the Duc in Altum church in Magdala, Israel. It is a close-up of Jesus' sandal-covered feet, with the bottom of his tunic nearly touching them. A woman's hand is coming in from the left side of the image, just inches from the ground, reaching out to touch the *tzeetzeet* (tzitzit) gently peeking from underneath Jesus' garment.

Because of her twelve-year bleeding problem, the woman in Mark 5:25–34, no doubt, had been relentlessly assailed with condemning cries of "Unclean! Unclean!" from the bustling crowd. Despite trying so many times, she couldn't find anyone who could end her misery. But she trusted that the Anointed One could. And there he was. She crawled along the dusty road outside the synagogue in Galilee because she knew that if she could touch even a thread, she would be healed. The mural depicts a spark of light as she touched the tassel and was instantly made whole, delivered, freed, and cleaned. She had encountered the Master's healing touch, and her life would never be the same. And just as he was with her, he is close to you. He's always near. Stretch out your hand and let his proximity change your life.

How have you encountered the Son of God?

JANUARY 2

# הֶסְפֵּד—*Hehspehd*

## “Traditional Beating of the Chest”

“The tax collector…beat his breast, saying, ‘God, be merciful to me, a sinner!’”
LUKE 18:13 ESV

*Hehspehd* (hesped) continues today at Jewish funerals and on the Day of Atonement. It is when forgiveness is sought by beating one’s chest while chanting the Al Chet (a list of fifty-three sins).

Luke 18:9–14 records Jesus’ parable of the Pharisee and the tax collector. Both men go to the temple to pray, yet they have radically different heart postures. The Pharisee called attention to himself, announcing to anyone within earshot just how righteous he was by essentially saying, “Thank God I’m not a dirtbag like all these other sinners!” The tax collector, on the other hand, approached God with the right attitude. Acutely self-aware and beating his chest, he cried, “Lord, have mercy on me, a sinner” (v. 13, author’s paraphrase). In fact, Jewish tradition says that he beat his heart (lev) as a sign of deep grief—mourning over his transgressions. He knew he brought nothing to the table and surrendered himself to the mercy of the creator of the universe.

Without a humble spirit, God’s grace is nowhere to be found. As you approach him in prayer, ensure you know who you are and who he is and certainly make sure your heart is in the right place.

Thank you, Lord, for washing me in your mercy.

# עֲקֵדָה—*Ahkaydah*

## "Binding of Isaac"

By faith Abraham, when he was tested, offered up Isaac.
HEBREWS 11:17 ESV

The patriarch Abraham began his faith journey when he believed the Lord and was credited with righteousness (Genesis 15:6). Abraham's faith was tested at least twelve times; some tests were big, some not so big. But no test was as gargantuan as the command to sacrifice his son Isaac—the son of promise. The *Ahkaydah* (Akedah) is a prayer chanted on Rosh Hashanah, the Jewish New Year. It celebrates God's faithfulness and provision to his people based on Abraham's fervent trust in the Lord.

Abraham believed that what he believed was really real—so much that he obediently marched Isaac to Mount Moriah, intent on slitting his beloved son's throat. As he and Isaac hiked up the mountain, a ram silently climbed up the other side unseen. In the background, God was working his provision as Abraham, in the foreground, was being obedient. Although he had no idea how God would provide, Abraham trusted anyway. He trusted God's promise of innumerable descendants through Isaac, even when the process seemed impossible. God doesn't owe us explanations. We're not called to understand. We're called to trust.

Lord, help me develop faith as strong as Abraham's: willing to trust and obey you even when your command scares me to death.

# מַ֫יִם חַיִּים—*Mayeem Khahyeem*

## "Living Water"

"Whoever drinks of the water that I will give him will never be thirsty again."
JOHN 4:14 ESV

John 4 records Jesus leaving Judea, headed for Galilee. John 4:4 tells us he "had to" go through Samaria. Jews consistently took the long way around Samaria to get to Galilee because the hatred between Jews and Samaritans was ferocious. If a Jew's foot dared touch Samaritan soil, that Jew would become "unclean" (Leviticus 5:1–5), which required the appropriate sacrifice.

But Jesus had a divine appointment with a woman at a well in Samaria. It eclipsed any cleanliness law. They met at high noon, in the fiercest heat of the day, when the other women drawing water had already come and gone. This one had a scandalous reputation, was living in sin, felt completely unwanted, was racked with guilt and shame, and avoided all human contact. Yet here she was having a conversation with this rabbi who trekked across "unclean" soil to see her, an "unclean" woman, and to provide her *mayeem khahyeem* (mayim chayim) so she would never thirst again. Every single soul matters! You matter! Despite any of the Deceiver's lies, you matter. Despite your background or past, you matter.

Jesus washes away every dividing line because you are wanted. Are you thirsty today? Drink and be filled.

# תַּלְמִיד—*Tahlmeed*

## “Disciple; Pupil”

Jesus told his disciples, “If anyone would come after me, let him deny himself and take up his cross and follow me.”
MATTHEW 16:24 ESV

Traditionally, an Old Testament *tahlmeed* (talmid) sought out a rabbi to study under—to be discipled by. This is what Paul’s parents would have done with Gamaliel: “Please, Rabbi Gamaliel, take on the teaching of Torah to our son.” But Jesus showed up and turned the system upside down by calling twelve ordinary men to study under, emulate, and follow him. Peter, James, John, and the boys did not fully comprehend what that meant until Jesus ascended to the Father. Do you?

Jesus said there are three demands of a *tahlmeed*. First, deny self. We are to let go of self-gratification and replace it with pleasing God. Do you spend too much time serving the one in the mirror? Second, take up Christ’s cross. Every first-century hearer knew that symbolized suffering, humiliation, and death. It is an all-in acceptance of the challenges and sacrifices that accompany following Jesus. Are you all in? Finally, follow him. Decide second by second for the rest of your life to be like Jesus—to live a life of compassion and truth. Are you following him today?

Jesus, help me truly be a *tahlmeed* by surrendering to a life of radical followership.

JANUARY 6

# חֶסֶד—*Khehsehd*

## "Steadfast Love; Loving-Kindness"

Give thanks to the LORD, for he is good,
for his steadfast love endures forever.
PSALM 136:1 ESV

*Khehsehd* (hesed) is one of the most theologically important words in the Old Testament. It appears 248 times, and no English word can capture its fullness. If we threw *mercy*, *loyalty*, *steadfastness*, *kindness*, *covenant*, *fidelity*, and *faithfulness* into a giant bucket called love and mixed it up in the KitchenAid, we would have *khehsehd*.

Psalm 136 is dominated by the psalmist's thanksgiving for the Lord's *khehsehd*. Line by line, he declared why God's steadfast love never ends: because of who God is (vv. 1–4), what he created (vv. 5–9), what he did to unshackle Israel from Egypt (vv. 10–16), what he did to his people's enemies (vv. 17–22), his redeeming memory (v. 23), his deliverance (v. 24), and his provision (v. 25). He is who he says he is, and he can do everything he says he can do. Undergirding it all, the psalmist declared twenty-six times, "His steadfast love endures forever." God's *khehsehd* bore its most glorious fruit when Jesus proclaimed, "It is finished," and took his last breath (John 19:30). Our eternities with him were sealed when his deliverance, remembrance, provision, and unending love were nailed to the cross.

Father God, I praise you every day because your *khehsehd* is unending.

# יהוה—YHWH

## "The Lord; Yahweh"

God said to Moses, "I Am Who I Am."…God also said to Moses, "Say this to the people of Israel: 'The Lord, the God of your fathers,…has sent me to you.' This is my name forever."
Exodus 3:14–15 esv

Of the many names used in the Old Testament, YHWH, usually translated "Lord," is the personal name of the covenant-making, promise-keeping God of Abraham, Isaac, and Jacob. The four Hebrew consonants for "YHWH" form what academics call a tetragrammaton, referring to the four Hebrew letters יהוה (from left to right, *HWHY*). The word's pronunciation is unknown because ancient Jews considered God's name too holy to utter. Instead of speaking his name, they said, "Adonai," which means "Lord."

God's words to Moses in Exodus 3:14 are best translated, "I will cause to be that which I cause to be." This phrase encompasses his self-existence, love, holiness, transcendence, omnipotence, omniscience, omnipresence, goodness, faithfulness, justice, mercy, grace, sovereignty, simplicity, and immutability. But the most mind-blowing thing about YHWH is that, despite our failures, he wants to be in a relationship with you, me, and every man or woman who has ever lived or will ever live.

Father, I struggle to really understand who you are, but help me rest in the truth that you love me.

# שַׁבָּת—*Shahbaht*

## "Sabbath"

When Jesus saw her, he called her over and said to her, "Woman, you are freed from your disability."
LUKE 13:12 ESV

In about 1500 BC, God graciously gave us one day per week to refrain from work and keep holy, separate, distinct, and consecrated. But then the big shots started defining work. Jesus entered the scene centuries later when there were already hundreds of prohibited activities. By AD 200, there were thirty-nine categories and hundreds of subcategories defining prohibited work.

One *Shahbaht* (Shabbat), Jesus encountered a woman with a disabling spirit. He healed and freed her from eighteen years of bondage. Can you imagine her delight? The sheer joy? It was a mountaintop moment. Then the synagogue ruler, the killjoy of all killjoys, essentially told the crowd, "We're only open for healing nine o'clock to five o'clock Sunday through Friday. Y'all need to come back during regular office hours."

In response, Jesus effectively said, "Do you people really think you're tracking with God's intention for the Sabbath? All these prohibitions are shackles around people's necks." Jesus' words and actions illustrate that God's love and compassion always wreck the legalistic fences humans erect. He sees individuals' suffering and responds with grace and healing, emphasizing the spirit of the law over its letter.

Father, bring to light the areas in my life where I'm prioritizing rules over relationships.

# בְּרִית מִילָה—*B'reet Meelah*

## "Covenant of Circumcision"

Neither circumcision counts for anything, nor uncircumcision, but a new creation.
GALATIANS 6:15 ESV

In Genesis 17, God took a giant, gracious leap toward humanity with an incredible series of promises to Abraham. The outward sign of these promises is circumcision. For more than four thousand years, Jews have looked on the *B'reet Meelah* (Brit Milah) as the entrance of a Jewish male into God's covenant community. The early church struggled with whether adherence to the Jewish law, embodied by circumcision, was a mandatory ingredient for salvation. In Galatians, Paul clarified that these external rituals are worthless compared to the heart and mind transformation that happens when we become a new creation in Christ.

Becoming a new creation means that the old you, with your bent toward sin, gets a new nature, one that's aligned with God's will. This is not some simple surface-level change. Rituals, traditions, and outward appearances do not define you as a Christ follower. Deep spiritual transformation that permeates every arena of your life through the indwelling of the Holy Spirit defines you. As new creations, we walk by love, grace, and a renewed relationship with God. We don't cling to a legalistic set of rituals.

Lord Jesus, empower me to walk in the newness of life that your sacrifice provides.

## JANUARY 10

# כְּתֻבָּה—*K'toobah*

## "Marriage Covenant"

Wives, submit to your own husbands, as to the Lord.
Ephesians 5:22 ESV

When Susan and I were married, we signed a *k'toobah* (ketubah) immediately before the ceremony. Today, if I do something that upsets her, she laughs and says, "I guess I can't leave because I signed that thing at our wedding."

Although the Bible outlines various laws and traditions about marriage, the *k'toobah* is not specifically mentioned. The oldest *k'toobah* found dates from about 400 BC. It is a covenant document (codifying the oath referenced in Malachi 2:14) that specifies the financial terms of the marriage, identifies several protections for the wife, and names her as the beneficiary should the husband die.

In Ephesians 5, Paul simplified marriage by focusing on the spirit undergirding it. To the wife, he said to submit to your husband's headship (v. 22). To the husband, he said to love your wife sacrificially (v. 25). The wife's submission is not about inferiority. She should foster harmony and unity by willingly helping and supporting. The husband's love is Christlike—selfless and sanctifying. The more wives submit, the more husbands will love sacrificially. The more husbands love like Jesus, the more wives will submit.

Father God, let Christian marriage be a beautiful witness to the world of godly submission and Christlike sacrifice.

# כִּפָּה—*Keepah*

## "Head Covering"

After this, the church all over Judea, Galilee, and Samaria experienced a season of peace. The congregations grew larger and larger, with the believers being empowered and encouraged by the Holy Spirit. They worshiped God in wonder and awe, and walked in the fear of the Lord.

ACTS 9:31 TPT

A *keepah* (kippah; in Yiddish, *yarmulke*) is the head covering worn by Jewish men. I was raised in a synagogue with boxes of *keepote* (kippot, plural) by every exterior door so we could put one on when entering the building. Although there is no biblical command to wear one, I was taught it was a sign of walking with reverence, awe, and humility before the Lord.

Through the ministry of the Holy Spirit, the early church "walked in the fear of the Lord." What does that formula look like in the twenty-first century? It's a majestic mix of (1) being a born-again Christ follower, (2) having an all-encompassing recognition of the eternal presence of the Holy Spirit, (3) cultivating full appreciation of how undeserving we humans are, and (4) possessing overwhelming gratefulness for God's mercy and grace in our lives, which results in (5) living in obedience to him.

Are you walking with your *keepah* on—living a life with reverence, awe, humility, and obedience before the Lord?

# יְהוֹשֻׁעַ—*Y'hoshooah*

## "Jesus"

God has highly exalted him and bestowed on him the name that is above every name, so that at the name of Jesus every knee should bow…and every tongue confess that Jesus Christ is Lord.
PHILIPPIANS 2:9–11 ESV

In Philippians 2:9–11, Paul reminded us of the magnitude of Jesus' name. The name of Jesus, which in Hebrew is *Y'hoshooah* (Yeshua), is powerful. It means "Yahweh saves," which is a flashing sign that he came to rescue us from our sin and provide eternal life. Every time Peter, John, Andrew, and the boys said, "Hey, *Y'hoshooah*," their minds would have flooded with thoughts of hope and deliverance.

When you utter the name Jesus, you acknowledge his divine role in your salvation. However, speaking the name isn't enough—it is to be revered. "Every knee should bow…and every tongue should confess that Jesus Christ is Lord" (vv. 10–11) means that the day will come when everyone everywhere will recognize the authority of Jesus Christ. Acknowledge him now or acknowledge him later, but his name will ultimately be declared as the highest name of all. As you consider and reflect on the name Jesus, remember everything packed into it.

You are probably quick to acknowledge and embrace Jesus as your Savior, but do you surrender to his lordship over every area of your life?

# שׁוּב—*Shoov*

## "Repent"

"He arose and came to his father."
Luke 15:20 ESV

Without repentance, there is no forgiveness of sin. It is a critical component in our salvation. Repentance always involves a 180-degree turn—90 degrees away from the sin and another 90 degrees toward God. When we *shoov* (shuv) away from our junk and *shoov* to the Lord, he is always faithful to forgive.

Of the several principles in the parable of the prodigal son (Luke 15:11–32), I love the image of repentance Jesus painted. The son moved away, lived a wild and reckless life, squandered all he was given, and found himself in the proverbial bottom of the pit. When he got his head right, he got up (first 90 degrees), putting the sin behind him. When he came back to his father (second 90 degrees), he completed the U-turn. And, of course, his loving father embraced and forgave him. When you find yourself in a moment or even a season of wandering away, remember your heavenly Father's greatest desire is that you return to him. For a repentant child, God's mercy and grace are always greater than the depth of the sin.

Lord, thank you that no matter how many miles I run away from you, I could never run out of the reach of your loving arms.

# Chutzpah

## "Gall; Nerve"

I am not ashamed of the gospel, for it is the power of God for salvation to everyone who believes, to the Jew first and also to the Greek.

ROMANS 1:16 ESV

The Yiddish language is derived from the German and Hebrew languages. *Chutzpah* is rooted in the Hebrew word חָצַף (*khahtzahf*), which is a combination of the words *hasty*, *harsh*, *urgent*, and *insolent*. Over time, *chutzpah* has come to mean "gall," "nerve," "audacity," and "boldness." It is to be bold enough to do or say something risky and often a thousand miles outside traditionally accepted norms. In *The Joys of Yiddish*, Leo Rosten joked, "*Chutzpah* is that quality enshrined in a man who, having killed his mother and father, throws himself on the mercy of the court because he is an orphan."[2]

Of all the people in Scripture, Paul was the poster child for major-league, Jesus-infused, take-no-prisoners chutzpah. Why? Because he knew the gospel message powers salvation for humankind despite it being absurd to the gentiles and a giant stumbling block to Jews (1 Corinthians 1:23). He'd seen countless hearts, minds, and lives radically changed by the Messiah whom the gospel was centered on—Jesus of Nazareth.

Do you have the chutzpah to share your Jesus story with people who may very well reject it and you?

2 Leo Rosten, *The Joys of Yiddish* (Three Rivers Press, 2001), 81.

# תּוֹרָה—Torah

## "Law"

"Do not think that I have come to abolish the Law or the Prophets; I have not come to abolish them but to fulfill them."
MATTHEW 5:17 ESV

Most often, *Torah* refers to the first five books of the Old Testament, but it can also refer to the entire Old Testament. When Moses came down from Mount Sinai after meeting with God for forty days, he brought with him much of the civil law required for righteous living in a society whose God was the Lord. It was a gift. He later wrote in Deuteronomy 4:8, "What great nation is there, that has statutes and rules so righteous as all this law that I set before you today?"

Because of men and women's gnat-straining sinfulness (Matthew 23:24), the gift of the Torah grew into a noose squeezing the people's necks. For example, "Remember the Sabbath day, to keep it holy" (Exodus 20:8) morphed into hundreds of man-made rules defining what constituted work. Into that culture, Jesus proclaimed, "I didn't come to trash the Torah. I came to fulfill it" (Matthew 5:17, author's paraphrase). Jesus as Messiah challenges the entire Old Testament to be reinterpreted. He ends, or completes, the law as the means of getting right with God (Romans 10:4).

Holy Spirit, allow me to understand the beauty and value of the full counsel of God's Word.

# הַלְלוּ—*Hahl'loo*

## "Praise"

"Hosanna! Blessed is he who comes in the name of the Lord!"
MARK 11:9 ESV

Hallel (derived from the word *hahl'loo*) is a group of psalms sung during festivals that praise God for his many redeeming acts. The Talmud describes Hallel as having five foundational redemptive motifs: the Hebrews' exodus from bondage in Egypt, God's parting of the Red Sea to facilitate their crossing, his provision of the Law at Sinai, the resurrection of the dead, and the birth pangs of the Messiah.

At Jesus' triumphal entry, the shouts of joy from the crowds came from the last psalm of Hallel, Psalm 118:25–26: "Save us…! Blessed is he who comes in the name of the LORD!" We get the word *hosanna* from the Hebrew word for "save us." Then on Tuesday of Passion Week, Jesus confronted the Jewish leadership by assigning the words of Psalm 118 to himself: "The stone that the builders rejected has become the cornerstone; this was the Lord's doing, and it is marvelous in our eyes" (Mark 12:10–11). Jesus was the one who came in the name of the Lord. He was the rejected stone that became the cornerstone. How amazing is it to think that all Jerusalem sang the redeeming words of Hallel just hours before the greatest act of redemption in human history?

Lord Jesus, thank you for being the cornerstone, the most important building block of life.

# כַּפֹּרֶת—*Kapporehth*

## "Mercy Seat"

Jesus' God-given destiny was to be the sacrifice to take away sins,
and now he is our mercy seat because of his death on the cross.
ROMANS 3:25 TPT

Exodus 25:17 reads, "You shall make a mercy seat of pure gold" (ESV). The *kapporehth* was the solid gold cover of the ark of the covenant that was symbolic of God's throne. The presence of the Lord dwelled there. On the Day of Atonement, the high priest sprinkled goat blood across it to satisfy the righteous demands of God and make atonement for the sins of Israel until the next year.

The mercy seat in the holy of holies was where reconciliation between sinful humanity and a holy God occurred. In Romans 3:25, Paul called Jesus our mercy seat by using the Greek word *hilastērion* for the Hebrew word *kapporehth*. It is stunning that Jesus, as the *hilastērion*, personified in reality what was only symbolized in the *kapporehth*. Be encouraged to acknowledge, accept, and live in Jesus' epic sacrifice for your sins. Allow his stunning act of love and grace to inspire you to walk in gratitude and obedience to God. Reflect on the gravity of your sin and the price paid to redeem and reconcile you.

Jesus, thank you for taking the hit that was mine to take.

# תְּפִלִּין—*T'feeleen*

## "Phylacteries"

"I will put my law within them, and I will write it on their hearts."
JEREMIAH 31:33 ESV

For twenty-five hundred years, Jews have wrapped their heads and arms in *t'feeleen* (tefillin)—small square boxes with leather straps. Inside each box is a parchment with the passage containing this command: "Bind [God's words] as a sign on your hand, and they shall be as frontlets between your eyes" (Deuteronomy 6:8). As an external reminder that God's Word should be on their minds and hearts, one box is placed on the forehead, and the other is placed two fingerbreadths above the elbow on the bicep of the weak arm, with the box facing the heart.

However, Jeremiah talks about a coming new covenant when God promises to put his law in us. The external became internal fifty days after Jesus' resurrection when the Holy Spirit came (Acts 2). His indwelling presence in your life as a believer allows God's Word to saturate you to the core. He will guide you into truth and set aflame that truth inside you. He illuminates the Word and allows you to understand it as never before (1 Corinthians 2:12).

Lord, I ask today that your Holy Spirit guide me to understand your Word as you intend it to be understood.

# כַּשְׁרוּת—*Kahshroot*

## “Dietary Laws”

“Do you not see that whatever goes into a person from outside cannot defile him, since it enters not his heart but his stomach, and is expelled?” (Thus he declared all foods clean.) And he said, “What comes out of a person is what defiles him.”
Mark 7:18–20 esv

In the *kahshroot* (kashrut), why is eating hedgehogs and lizards unsuitable but eating frogs okay? Why are bass permitted while sharks are forbidden? The best evidence is that God gave the dietary laws to keep the Israelites healthy, to prevent them from consuming animals associated with pagan worship rites, and to set Israel apart as a holy and unique people among the nations.

Yet we can unequivocally say that in the fifteen hundred years between God giving the law at Mount Sinai and Jesus’ words in Mark 7, the laws had effectively become more important than the meaning undergirding them—and the Lawgiver himself. Jesus, with his profound teachings, explicitly overturned the *kahshroot* by declaring all food suitable and clarified that sin and food are unrelated. He emphasized that disobedience and wickedness emanate from the heart and are what truly defile us, not eating a ham-and-cheese sandwich. It’s a heart thing and always has been.

Where have you allowed the letter of the law to sneak in and usurp the spirit of the law?

# חֲזַק וֶאֱמָץ—*Chahzahk Veh'ehmahtz*

## "Strong and Courageous"

"Be strong and courageous, for you shall cause this people to inherit the land that I swore to their fathers to give them. Only be strong and very courageous, being careful to do according to all the law that Moses my servant commanded you.…Be strong and courageous. Do not be frightened, and do not be dismayed, for the LORD your God is with you wherever you go."
JOSHUA 1:6–7, 9 ESV

In Joshua 1:1–9, Yahweh (the LORD) commissioned Joshua as the leader of Israel. The Lord emphatically encouraged Joshua to be strong and courageous three times—not based on who Joshua was but based on who Yahweh is.

"Be strong and courageous" in Joshua 1:6 is based on Yahweh's promise of land; in verse 7, it's based on the priority of Yahweh's law; and in verse 9, it's based on Yahweh's unfailing presence. Arguably, the entire charge to Joshua is based on Yahweh's eternal presence. As a Christ follower and leader—whether pastor, small group leader, ministry leader, student leader, seniors' leader, or a leader in your family—rest on God's promises, his Word, and his presence. Be strong and courageous in your leadership, knowing that Yahweh undergirds it and is your ever-present source and strength.

Yahweh, thank you for turning my weaknesses into leadership by your strength.

# מוֹאֲבִיָּה—*Moahveeyah*

## "Moabite Woman"

The book of the genealogy of Jesus Christ.…Boaz [was] the father of Obed by Ruth…and Jacob the father of Joseph the husband of Mary, of whom Jesus was born, who is called Christ.
MATTHEW 1:1, 5, 16 ESV

Ruth was a Moabite widow who displayed incredible loyalty to her Israelite mother-in-law, Naomi. They traveled from Moab to Naomi's hometown of Bethlehem, where Ruth met and married Boaz. Their son, Obed, became the grandfather of King David, and many generations later in their lineage, Jesus was born.

Ruth is one of four women (other than Mary) included in Jesus' genealogy in Matthew. Not a big deal, right? Wrong. Ancient Jewish genealogies never mentioned women. They always traced heritage from father to son. And these four sure had issues: None of them were Jewish; Rahab was a prostitute; the wife of Uriah—Bathsheba—committed adultery; Tamar conceived via her father-in-law, Judah, while disguised as a prostitute; and Ruth was a cursed Moabite. Jesus' genealogy illustrates the truth that God can, does, and will use the good, bad, and ugly to get done whatever he wants to get done. This is a majestic image of the outworking of his sovereignty and grace-filled providence.

Lord, thank you for showing me in your Word that you use broken people like me to accomplish great things for your sake.

# שְׁכִינָה—*Sh'kheenah*

## "Divine Presence"

The Word became flesh and dwelt among us.
JOHN 1:14 ESV

*Sh'kheenah* (shekinah) is God's manifest presence dwelling with his people. In short, the foundation of the Lord's covenant with Israel at Sinai is this: "Obey My voice, and I will be your God, and you will be My people" (Jeremiah 7:23 NASB). Exodus 25:8 reads, "That I may dwell in their midst" (ESV). And Exodus 29:45 reads, "I will dwell among the people of Israel."

Paul explained *sh'kheenah* in new covenant terms: God "emptied himself,…being born in the likeness of men" (Philippians 2:7). John recorded the ultimate expression of *sh'kheenah* in John 1:14: "The Word became flesh and dwelt [in Greek, *skēnoō*] among us." The similarity between the Hebrew *sh'kheenah* and the Greek *skēnoō* tells us that John had God's dwelling with Israel in mind as he penned his gospel. The Word becoming human in the first century and hanging out with us are akin to God's presence with Israel prior to Jesus' birth. Have you ever felt like God doesn't understand your problems? He does. He walked as a man for thirty-three years. He is intimately aware of every struggle you will ever have. You can come to him with confidence that he understands it all and loves you.

Jesus, thank you for coming as a human like me and empathizing with all my experiences.

# פָּרֹכֶת—*Pahrokheht*

## "Veil"

The veil of the temple was torn in two from top to bottom.
MARK 15:38 NKJV

Beginning in Exodus 25, God laid out the blueprints for building a "portable temple" called the tabernacle so he could dwell with the people. According to God's pattern, a curtain-like *pahrokheht* (parochet) was to be hung to separate the Holy Place from the Most Holy Place, keeping sinful people out (26:31–33). Because he would dwell in the Most Holy Place, he instructed that the ark of the testimony containing the Ten Commandments be put in it (v. 33). Exodus 25:22 tells us this was where God met with Moses.

When Solomon built the First Temple, the ark was placed in its Most Holy Place. The high priest was the only one allowed to enter the Most Holy Place and only on Yom Kippur, the year's holiest day. A thousand years later, when Jesus hung on the cross and took his last breath (Mark 15:37), the veil tore in half from top to bottom, opening up the Most Holy Place to everyone. Jesus clearly bridges the distance between sinful humanity and a holy God, providing all humankind with direct access to him for all time. Jesus' sacrificial death makes an intimate, personal relationship with the Creator possible.

Lord, thank you for providing me with my own personal hotline to you.

# חָמֵץ—*Khahmaytz*

## “Leavened”

Jesus said to them, “Watch and beware of the leaven of the Pharisees and Sadducees.”
MATTHEW 16:6 ESV

When making bread, it takes a quarter teaspoon of yeast (leaven) per cup of flour. I’m not a math genius, but that’s 1 part leaven to 192 parts flour. When water is added, the gas produced by the leaven instantly causes thousands of little bubbles to spread throughout the dough—and bingo, it rises and becomes *khahmaytz* (chametz).

In Matthew 16:5–12, Jesus, the greatest communicator ever, used this common household item as a warning to his guys. His choice of the word *beware* is critical. It means “to be on guard.” He illustrated a foundational truth about the nature of deception; the deceived is unaware that the deceiver is deceiving them. In this case, the warning regards false teaching and the nefarious way it spreads, just like leaven (v. 12). We would do well to heed the warning also. How? Measure the content of the preaching you listen to. Is it Jesus focused? Gospel centered? Does it align with Scripture? Does it include repentance? Is it merely a glorified motivational speech? Observe the life of the preacher. In Matthew 23, Jesus essentially told the crowd, “The scribes and Pharisees don’t practice what they preach. Hypocrites!”

Lord, give me discernment to recognize your truth.

# קָדוֹשׁ—*Kahdosh*

## "Holy"

As he who called you is holy, you also be holy in all your conduct.
1 Peter 1:15 esv

*Holiness*. It is a word rarely preached from pulpits today. Yet historically, Christians didn't shy away from using the word. Spurgeon said, "I believe the holier a man becomes the more he mourns over the unholiness which remains in him."[3]

God first mentioned holiness at the end of creation. He "blessed the seventh day and made it holy" (Genesis 2:3). He deemed it *kahdosh* (kadosh). He consecrated it. The word shows up again in Exodus, when God was preparing a people to be in covenant with himself. He trained them to be different, unique, and set apart from the nations. In Leviticus 11:44, God said, "I am the Lord your God. Consecrate yourselves therefore, and be holy, for I am holy." As a Christ follower, my lifestyle ought to be different from that of those who are not following Christ—or the cross means nothing. Okay, but what does that look like? Years ago, someone asked me to write a job description for being a Christian. I said, "Live a lifestyle that (1) conforms to the Beatitudes (Matthew 5:3–11) and (2) displays the fruit of the Spirit (Galatians 5:22–23)." Does your life reflect consistent growth in conforming to God's character?

God, let me live according to your standards rather than the world's.

3 Charles Haddon Spurgeon, "The Sine Qua Non," April 16, 1870, The Spurgeon Center for Biblical Preaching at Midwestern Seminary, transcript, spurgeon.org.

# פָּרוּשׁ—*Pahroosh*

## "Pharisee"

Nicodemus also, who earlier had come to Jesus by night, came bringing a mixture of myrrh and aloes.
John 19:39 ESV

The Pharisees were a separatist sect in Judaism from 150 BC until AD 135. They were the legalistic loudmouths who meticulously adhered to the law. Over the years, they even developed a massive volume of oral traditions that they added to the written law. Nicodemus was a *Pahroosh* (Parush) and "member of the Sanhedrin" (John 3:1 AMP). He was also clearly searching for truth. In the stealth of night, he secretly had a one-on-one with Jesus (v. 2), questioning him about being born again. Nicodemus wanted to decide for himself if Jesus was the real deal.

In John 7, the evangelist recorded Nicodemus subtly defending Jesus' right to a fair trial according to Jewish law (vv. 51–52). I believe this is an image of the Lord slowly softening this Pharisee's heart. God can soften even the hardest heart. Even yours. In John 19, after Jesus' death on the cross, Nicodemus delivered a boatload of myrrh and aloes to prepare Jesus' body for burial. He had probably been a secret believer for a while, but after the crucifixion, he'd seen enough. It was time to stand up for his King. Will you?

Take a stand for Jesus—even in the face of vehement opposition.

# שְׁמַע—*Sh'mah*

## "Hear"

"Hear, O Israel: The LORD our God, the LORD is one."
DEUTERONOMY 6:4 ESV

You may very well be familiar with the *Sh'mah* (Shema) as the most basic expression of Jewish faith. And you would be spot-on. Moses penned this battle cry of Judaism into a radically polytheistic world. With all these different gods everywhere, Yahweh (the LORD) would be the single object of Jewish faith. However, there is a glimpse of the Trinity in this verse. The word *God* is plural, and shockingly, this grammatically plural *God* is then described as one.

The triune nature of God is majestically mysterious. God is one in essence and three in person: Father, Son, and Holy Spirit. These three persons are distinct yet coequal, coeternal, and consubstantial (made up of the same God stuff). Even so, the Father is not the Son, the Son is not the Holy Spirit, and the Holy Spirit is not the Father, but all three are fully God. The Father is our Creator, Provider, and Sustainer; the Son is our Redeemer, Savior, and Reconciler; and the Holy Spirit is our Comforter, Guide, and Illuminator. In your prayer time, focus on each person of the Trinity. Thank the Son for his sacrifice and salvation, the Holy Spirit for his comfort and guidance, and the Father for his creation and provision. Intentionally pursue growth in your relationship with each person of the Trinity.

God, thank you for revealing yourself to me more and more each day.

# מְזוּזָה—*M'zoozah*

## "Doorpost"

In [Jesus] we have redemption through his blood.
Ephesians 1:7 ESV

A *m'zoozah* (mezuzah) is a small box affixed to the doorframe of all exterior doors (sometimes interior doors too) in a home. Inside is a parchment scroll with the words of Deuteronomy 6:4–9 written on it. On the back side of the parchment, the Hebrew word *Shahdai* (Shaddai), meaning "Almighty," is written. According to the second-century Jewish mystical commentary the Zohar, the three Hebrew consonants in *Shaddai* are an acronym that translates to "Guardian of the Doors of Israel."[4]

In Exodus 12, the Hebrews were instructed to wipe lamb's blood on their doorposts to protect them from the angel of death, who was coming for all the firstborn sons in Egypt. It was the blood of the lamb that saved them. As Christ followers, we have also been protected, delivered, rescued, and redeemed by the precious blood of the Lamb—Jesus of Nazareth. The Greek word for "redemption" implies being freed from slavery at a price, the sacrificial blood of Christ being the fee. You are no longer a slave to sin because the blood of the Lamb has delivered you from the shackles of bondage. In the words of the Zohar, God Almighty has provided a way, and Jesus is the Way.

Lord Jesus, thank you for buying me back with your blood.

4 Ronald L. Eisenberg, *The JPS Guide to Jewish Traditions* (The Jewish Publication Society, 2004), 581.

# טוּ בִּשְׁבָט—*Too Beesh'vaht*

## "15th of Shevat"

"Look at the fig tree, and all the trees. As soon as they come out in leaf, you see for yourselves and know that the summer is already near."
LUKE 21:29–30 ESV

*Too Beesh'vaht* (Tu Bishvat) is a minor holiday celebrated on the fifteenth day of the Hebrew month of Shevat (usually late January). It's known as the New Year of the Trees because it marked the beginning of the tithing cycle for produce.

In Luke 21, Jesus began discussing future events—the destruction of the temple and Jerusalem, war, persecution, and his second coming. The disciples asked, "When?" They had become masters at pressing Jesus with *when* questions. When will this happen? When will that happen? And Jesus was the master at answering by taking ordinary things in everyday life and creating timeless lessons with them. Jesus, in simple terms, said that we'll know summer is on the way by recognizing that spring is here when the trees are starting to bloom. Effectively, he said, "You won't have a calendar date, but keep your antenna up and look for the signs I just gave you. When they happen, I'm on the way back." Are you living faithfully in anticipation of his coming kingdom?

How does the promise of Jesus' return affect your daily decisions and priorities?

# מִקְוֶה—*Meek'veh*

## "Ritual Bath; a Gathering [of Water]"

We were buried therefore with him by baptism into death, in order that, just as Christ was raised from the dead by the glory of the Father, we too might walk in newness of life.
ROMANS 6:4 ESV

The *meek'veh* (mikvah) is the gateway to purification and renewal in Judaism. It is a ritual bath with incredibly stringent building and water requirements. In ancient Judaism, *meek'vahote* (plural) were built into the ground. Today, they are built into the ground or constructed as a permanent part of a building. Anytime one becomes ceremonially unclean (touching a corpse, menstruating, having skin diseases), immersion in a *meek'veh* is required for ritual purity. Once immersed, the person is deemed "clean" and can reengage in the ceremonial life of the Jewish community.

Christian baptism is an external symbol of internal rebirth, symbolizing the washing away of sins and the cleansing of the believer by the blood of Christ. Although it is not salvific, it is typically an indicator of a believer's entrance into the community of faith. Echoing the life-changing quality of the *meek'veh*, being fully immersed paints a beautiful image of dying to your old ways of life and rising up out of the baptismal waters to walk in a new life with Jesus.

How are you walking in the newness of life?

# רוּחַ הַקֹּדֶשׁ—*Rooahkh hah-Kodehsh*

## "The Holy Spirit"

"When he comes, he will convict the world concerning sin and righteousness and judgment."
JOHN 16:8 ESV

David wrote Psalm 51 when Nathan came and laid the hammer down on his sordid affair with Bathsheba (2 Samuel 12:1–15). It records David's penitent words as *Rooahkh hah-Kodehsh* (Ruach ha-Kodesh) convicted him of his sin. He cried, "Have mercy on me;...blot out my transgressions. Wash me...and cleanse me!... Renew a right spirit within me" (Psalm 51:1–2, 10). Then he begged God not to leave him: "Cast me not away from your presence, and take not your Holy Spirit from me" (v. 11).

A thousand years later, Jesus said the Holy Spirit "will convict the world concerning sin" (John 16:8). He convicted David. He did not condemn him. Guilt, shame, and condemnation come from the Deceiver because he is a liar and hates you. Conviction, not condemnation, comes from the Holy Spirit because he loves you and wants to help conform you to the image of the Son (Romans 8:1, 29) through repentance, confession, and forgiveness. This is a beautiful image of God pointing out our need for him, coupled with his grace in applying Jesus' blood to satisfy the need.

Jesus, thank you for sending your Holy Spirit to help me be more like you every day.

# שִׁבְעָה—*Sheev'ah*

## "Seven"

We take delight in the thought of leaving our bodies behind to be at home with the Lord.
2 Corinthians 5:8 TPT

After the funeral, the family of a deceased person "sits *sheev'ah* (shiva)" for seven days, a time when they refrain from working, bathing, cutting their hair, listening to music, having sex, wearing leather, and doing anything pleasurable. Rather than sitting on comfortable furniture, they sit on plain, short wooden stools. It is a time for extreme mourning while they receive support and comfort from their community.

Three daily prayer services are held in the *sheev'ah* home, the Talmud is often studied, and certain mourners' prayers are chanted. In Jewish thought, these things deliver merit to the soul of the deceased and earn them a higher place in the next world. But for born-again believers, 2 Corinthians 5:8 is crystal clear—at the moment of physical death, we are immediately "at home with the Lord," dwelling with him. This is a glorious truth made by the Word of God. This "home" is death-free, mourning-free, pain-free, disease-free, worry-free, anxiety-free, tear-free, and need-free, and it's full of love, joy, peace, health, energy, worship, glory, praise, light, and Jesus.

Lord Jesus, thank you that I can face the trials of this life with courage and confidence because you have prepared a perfect eternal home for me.

# בַּר מִצְוָה—*Bahr Meetz'vah*

## "Son of the Commandment"

If anyone is in Christ, he is a new creation. The old has passed away; behold, the new has come.
2 Corinthians 5:17 ESV

The *bahr meetz'vah* (bar mitzvah) is a Jewish boy's coming of age. In modern culture, he leads a Sabbath service, reads from the Torah, gives a speech, and has a huge shindig afterward. The *bahr meetz'vah* is the moment when his culture declares him to be a full-blown member of the Jewish community with all the rights and obligations that come along with it. The commandments of the Torah are now his to keep. From this day on, he will wear tefillin (phylacteries) and a tallit (prayer shawl). His membership in the Jewish covenant community is conferred by declaration rather than conviction.

As heartfelt and moving as a *bahr meetz'vah* celebration can be, our membership in God's covenant community is conferred by grace alone through faith alone in Christ alone. Accepting the gospel message is a deeply personal decision. Being "in Christ" is an individual sport. Each "new creation" is individually crafted. You can't have your mama's faith or your community's faith. You can only have your faith. When your faith is combined with Jesus' grace, you are incorporated into his church and individually reconciled to him.

Have you personally decided to follow Jesus?

# בְּרִית—*B'reet*

## "Covenant"

On that day the Lord made a covenant with Abram.
Genesis 15:18 esv

In Genesis 3, Adam and Eve bought the Adversary's lie and wrecked their intimate fellowship with God. The rest of the Bible is the story of God putting it all back together. The Old Testament records the unfolding of God's redeeming plan, the history of salvation that was rolled out through a series of covenants with Noah, Abraham, Moses, and David. In the Abrahamic *b'reet* (b'rit), God promised to build a great nation through Abraham, make him famous, and, through his lineage, bring a great blessing to all the families of the earth. Land was also part of the promised blessing from God.

The ancient custom between two covenanting parties was to split animals in half and walk a path between them. The agreement was that should either party break the pact, they would likewise be split in half. In God's covenant with Abraham, God alone passed through, indicating that he would unconditionally fulfill the terms of the covenant (Genesis 15:17). Effectively, God declared, "This deal doesn't hinge on your performance—it hangs on my faithfulness." And God's faithfulness finds its ultimate fulfillment in "Jesus Christ, the son of David, the son of Abraham" (Matthew 1:1).

Father God, despite my disobedience, thank you for your covenant-keeping faithfulness.

# טַלִּית—*Tahleet*

## "Prayer Shawl; Cloak; Sheet"

"Do this in remembrance of me."
LUKE 22:19 ESV

The *tahleet* (tallit) is the prayer shawl with tzitzit (tassels) on each corner that is traditionally worn by Jewish men during most worship services. The tassels serve as a reminder "to look at and remember all the commandments of the LORD, [and] to do them" (Numbers 15:39). Gematria is a Jewish method of interpreting the Old Testament that assigns numerical values to each letter of the Hebrew alphabet. Providentially, the numeric value of the word *tzitzit* is six hundred, and each tassel has eight threads with five knots: 600 + 8 + 5 = 613. How many commandments do you think are in the Torah? Drumroll please…613.

The very essence of Christianity is also remembering, remembering who Jesus is and remembering his redeeming work on the cross. At the Last Supper, Jesus broke the bread and said, "This is my body, which is given for you. Do this in remembrance of me" (Luke 22:19). He wants you to always remember that he sacrificed for your forever. Your salvation was free to you, but it wasn't free. "You were bought with a price" (1 Corinthians 6:20). In your Christian life, let the cup and the bread—or even the cross hanging around your neck or the "Jesus fish" on your car—all serve as constant reminders that your eternity was expensive.

Lord Jesus, thank you for giving your life to secure my forever.

# שָׁלוֹם—*Shahlome*

## "Peace; Welfare"

Be anxious for nothing, but in everything by prayer and supplication, with thanksgiving, let your requests be made known to God; and the peace of God, which surpasses all understanding, will guard your hearts and minds through Christ Jesus.

PHILIPPIANS 4:6–7 NKJV

One of God's desires for his people is *shahlome* (shalom). The words in Jeremiah 29 are the Lord's words that Jeremiah penned in a letter to those in Babylonian captivity. Amid the chaos and pain the Israelites experienced by being ripped away from home and marched in chains to a foreign, pagan land, God reassured his people that he had "plans for peace and well-being and not for disaster" (Jeremiah 29:11 AMP), plans to give them hope and a future.

The Lord doesn't promise us a pain-free life. He didn't in Jeremiah's time, and he doesn't now. He never says there won't be tornadoes, hurricanes, or tsunamis. God's Word in Philippians encourages us not to be riddled with anxiety but to turn to him in prayer and gratitude. If we do that, verse 7 promises us peace—not just any old peace but the most amazing, inexplicable, mind-blowing, blood-pressure-reducing peace imaginable.

Lord, please help me not to get stressed out but to trust your sovereignty. Give me the unexplainable peace Paul talked about in Philippians 4.

# גֹּאֵל—*Go'ayl*

## "Redeemer"

When the fullness of time had come, God sent forth his Son, born of woman, born under the law, to redeem those who were under the law, so that we might receive adoption as sons.
GALATIANS 4:4–5 ESV

In the book of Ruth, we're introduced to an honorable man named Boaz, who was a close relative of Ruth's deceased husband, Mahlon. Boaz fulfilled the role of a redeeming kinsman—a *Go'ayl* (Goel)—and married Ruth. A redeeming kinsman is a close relative who has the ability and privilege of rescuing or redeeming the family's property or people.

God's providential hand was all over this family's lineage. Ruth and Boaz had a baby boy named Obed, who "just happened" to be King David's grandpa. Then, twenty-eight generations later, from David's line, the Savior of the world, Jesus, was born in Bethlehem—the very place where Boaz lived, redeemed and married Ruth, and raised Obed. Though you and I were born shackled to sin and desperately in need of redemption, Jesus was born at the perfect time on a mission to redeem us. We were "under the law" (Galatians 4:4), completely unable to escape its condemnation. Bondage-breaking, authentic freedom and a new family are found in his redeeming blood.

Lord, I thank you today for purchasing and adopting me into your family.

# אֱמֶת—*Ehmeht*

## "Truth"

"I am the way, and the truth, and the life."
John 14:6 ESV

Psalm 86, commonly attributed to David as Saul hunted and persecuted him, records several appeals to the Lord. In verse 11, David cried out, "Teach me your way, O Lord, that I may walk in your truth." In other words, "Help me live a life in obedience to your Word." In John 14, Thomas asked Jesus essentially the same thing: "Wait, what? Rabbi, help us! We're lost." And Jesus was like, "C'mon, man." He said, "I am the way, and the truth, and the life."

This is a giant truth in Scripture. Jesus is the way, the only way, because he is the very personification of truth. Jesus himself said he came into the world to "bear witness to the truth" (18:37). *Ehmeht* (emet) is that which conforms to reality, and Jesus is the ultimate reality and fulfillment of all God's promises. Because he embodies truth and is the only way to the Father, he also embodies life—everlasting life. If our appropriate starting point is that we deserve eternal death, the fact that life is even a possibility reeks of God's mercy and grace.

Jesus, thank you for opening my eyes to the salvation that only you offer.

# לֵב—*Layv*

## "Heart"

If you confess with your mouth that Jesus is Lord and believe in your heart that God raised him from the dead, you will be saved. For with the heart one believes and is justified, and with the mouth one confesses and is saved.
Romans 10:9–10 ESV

Eight hundred years before Jesus, the prophet Jeremiah declared the *layv* (lev) deceitful and desperately sick (Jeremiah 17:9). In ancient Hebrew thought, the heart was the center of everything that makes a person a person—the seat of intellect, emotion, feelings, character, personality, everything.

It's this same cataclysmically wicked heart that Paul said we activate to believe. You and I are justified through belief in the gospel and trust in Jesus by faith. The confession from your mouth and the belief in your heart are not two separate rungs on the ladder of your salvation but one single step. Confession and belief should never come down to head knowledge plus a dash of some "magical" word formula. It is an all-in, with-everything-you-are, with-everything-you-do commitment to Christ. Consider how you can maintain a lifestyle of recognizing Jesus as Lord in every aspect of your life—not just in words but in actions.

Father, help me always make sure my head and heart are in the right place.

# מוֹדֶה אֲנִי—*Modeh Ahnee*

## "I Gratefully Thank"

The steadfast love of the LORD never ceases; his mercies never come to an end; they are new every morning; great is your faithfulness.

LAMENTATIONS 3:22–23 ESV

The *Modeh Ahnee* (Modeh Ani) is a prayer Jews recite every morning before getting out of bed. The words I grew up saying are "I gratefully thank you, O living and eternal King, for you have returned my soul within me with compassion—abundant is your faithfulness!" Connecting their morning and evening prayers, many observant Jews add David's words in Psalm 31:5 to their evening prayer: "Into your hand I commit my spirit." In Jewish thought, our souls metaphorically go to heaven when we fall asleep, so every morning, Jews thank God for his unending love, mercy, and faithfulness and for reconnecting body and soul. The *Modeh Ahnee* recalls Jeremiah's words in Lamentations 3, proclaiming that God's mercy reboots with every sunrise because his faithfulness is great.

Jesus' last words, recorded by Luke, echo Psalm 31:5: "Father, into your hands I commit my spirit!" (Luke 23:46). As Christ followers, we would be well served to begin every day with thanksgiving in our hearts and minds for what Jesus did for us on the cross. He willingly died to pay a penalty that was ours to pay. Do you thank him daily?

Lord, thank you for protecting me through the night and providing me with new mercies every day.

# עוֹלָם הַבָּא—*Olahm Hahbah*

## "The World to Come"

Now the righteousness of God has been manifested apart from the law, although the Law and the Prophets bear witness to it—the righteousness of God through faith in Jesus Christ for all who believe.

Romans 3:21–22 ESV

*Olahm hahzeh* is "this world," in contrast with *olahm hahbah* (olam haba), which is "the world to come." In Jewish thought, the world to come is the place of reward for the righteous. In the world to come, a Jew will experience the amount of goodness they brought into this world. In other words, their position in *olahm hahbah* depends on their obedience to the law, good works, and Bible study in *olahm hahzeh.*

The reality is that our sinful nature renders us unable to perfectly keep the law and achieve righteousness on our own. But praise the Lord that when we repent, believe through faith in Jesus, and surrender our lives to him, we are declared righteous because of Christ's finished work on the cross and will live with him for eternity in heaven. So in your struggles, let this remind you to rely on his righteousness rather than your own. Turn to him in prayer and ask for his guidance in every area of your life.

Lord, help me trust that your righteousness is more than enough.

# נָזִיר—*Nahzeer*

## “Nazarite”

We have four men who have taken a vow; take them and purify yourself along with them and pay their expenses, so that they may have their heads shaved.
ACTS 21:23–24 NET

Nazarites were people who vowed to abstain from haircuts, alcohol, anything related to grapes, and contact with a corpse. The *Nahzeer* (Nazir) vow is primarily described in the Old Testament, with Samson (Judges 13–16) being the most notable adherent.

When Paul landed in Jerusalem in Acts 21:17 and met with James and the elders in the Jerusalem church, they told him that some overzealous Jewish believers were freaked out by his reputation of being indifferent to Jewish law and customs. Paul was asked to join in the purification rites of four Nazarites and pay their “haircut bill”—all to placate these zealous Jewish Christians. Did Paul shackle himself back to the law by following it in this instance? Absolutely not! Paul’s every breath revolved around winning people to the Lord. He was willing to do anything short of sin to lead people to Jesus. For gentiles, he became like a gentile. For the weak, he shared in their weakness. All this was to win to Christ as many as God put in front of him (1 Corinthians 9:19–23).

Lord, let me be willing to exit my comfort zone for the sake of the gospel.

# צוֹם—*Tzoom*

## "Fast"

"When you fast, don't make it obvious, as the hypocrites do, for they try to look miserable and disheveled so people will admire them for their fasting."
MATTHEW 6:16 NLT

In twenty-first-century American culture, fasting has become trendy. Biblically, fasting is refraining from eating and drinking for a specified amount of time. The Torah only mandates that the Israelites *tzoom* (tsum) on Yom Kippur (the Day of Atonement). However, it appears elsewhere, typically alongside mourning or sorrow or to prevent impending disaster. Authentically, it's a sacrificial act where we deny ourselves, learn self-discipline, and center our attention on God in prayer, expressing our need for him.

By Jesus' time, people, including the Jewish leadership, had twisted a beautiful, God-focused fifteen-hundred-year-old commandment (Leviticus 23:27) into something to boast about. I remember growing up and watching my parents remind everybody that we were fasting for the entire twenty-four hours of Yom Kippur each year. We made sure everyone knew how hungry we were but that our "incredible holiness" was more important than our hunger. This is the attitude that Jesus abhorred. He essentially said, "Comb your hair, brush your teeth, put on your makeup, stop frowning, stop the fake hunger pangs, get over yourselves, and focus on your heavenly Father."

Lord, inspect my motives and expose any insincerity in my prayer and worship life.

# יְבָרֵךְ—*Y'vahrekh*

## "To Bless"

"Bless those who curse you, pray for those who mistreat you."
LUKE 6:28 CJB

Like a job description for a Christian, Jesus' Sermon on the Plain (Luke 6:17–49) emphasizes love, grace, and humility, teaching us to love our enemies. Jesus was incredible at turning the status quo upside down, and his message here paints kingdom living and values in stark contrast with cultural norms and worldly values.

The world says, "If someone hates you, hate them back more." Christ followers respond, "I love you. How can I serve you?" The world says, "If someone curses you (wishes evil on you), retaliate with more evil." Christ followers respond, "'May the LORD bless you and protect you' (Numbers 6:24 NLT). Is there anything specifically that I can pray about for you?" Christians should be different. We should act differently, speak differently, and respond differently. We simply cannot be the same on the "saved" side of the cross as we were on the "lost" side. If we act, speak, and react as the world does, the world's logical conclusion is that Jesus makes no difference. Can you blame them? Do not cheapen the cross. Your Savior paid a mighty cost to transform you.

I was one way, Lord. And now I'm radically different. And you were the in-between. Thank you!

# חַי—*Chai*

## “Life”

“I have come so that they may have life, and have it abundantly.”
John 10:10 LEB

Countless other living things were created and given the capacity to breathe before humans. However, there was something special about humans. Something different. God “blew into his nostrils the breath of life, and the man became a living creature” (Genesis 2:7). This was unique. Humans are living spiritual beings, created to exist forever with God. And then it happened…

- The Deceiver entered the game to “steal and kill and destroy” (John 10:10).
- Adam and Eve were deceived and sinned.
- Fellowship with God broke, and death loomed for Adam and Eve.
- But this did not sneak up on God!

God’s ultimate desire is to have an eternal personal relationship with every person ever born. When he came to earth, the Son of Man (John 3:13), Jesus, declared his mission statement: “I have come so that they may have life, and have it abundantly” (10:10). This promised abundant Christian life is not about physical health or material wealth but speaks to salvation—the gift and assurance of eternal life that every believer receives from Jesus. It is a life filled with meaning, purpose, joy, peace, and hope for a magnificent future.

Father God, thank you for breathing your precious eternal life into me.

# מַצָּה—*Mahtzah*

## "Unleavened Bread"

Cleanse out the old leaven that you may be a new lump, as you really are unleavened. For Christ, our Passover lamb, has been sacrificed. Let us therefore celebrate the festival, not with the old leaven, the leaven of malice and evil, but with the unleavened bread of sincerity and truth.
1 Corinthians 5:7–8 esv

*Mahtzah* (matzah) is unleavened bread baked before the dough has had time to rise. It is the classic symbol of the Passover holiday since it looks back to when the Israelites left slavery in Egypt so quickly that there was not enough time to let the dough rise. At the Passover meal, *mahtzah* and maror (bitter herbs) are eaten together to symbolize the affliction Jews faced in Egypt. In addition, all leaven is removed from the home.

In 1 Corinthians 5:7–8, Paul used leaven to proclaim a timeless truth about the life of a Christian. Just like Israel was commanded to cleanse their homes of leaven, Christ followers are called to cleanse our lives of sin and commit to live according to God's Word. Rest in the truth that the sacrifice of Jesus as our Passover Lamb makes us a new creation. Celebrate the newness of life by walking in "sincerity and truth," rejecting "malice and evil," and living a life of Christlikeness.

Lord, let me celebrate the newness you freely gave me and help me live an "unleavened" life of purity.

FEBRUARY 16

# כִּסֵא שֶׁל אֵלִיָּהוּ—*Keesay Shehl Ayleeyahoo*

## "Chair of Elijah"

"I tell you that Elijah has already come...." Then the disciples understood that he was speaking to them of John the Baptist.
MATTHEW 17:12–13 ESV

Jewish tradition considers the prophet Elijah to be the guardian and protector of newborn Jewish boys (grounded in 1 Kings 17:17–24), and the Talmud states that he is present at every Brit Milah (circumcision). Therefore, it is customary at a circumcision for a special, ornate chair to be placed facing west and traditionally left vacant for Elijah.

Another major reason Elijah is present at each Brit Milah is the belief that he will herald the birth of the Messiah. The Lord said, "I will send you Elijah the prophet before the great and awesome day of the LORD comes" (Malachi 4:5). Jewish belief is that this marks the Messiah's coming. When Jesus' guys asked him about this, Jesus identified John the Baptist with Elijah (Matthew 17:12–13). John took on the prophetic voice of Elijah and announced the Messiah's coming. It is sad that so many missed him when he came, but it is utterly heartbreaking that, after two thousand years, so many still miss him.

Father, give me the boldness and compassion to share Jesus with my friends and family who have missed him.

# עֲמִידָה—*Ahmeedah*

## "Standing"

"Stand up. Praise Yahweh your God from everlasting to everlasting."
NEHEMIAH 9:5 HCSB

In Judaism, prayer is highly structured and liturgical. It is seen primarily as fulfilling an obligation to God, and the *Ahmeedah* (Amidah) is the focal point of fulfillment in each of the three daily services. It consists of nineteen prayers and is always recited while standing. The structure involves taking three steps back, then taking three steps forward (metaphorically drawing near to God), and bowing twice. The worshiper then recites three prayers of praise to God, thirteen prayers of requests, and three prayers of thanks before bowing twice more. It's wrapped up by taking three steps back again so as to never turn your back on God. On the Sabbath, there is only one prayer in the middle section because the focus on Sabbath is with thanksgiving more than petitioning.

I encourage you to integrate *Ahmeedah*-like principles into your life. Cultivate a habit of praise, petition, and gratitude. Begin every day praising God. During the day, ask him to help you align your life with his will. And end the day thanking him for every good thing.

Thank you, Lord, that you are a God with whom I can have a deeply personal and intimate relationship. Thank you that fellowship with you is dependent not on structure and obligation but on Jesus' finished work on the cross.

# שׁוֹפָר—*Shofahr*

## "Trumpet"

The trumpet will sound, and the dead will be raised imperishable, and we will be changed.
1 Corinthians 15:52 NASB

Rosh Hashanah is called the Day of Blowing because it is memorialized with one hundred blasts from the ram's-horn trumpet. The trumpet was also blown for several other reasons—at Mount Sinai, to announce the Year of Jubilee, to announce a death, to welcome the Sabbath, and at the crowning of a king.

The trumpet will also be blown to announce the resurrection of the dead. When the dead in Christ rise at Jesus' second coming, it will be inaugurated with the mightiest *shofahr* (shofar) blow ever. This magnificent promise of resurrection and transformation allows us to live with hope and assurance in a world full of uncertainty. Knowing that we will be raised and given imperishable, glorified bodies tailor-made for a new earth encourages us to live without fear, trusting in God's sovereign plan for our lives. When anxiety or worry about the future rears its ugly head, remind yourself of God's rock-solid guarantee of resurrection. Reflect on his promises and let them provide you with profound peace, joy, and confidence.

Lord Jesus, when I get scared about the godlessness and depravity in the world, help me focus on the promise that in the end, we win.

# קִדּוּשׁ—*Keedoosh*

## "Sanctification"

"Sanctify them in the truth; your word is truth."
JOHN 17:17 ESV

The *keedoosh* (kiddush) is a joyful and celebratory blessing recited on Friday evenings, declaring Shabbat (Sabbath), the seventh day of the week, sanctified—holy and unique. It is performed a second time over a cup of wine at the beginning of the Shabbat meal. *Keedoosh* is also said at Sabbath morning receptions, at the beginning of a new month, and on holidays.

John 17 records the High Priestly Prayer, which is Jesus' intercessory prayer conversation with his Father about sanctifying his disciples. He asked his Father to "sanctify them in the truth," referring to his followers. And he declared, "Your word is truth." To be sanctified is to be set apart for special use. So Jesus was petitioning his Father to take those who are his then and now (and this joyfully includes you) and separate them from the ways of the world and into his ways—into a way of life that conforms to the image of his Son. The vehicle of sanctification is God's Word, and it is not a once-and-done event. As a believer, sanctification is the lifelong process of becoming more Christlike.

How can you develop a routine of seeking God's truth before relying on your own understanding or the insights of others?

# מִנְיָן—*Meen'yahn*

## "Number"

They were devoting themselves to the teaching of the apostles and to fellowship, to the breaking of bread and to prayers.
Acts 2:42 LEB

The tradition of a *meen'yahn* (minyan), which is the requirement that at least ten adult Jewish men are needed to have a worship service, is not found in the Bible. It stems from the ten of twelve spies who, after snooping on Canaan, returned to Moses with a negative after-action report. This group of ten was called a "congregation" (Numbers 14:27 KJV). This verse is the origin of the concept of *meen'yahn*. There are several other *meen'yahn* rules to follow. For instance, if the service begins with ten but some leave, it can only continue if at least six are left. Five, no. Four, no. Six, yes.

When the church was born in Acts 2, Peter preached the gospel, and three thousand folks were saved. Verse 42 tells us they continued to gather together, share a message, fellowship, take communion, and pray. That sounds like a God-honoring worship service to me. And guess what? There was no minimum number to contend with. There was no canceled service because only four people showed up. They trusted that God had exactly who he wanted in attendance.

Lord, thank you for every single individual who attended church last Sunday. I trust that it was exactly the number you expected.

# טָמֵא—*Tahmay*

## "Unclean"

Jesus answered them, "Healthy people don't need a doctor—sick people do."
LUKE 5:31 NLT

The Lord told Aaron, "You will distinguish between the holy and the common, and between the unclean and the clean" (Leviticus 10:10 CJB). Biblically, clean and unclean relate to a person's state of ritual or moral purity. Leviticus 11–15 describes the many things that defile a person, making them ritually unclean. Under the old covenant, a person who became unclean was unfit to be in God's presence (or his people's presence) and must take the appropriate steps to ceremonially clean themselves to be restored to fellowship.

In Luke 5, the religious leaders asked Jesus' guys why their rabbi hung out with dirtbags, tax collectors, and other unclean folks. Jesus answered,

> Healthy people don't need a doctor—sick people do. I have come to call not those who think they are righteous, but those who know they are sinners and need to repent. (vv. 31–32 NLT)

The idea that you and I need to get ourselves cleaned up before coming to the Lord is completely antithetical to the gospel. Churches should be Holy Spirit hospitals, not places for self-righteous huddles. If you feel broken, shackled to sin, dirty, worthless, and unclean, you are exactly the one Jesus is calling.

Every time you wash your hands today, remember how Jesus' sacrifice cleanses you.

# חָטָא—*Khahtah*

## "Sin"

Everyone has sinned; we all fall short of God's glorious standard.
ROMANS 3:23 NLT

*Khatah* (chata), *sin*. I hate the word! *Khatah*'s basic meaning is "to be culpable of a moral transgression." And it always comes with a break in the relationship between offender and offended. In Jewish thought, we sin solely because perfection is impossible. In Judaism, human nature is not intrinsically sinful because humankind was unaffected by the fall.

However, the evidence from God's Word and all human history says perfection is impossible strictly because we are, in fact, inherently sinful. We choose poorly because our sinful nature taints our free will. We sin because we are sinners, and sin carries a death sentence. Praise the Lord, then, for Romans 3:24: "God, in his grace, freely makes us right in his sight. He did this through Christ Jesus when he freed us from the penalty for our sins." Despite sin's destruction of our fellowship with God, God graciously reconciles it through Jesus. Reflect on what it means to you personally that you are made right by God's gift of grace. What impact does his grace have on your daily walk?

Lord, I praise you today that the burden of earning your favor is not on me, a sinner. Your grace is more than enough.

# שִׂמְחָה—*Seem'khah*

## "Joy"

Rejoice in the Lord always. Again I will say, rejoice!
PHILIPPIANS 4:4 NKJV

In Jewish culture, a *seem'khah* (simcha) is a joyful occasion celebrated with friends and family. The birth of a child, the Brit Milah (circumcision) of a baby boy, a bar or bat mitzvah, and a wedding are all *seem'khot* (simchot, plural) in Jewish life. They are often celebrated by sharing a meal, expressing gratitude, praying, and dancing.

The New Testament's message of steadfast devotion, faith, and hope in Jesus is centered around rejoicing even while suffering through relentlessly difficult seasons of life. Paul wrote the letter to the Philippians from a Roman prison, yet he used the words *rejoice* and *joy* sixteen times. Only *Jesus* and *Christ* occur more frequently in the letter. The apostle rejoiced while in chains and staring through prison bars because inner peace and joy exist independent of external circumstances. When Paul encouraged you to rejoice, he was not simply encouraging you to be happy. Happiness is not joy. Happiness is based on feelings, is fleeting, and is bound by time and circumstances. Joy is a permanent state of being and hinges on being "in the Lord."

Father God, teach me to grasp the difference between happiness, which can be gone instantly, and the deep abiding joy that only results from knowing you.

# תְּפִלָּה—*T'feelah*

## "Prayer"

"When you pray, do not keep on babbling like pagans, for they think they will be heard because of their many words."
MATTHEW 6:7 NIV

Deeply intimate time spent in personal *t'feelah* (tefillah) with the Lord was central in the lives of God's people—from Abraham and Isaac to Elijah and the other prophets. Over time, formal liturgy squeezed the intimacy with God that had existed for so long. By AD 100, the rabbis taught that studying the Torah was superior to prayer, as if the two were meant to be mutually exclusive. In Judaism today, there are three formal daily prayer services, corresponding to the two daily temple sacrifices and the evening burning of the fatty portions of sacrificed animals.

Jesus had much to say about constantly communicating with our heavenly Father. In Matthew 6:7, he told his followers that it's not about going on and on with a bunch of "churchy" language and word counts. It's not about "meaningless repetition" (v. 7 AMP). Don't pray "like those people who don't know God" (v. 7 NCV). He said, "Don't fall for that nonsense. This is your Father" we're talking about (vv. 7–13 MSG). And then our Savior gave us the Lord's Prayer (vv. 9–13) as an eternal prayer template to tailor to our praises and needs.

Pour your heart out to God using the Lord's Prayer as your template.

# מִשְׁנָה—*Meesh'nah*

## "Repeated Study"

"Why do your disciples break the tradition of the elders? For they do not wash their hands when they eat."
MATTHEW 15:2 LEB

The *Meesh'nah* (Mishnah), written at the beginning of the third century, is a collection of oral traditions and written works that provide insight into early rabbinic Judaism. It began with the oral law, which Jews believe God gave Moses simultaneously to explain the written law. The oral law, never to be written, was passed down orally from generation to generation. Only after the destruction of the Second Temple was it decided that it could be written. Because the Pharisees believed that both the oral and written law given to Moses were divinely inspired, to them, both were God's Word and carried equal authority.

When the Pharisees and scribes asked Jesus why his disciples broke "the tradition of the elders," they believed the disciples violated God's inspired Word. Jesus got to the real issue by saying they shouldn't be "teaching as doctrines the commandments of men" (v. 9). Man's word is never equal to God's. Have you allowed tradition to become as binding in your life as Scripture? Has religious routine become the driver in your spiritual life?

Lord, let my worship be from a Jesus-transformed heart, not from traditions or external rituals.

# תַּלְמוּד—*Tahlmood*

## "Learning"

"On these two commandments depend all the Law and the Prophets."
MATTHEW 22:40 ESV

During the two hundred to three hundred years following the writing of the Mishnah, the rabbis continued to write and teach. The Mishnah and its diverse commentaries form the two volumes of the *Tahlmood* (Talmud)—the Babylonian *Tahlmood* and the Jerusalem *Tahlmood*. They contain nearly ten thousand pages of teachings covering Jewish law and tradition.

The *Tahlmood* also gives us a glimpse into the first-century world of Jesus the Messiah. Jesus' Jewishness has become an incredibly hip topic in the last fifty years. Yes, of course he was Jewish, raised in a Jewish home under the umbrella of Jewish law. However, never forget that he was a revolutionary. Jesus said, "Love the Lord your God.…Love your neighbor as yourself" (Mark 12:30–31). Then, he hit them with the words of a holy rebel: "On these two commandments depend all the Law and the Prophets" (Matthew 22:40). The idea that love trumped the law was radical and extremist. At that point, the people had the Old Testament and the full body of oral law, and Jesus simply said, "Love God and love people." How does your love for God influence how you interact with people you find hard to love?

Father God, let me live a life of radical love as a reflection of you.

# עֵץ הַדַּעַת טוֹב וָרָע—*Aytz Hahdah'aht Tov Vahrah*

## "Tree of the Knowledge of Good and Evil"

"You may eat any fruit in the garden except fruit from the Tree of Conscience—for its fruit will open your eyes to make you aware of right and wrong, good and bad. If you eat its fruit, you will be doomed to die."
GENESIS 2:16–17 TLB

Adam had it made. He just didn't realize how good it was. He was in an intimate relationship with the Creator. He didn't have her yet, but he was about to meet the love of his life, Eve. Life was good—very good! He had full dominion with one caveat: God essentially said, "It's all yours, but don't eat from that one tree over there."

One rule, not hundreds. Just one. But with 100 percent untainted libertarian free will, he and Eve made a disastrously horrible decision and ate from the prohibited tree (Genesis 3:6), became morally aware, and were given a death sentence. From that point, all humanity was infected with sin. But wait! "The wages of sin is death, but the free gift of God is eternal life through Jesus Christ our Lord" (Romans 6:23).

Jot down a few ways you can be more mindful of the consequences of sin in your life and a few promises of embracing the gift of eternal life in Jesus.

# עֵץ חַיִּים—*Aytz Khahyeem*

## "Tree of Life"

How blessed are those who wash their robes, so that they have the right to eat from the Tree of Life!
REVELATION 22:14 CJB

The Tree of Life appears in Genesis 2 at the end of creation, four times in Proverbs, and not again until Revelation. The Tree of Life was intended for people to enjoy, representing God's provision and eternal life. In Genesis 3:6, though, humans rejected God and chose to be autonomous, thus rendering themselves ineligible to share in its fruit.

From the beginning, God's design was for people to be with him forever—not necessarily to be physically immortal on the earth but to make the transition from physical life to eternal life with God painless and seamless. Humans wrecked it for themselves by eating from the other tree. Yet God didn't leave us hopeless. Revelation 22:14 tells us that those who follow Jesus have a right once again in the new earth to share in the Tree of Life's fruit. Praise the Lord that this future hope has been a present reality since the events of that first Easter weekend when Jesus, the ultimate Tree of Life, opened the door to reclaim what was lost in the garden—eternal life with God.

Jesus, thank you for being my Tree of Life, allowing me to bear fruit for your sake.

# הָוֹן—*Hone*

## "Wealth"

The wealth of rich people is like a city that makes them feel safe. They think of it as a city with walls that can't be climbed.
PROVERBS 18:11 NIRV

The Hebrew word *hone* is used often in Psalms and Proverbs and is almost always depicted as a by-product of wickedness. Proverbs 18:11 is juxtaposed with verse 10, which speaks about God as the safe place or refuge for the righteous. Clearly, wealth is not inherently evil, but it cannot replace the Lord as the foundation for security.

Jesus addressed the impact wealth can have on a person: "It is easier for a camel to go through the eye of a needle than for a rich man to enter the kingdom of God" (Mark 10:25 AMPC). Was Jesus saying wealth excludes a man or woman from salvation? By no means, but it sure can get in the way. It's easy for your stuff to seize control of your heart and make it harder to focus on God. Having wealth and possessions is not evil; just don't allow your things to have you. Keep the pecking order straight—God is first, and everything else is a bonus. Have you relied on your savings, job, or status for security, or do you trust God to provide?

What things have you allowed to get in the way of your trust in God?

# גּוֹיִם—*Goyeem*

## "Gentiles"

"God shows no favoritism. In every nation he accepts those who fear him and do what is right."
ACTS 10:34–35 NLT

The term *goyeem* (goyim) literally means "nations" or "peoples," but it's typically used to refer to non-Jews or pagan peoples surrounding Israel. They are also called strangers or foreigners. Yet there are a few subtle hints of the gentiles' inclusion in the people of God. However, under the old covenant, the idea is nearly always that non-Jews benefit only indirectly from God's covenant with Israel.

The blood of Jesus inaugurated "a new and life-giving way through the curtain" (Hebrews 10:20) into God's presence for everyone who believes and surrenders their life to him. Whether Black, White, blue, green, Jew, gentile, Muslim, Hindu, slave, free, male, female, Democrat, Republican, wealthy, or homeless, God "shows no favoritism" (Acts 10:34). Embrace God's impartiality by serving everyone with love and respect regardless of their background, recognizing that all are of equal value in God's economy. Doggedly pursue a life of righteousness, understanding that God accepts everyone who fears him based only on Jesus' righteousness, not on their cultural or ethnic identity. How can you intentionally and daily reflect God's impartiality, particularly with people who don't look like you?

Lord, remove any prejudices I have that prevent me from sharing your love with others.

# מַעֲשֵׂר—*Mah'ahsayr*

## "Tithe"

"Woe to you, scribes and Pharisees, hypocrites! For you pay tithe of mint and anise and cummin, and have neglected the weightier matters of the law: justice and mercy and faith. These you ought to have done, without leaving the others undone."
MATTHEW 23:23 NKJV

The origin of the tithe in the Old Testament was simple. A tenth of crops, fruit, and herds were to be taken to the house of the Lord for the Levites. Seems pretty simple—but apparently not. Bust out the theological tweezers! Over the years, tons of ridiculous additional rules and regulations were tacked on. All this transformed a meaningful, God-ordained principle into a burdensome noose around the necks of the people.

Things get out of hand when we concern ourselves with one thing (which may be important) and completely ignore the other thing that is clearly much more important. This is what Jesus consistently hammered the Pharisees for. The law didn't even require the tithing of herbs and spices, but the Pharisees always had to take everything to the extreme, completely missing that authentic worship isn't simply fulfilling some list of external religious duties. It's about prioritizing justice, mercy, and faithfulness in your life for the sake of Christ.

Identify the areas in your life where you may nitpick minor details but neglect the important matters of your faith.

# עֲנָוָה—*Ahnahvah*

## "Humility"

Do nothing out of selfish ambition or conceit, but in humility consider others as more important than yourselves.
PHILIPPIANS 2:3 CSB

In Numbers 12:3, Moses is called the humblest man on the planet. In Zephaniah 2:3, the humble are obedient, and in Psalm 22:26, the humble chase after God. Humility has been a virtue from the beginning.

A life of humility does not equal a life of self-flagellating or demeaning yourself. It is being self-aware and God-aware—knowing who you are and who God is. It is cultivating a mindset that doesn't serve yourself but focuses on others. Years ago, a Christian business mentor told me, "You will get everything you want out of life if you help enough other people get what they want." In other words, prioritize the needs and interests of others over your own. Fight your inherent self-centered ambition and work to lift up the people around you. We have the perfect template for how to do this in the person of Jesus Christ. In the greatest act of humility ever, God left the majesty and glory of heaven, became a human being, and selflessly humbled himself to the point of a criminal's death. He did it for one reason—you!

What steps can you take today to ensure that you authentically value others above yourself?

# זֶרַע חַרְדָּל—*Zehrah Khahr'dahl*

## "Mustard Seed"

"The kingdom of heaven is like a grain of mustard seed that a man took and sowed in his field. It is the smallest of all seeds, but when it has grown it is larger than all the garden plants and becomes a tree."

MATTHEW 13:31–32 ESV

Rabbis often used the mustard seed to represent small things. In Palestinian agriculture at the time of Jesus, mustard was considered an incredibly invasive plant. It would grow up to ten feet tall and spread like crazy. Jesus was a master at using familiar objects to teach deep spiritual lessons. At this point in his ministry, he and his band of brothers must have looked insignificant (like a minuscule seed) to the Jewish leadership—just another rebel and his followers who would wander off into obscurity. Jesus' point was that from its small, inconsequential beginning with twelve guys, the kingdom would infiltrate the world, grow big and tall, and become an unstoppable force.

Clearly, little things can have huge impacts. Your small acts of faith and kindness can change someone's forever. How are you nurturing the mustard seeds of faith in your life? Are you a spiritual consumer, or are you contributing to the kingdom's growth in your community and beyond?

Lord, let my life be focused on kingdom multiplication.

# יָמִין—*Yahmeen*

## "Right"

Christ Jesus is the one who died, but even more, has been raised; he also is at the right hand of God and intercedes for us.
ROMANS 8:34 CSB

Jacob blessed his grandson Ephraim with his *yahmeen* (yamin) hand. In the sacrificial system, the right thigh, ear, thumb, and big toe were more valuable than their left-side counterparts. The right hand was seen as a symbol of strength. God's right hand always "shattered the enemy" (Exodus 15:6). Sitting at the right hand of a ruler was a position of honor and power in ancient cultures, including Judaism.

When Jesus is depicted as sitting at the right hand of God, it indicates his authority and divine status, confirming the Jewish concept of kingship and honor. Romans 8:34 paints an image of the Son of God in the throne room of heaven interceding on our behalf, constantly pleading our case. As Christ followers, we have been declared not guilty. However, we have an advocate who ensures that every case brought against us is thrown out of heaven's court. Knowing he is there continually interceding for us provides great comfort because it's another confirmation of his faithful love and care. You can face life's hardships with unwavering hope because Jesus actively intercedes for you twenty-four hours a day, 365 days a year.

Jesus, thank you for having my back.

# עָפָר—*Ahfahr*

## "Dust"

"If any place does not welcome you and people refuse to listen to you, when you leave there, shake the dust off your feet as a testimony against them."
MARK 6:11 HCSB

"Shake the dust off your feet" comes from the ancient Jewish oral tradition (later found in the Mishnah) that walking on gentile soil rendered a person unclean. Therefore, one needed to quickly get it off their feet.

In Mark 6, Jesus prepared his guys for their first mission trip. He conveyed authority over evil spirits, telling them to take only a walking stick, to allow townspeople to provide food and shelter, and to prepare themselves for rejection. If they were not welcomed or listened to, they were to "shake the dust" and hit the road.

Jesus' last words to his disciples, "You will be My witnesses" (Acts 1:8), travel down the corridor of time to you and me as a command. We're not in control of the result, but we are in total control of whether we share Christ. In our context, we must understand that the message will be rejected—probably more than it will be accepted. Adopt a "next" mindset while embracing the idea that persistence is sometimes needed when God is working on someone's heart.

How do you respond when someone rejects your efforts to share Jesus?

# רֶגֶל—*Rehgehl*

## "Feet"

Mary was sitting at Jesus' feet and listening to him teach.
LUKE 10:39 ICB

In Jewish culture, sitting at the feet of someone meant you were their disciple. It meant your every breath hinged on the next word out of their mouth. When all was said and done, you not only would have been a disciple but would have also been a disciple maker in their likeness. At Rabbi Gamaliel's feet, the apostle Paul was "educated according to the strict manner of the law" (Acts 22:3 RSV). Did Paul benefit from Gamaliel? Of course, but Mary sat at the feet of the King. What can we learn from her?

By sitting at Jesus' feet as she did, we declare that learning from God's Word is priority number one. Spending time in his Word and approaching it with humility prepares us with wisdom for life's challenges. Are you prioritizing time in God's Word? In our distraction-filled world, intentionally carving out time to be still with Jesus deepens the intimacy of our relationship with him and helps us experience his presence more fully. When life has you completely overwhelmed and riddled with anxiety, worry, or doubt, sitting at Jesus' feet provides a peace that surpasses all understanding.

How often do you prioritize spending time with Jesus, like Mary did, despite the busyness and distractions everywhere?

# אֱלֹהִים—*Ehloheem*

## "God"

In the beginning God created the heavens and the earth.
GENESIS 1:1 HCSB

The Bible is not a proof text for God's existence. It assumes he exists from the get-go. The word *Ehloheem* (Elohim) appears just a few words in and refers to who caused all creation. Packed into it is God's immense power and magnificent creativity. It appears more than twenty-six hundred times in the Bible. *Ehloheem* is plural, which points to God's enormous majesty and hints at his triune nature.

The Bible states eight times during creation, "God said" (Genesis 1:3, 6, 9, 11, 14, 20, 24, 26). Amazingly enough, whatever followed these words immediately came to fruition. Everything that has ever existed first came into being because God spoke. He spoke, and *poof*, time, space, and matter appeared and obeyed. If God can speak the universe into existence, he can also speak newness and transformation into your life. Trust in his ability to create beauty and order from chaos and to breathe light into the darkest areas of your life. His creation has meaning, purpose, and intentionality. You were carefully and purposely crafted in the image of *Ehloheem*. Therefore, your life has meaning and purpose as well. Live out your days discovering, embracing, and pursuing his calling on your life.

Father God, your words are powerful and inerrant. Lead me to trust you and walk with you forever.

MARCH 9

# רָב—*Rahv*

## “Rabbi”

They were astonished at his teaching, for he taught them as one who had authority, and not as the scribes.
MARK 1:22 RSV

The word *rabbi* (my great one) does not occur in the Old Testament. By the time of King David, *rahv* (rav) was used of a teacher and *rabbi* as the more formal “my teacher.” In New Testament times, *rabbi* had come to refer to a respected teacher or master. The designation of rabbi was typically reserved for someone who diligently studied under the tutelage of another rabbi for many years. Jesus, being the disruptor he was, offended the system and its leaders because he had no formal training or discipling. The Jewish leadership was under the delusion that he was unqualified. He didn’t have an MDiv from Tel Aviv University nor the appropriate hours as a rabbi’s apprentice, but I think being God trumps a PhD.

To provide the appearance of authority, scribes often quoted the famous rabbis. The people saw the disparity between them and Jesus and were astonished. They recognized Jesus’ authority, and it was from above. You, too, can rely on the authority of Jesus’ teachings as infallible, inerrant truth. Let it shape your worldview and guide your actions.

Lord, help me sort through the many voices in our culture and focus my heart and mind on Jesus’ words.

# כֶּבֶשׂ—*Kehvehs*

## "Lamb"

When he saw Jesus walking by, he said,
"Here is the Lamb of God!"
John 1:36 CEV

Close your eyes for ten seconds and think about a lamb. What do you see? I bet you have an image of a pure, sweet, fluffy, cuddly, cotton-bally, lovable animal that you just want to hug. That's not what a first-century Jew would see. At some point, every one of them had dragged a lamb into the temple and had its throat slit as an offering to the Lord. That little fluff ball they'd raised was a constant reminder of the consequences of sin.

Into that context, Jesus' public ministry began with John the Baptist's announcement: "Here is the Lamb of God!" Attaching the word *lamb* to him would have been incredibly odd to the people within earshot. However, Jesus' three and a half years of ministry, death, and resurrection brought understanding to John's words. The Lamb of God wasn't dragged to the altar; he went willingly to the cross for us. And Jesus, the perfect, pure, unblemished Lamb, calls us to a life of holiness. Embracing his purity motivates us to chase a life that reflects his character, runs away from sin, and longs to honor him in every sphere of life.

Lord, help me more willingly live a sacrificial life for you.

# הַבְדִּיל—*Hahv'deel*

## "Separate"

"The Sabbath was made for man, and not man for the Sabbath."
MARK 2:27 NASB

Originally a service of profound beauty, Havdalah closes out every Sabbath. The word *Havdalah* is deeply rooted in the Hebrew word for "separate"—*hahv'deel* (havdil)—as used in the creation narrative, emphasizing God's distinction between the sacred and the ordinary. The sanctity of the seventh day compared to the other six highlights this distinction.

However, over time, dozens of restrictions were added to Havdalah, like a noose around the neck of the service itself. The nonnegotiables were the recitation of three blessings and seven biblical verses, the consumption of wine or juice (but no water), and the use of braided two-or-more-wick candles or two single-wick candles held together. And if you forget to do it on Saturday, it can be observed no later than Tuesday. Ugh! Once again, the legalists spat on God's intent in an attempt to legislate everything. Jesus made it simple: "The Sabbath was made for man, and not man for the Sabbath." He encouraged us to refrain from majoring in the minors and to cling to God's intent, and he mercifully provided the Sabbath for us to rest and worship him. It is *for* us, not the other way around.

How have you turned the Sabbath into a burden rather than a gift meant to refresh and restore?

# בַּר אֱנָשׁ—*Bahr Ehnahsh*

## "Son of Man"

"The Son of Man has authority on earth to forgive sins."
MATTHEW 9:6 NIV

The phrase *Bahr Ehnahsh* (Bar Enosh) is used more than one hundred times in the Old Testament, particularly in Ezekiel. It most often indicates the particular prophet's humanity. However, its use in Daniel 7 is different. There, it is explicitly messianic. Daniel described what he saw:

> Behold, with the clouds of heaven there came one like a son of man, and he came to the Ancient of Days and was presented before him. And to him was given dominion and glory and a kingdom, that all peoples, nations, and languages should serve him; his dominion is an everlasting dominion. (Daniel 7:13–14 ESV)

For the folks who deny that Jesus claimed to be God, his use of the title Son of Man in Matthew 9 and his claim to forgive sins were clear declarations of divinity, for only God can forgive sin and effect spiritual reconciliation. You can trust him with every aspect of your life because he heals spiritually, emotionally, and physically. When tsunamis of life hit, approach the Son of Man with confidence, knowing only he has the authority and ability to heal, restore, reconcile, and forgive.

Jesus, thank you that your forgiveness is real and results in radical healing and restoration.

MARCH 13

# חֹתֶה גֶחָלִים—*Khoteh Gekhahleem*

## “Heap Burning Coals”

“If your enemy is hungry, feed him; if he is thirsty, give him something to drink; for by so doing you will heap burning coals on his head.”

Romans 12:20 esv

In Romans 12:9–21 Paul wrote about the earmarks of an authentic Christian. He encouraged loving good, hating evil, and loving each other. He encouraged joy, patience, a vibrant prayer life, generosity, hospitality, harmony, humility, and a peaceful spirit. The last issue he addressed in this teaching was a Christ follower’s relationship with an enemy. He told us God doesn’t need our help doling out justice. He can handle it just fine on his own. Paul basically advised, “If your enemy is hungry and thirsty, give ’em a sandwich and a Coke.” Then he incorporated a Jewish idiom from Proverbs 25:22 into verse 20 when he wrote, “You will *heap burning coals* on his head” (emphasis added).

“Burning coals” refers to stirring up the conscience of your adversary through kindness. Your kindness in the face of their sinfulness will often result in their repentance—sometimes even in their surrender to Christ’s lordship. Do you believe that kindness can result in the transformation of a stone-cold heart? Do you respond to conflict and confrontation with grace and mercy?

Lord, help me radically forgive those who hurt me.

# אֱלֹהִים חַיִּים—*Ehloheem Khahyeem*

## "The Living God"

"Those carrying their wooden idols are ignorant, they pray to a god that cannot save."
Isaiah 45:20 CJB

Isaiah consistently lays it on folks for worshiping dead pieces of wood as if the idols were God (Isaiah 44:9–20; 45:14–25). They're made by human hands, for heaven's sake. Jeremiah wrote, "There is no breath in them" (Jeremiah 10:14). But we serve *Ehloheem Khahyeem* (Elohim Chayim), who lovingly breathed life into us.

Our God conquered death in the person of Jesus Christ. He is alive! Everybody else's "guy" is dead and rotting in the ground—Muhammad, Buddha, Confucius, Joseph Smith, and all the rest. But our guy ran out of the tomb alive. Peter, preaching at Pentecost, said death couldn't hold Christ. Peter continued, "He wasn't abandoned to the grave, nor did his body experience decay. This Jesus God raised up. We are all witnesses to that fact" (Acts 2:31–32 CEB). The gospel is not about theology, not about doctrine, not about dunking or sprinkling, nor is it about the many things we mistakenly value too highly. The gospel is about a first-century rabbi named Jesus, who was willingly beaten and hung on a cross; experienced heart-stopping, no-brain-activity, 100 percent physical death; and walked 100 percent alive out of his tomb. He is alive today, and that changes absolutely everything.

Whom have you introduced to the living God?

# עַיִן תַּחַת עַיִן—*Ahyeen Tahkhaht Ahyeen*

## "Eye for an Eye"

"You have heard that it was said, 'An eye for an eye and a tooth for a tooth.'"
MATTHEW 5:38 ESV

Imagine Billy accidentally dents his neighbor John's car while backing out of his driveway. Fired up, John demands to dent Billy's car in return to set things straight. Does the demand for equal retribution seem fair? Will it lead to peace or more tension and pain? The intent of "eye for an eye" (Leviticus 24:20 NLT) was the principle that the punishment ought to fit the crime and that this would minimize crazy retaliation. Okay, fine, but how would Jesus respond? I believe he'd answer, "The legalists say, 'A thumb for a thumb.' But I say if someone dents your Camry, allow them to dent your Tesla too."

Perhaps a more intriguing question would be "How *did* Jesus respond?" His best buddy Peter said, "Although he was abused, he never tried to get even. And when he suffered, he made no threats. Instead, he had faith in God, who judges fairly" (1 Peter 2:23 CEV). How do you typically respond when you feel wronged? What can you do today to make certain you trust God rather than react out of anger or frustration?

Father, help me be willing to suffer mistreatment without a spirit of revenge.

# שֹׁמְרוֹן—*Shome'rone*

## "Samaria"

"A Samaritan on his journey came up to him, and when he saw the man, he had compassion."
LUKE 10:33 CSB

Jesus shared a story about a man injured and in a ditch on the road between Jerusalem and Jericho. A priest and a Levite jogged by and ignored him. But a Samaritan stumbled upon him and took great pity on the man. No way! The churchy elite ignored the man, and a filthy Samaritan helped? Jesus just must have been confused. You see, the tension between Samaritans and Jews that began around 950 BC was at its climax by Jesus' time. Jews looked at Samaritans as posers and half-breeds, and Samaritans considered Jews bigots. They hated each other. The Jews to whom Jesus told this parable would have never expected the Samaritan to help—beat up and rob, maybe, but not rescue.

How do you respond when you come across someone in need? Do you make a U-turn, or do you display compassion, even when it is a nuisance? Do you tend to look down on certain groups of people? Do you think everyone in heaven is going to look like you? In God's economy, there are only two demographic groups—lost sinners and saved sinners.

Lord, help me see past my little cocoon, see a need, and fill it.

# עָזְבוּ—*Ahz'voo*

## "Abandoned"

"If anyone loves me, he will keep my word. Then my Father will love him, and we will go to him and make our home within him."
JOHN 14:23 ISV

Ancient Jewish history is filled with countless accounts of Jews, often including their kings, abandoning God's Word and his commandments. One such king was Ahab, who reigned in the Northern Kingdom of Israel during the ninth century BC. Elijah challenged Ahab because he had "abandoned the LORD's commands and followed the Baals" (1 Kings 18:18 HCSB). It's like Elijah barked at Ahab with "Meet me in the parking lot at Mount Carmel and let's see who's who—Yahweh or Baal." Read 1 Kings 18:17–19:18 for the full account, but long story short, Yahweh laid it on Baal. The Kishon River flowed with the blood of the prophets of Baal and Asherah. The cause of the bloodshed? Ahab abandoning God's Word.

Does obeying the Lord cause salvation? Of course not. But Jesus said that if you love him, you'll listen to him. Your obedience to him is a tangible manifestation of your love for him. Check the person in your mirror and evaluate how closely he or she is following God's commands. As you conform more and more to his Word, he promises that you will feel his presence in stronger and more meaningful ways.

How does your obedience reflect the breadth and depth of your love for Christ?

# גַּת שֶׁמֶן—*Gaht Shehmehn*

## "Gethsemane; Olive; Oil Press"

Moving on a little farther, he threw himself prostrate on the ground in prayer, saying, "My Father, if it is possible, allow this cup to be taken from me. Yet let your will, not mine, be done."
MATTHEW 26:39 NCB

On the night of Jesus' arrest, he and his guys walked the short distance to an olive grove called Gethsemane to pray. Jesus knew what loomed on the horizon of his life, knew the onslaught of agony that was only hours away, knew that his flesh would be torn away from his body, and knew that square nails nearly three-quarters of an inch wide would pierce his wrists and ankles. He's God. Of course he knew.

Imagine the thoughts flooding the Son of Man's mind as he prayed among the olive trees, *If there's another way to do this, please*. But then he declared to his Father, "Let your will, not mine, be done." The Son always submitted to the Father's will, as should we. How can we have a "your will, not mine" mindset? It takes a life of prayer, a commitment to ever-growing obedience, and an unwavering trust that God knows better for us than we do.

Father, help me live a life aligned with your will.

MARCH 19

# Tsuris

## “Troubles”

“Do not be anxious for tomorrow, because tomorrow will be anxious for itself. Each day has enough trouble of its own.”
MATTHEW 6:34 LEB

*Tsuris* is a Yiddish word meaning “troubles,” “distresses,” or “aggravations.” It comes from the Hebrew *tzarot* (צָרוֹת). David wrote, “The troubles [*tzarot*] of my heart are growing and growing” (Psalm 25:17 CJB). During my teenage years, my mom often said things to me like, “I’ve had about enough of your tsuris,” meaning that my nonsense was driving her crazy. It’s comical that there is no singular for the word *tsuris*. Why? Because Jews don’t do troubles, distresses, or aggravations one at a time. LOL!

Jesus said not to drive yourself crazy about next week when today has enough tsuris already (Matthew 6:34). Worrying too much about the future is the thief of today’s joy and focus. Trust God for what’s going on in your life now and be there for your friends, family, and church today. Where is “there”? There is wherever you need to be. Surrender your concerns about the future to the Lord, knowing he’ll have your back then just as he has in the past. Make it a habit to let go of your tsuris by trusting God’s control over everything.

Lord, I’m struggling. Please give me the grace and provision I need for today.

# הַשֵּׁם—*Hahshaym*

## "The Name"

All the nations you have made shall come and worship before you, O Lord, and shall glorify your name.
PSALM 86:9 ESV

The word *Hahshaym* (Hashem) comes from *ha*, meaning "the," and *shaym*, meaning "name." So it's a reference to God as "the Name." Because of an aversion to speaking God's name, many Jews still consistently refer to him as *Hahshaym*. In the first eleven verses of Psalm 86, God's name is linked to trust, grace, goodness, forgiveness, steadfast love, a listening ear, prayer, greatness, worship, and wondrous works. Therefore, the psalmist shouted from the Judean hillside, "I praise You, O Lord my God, with my whole heart, and glorify Your Name forever" (v. 12 TLV). God is not a genie in a bottle to be rubbed only when you need something. We call on his hallowed name every day because we need his presence every day.

In the humblest act in human history, God's Son became human and sacrificed his life for your eternity. "God has highly exalted him and bestowed on him the name that is above every name" (Philippians 2:9 ESV). Let this foundational truth motivate you to praise and honor Jesus' mighty name in your daily walk, giving his will priority above your desires. Praise him right now for his cross-bearing love for you.

Gracious Lord, "Turn to me and have mercy. Give me, your servant, strength. Save me" (Psalm 86:16 NCV).

# זָכַר—*Z'kahr*

## "Remember"

"I will forgive their wickedness and will remember their sins no more."
JEREMIAH 31:34 NIV

The Old Testament is ripe with the theme of remembrance. God instructed Israel to remember the Sabbath (Exodus 20), remember the Passover (Deuteronomy 16), remember he is the one who provides power (Deuteronomy 8), and remember his past deeds (Psalm 77). This list of things to remember could literally fill this devotional. Praise God that he remembers too. He remembered his covenant with Abraham (Leviticus 26:42), his love for Israel (Psalm 98:3), and Rachel (Genesis 30:22). This list could also go on and on.

However, in Jeremiah 31, the prophet declared the word of the Lord, prophesying that a day was coming for a new covenant between God and his people. At that time, there would be permanent forgiveness, and God would dwell in us. That day arrived with the death, burial, and resurrection of Jesus Christ. The hallmark of this new covenant is that there is one thing that God will no longer remember—our sins. As a Christian, your sins are permanently done away with (Psalm 103:12) and put behind God (Isaiah 38:17). One of the most comforting truths in Scripture is that God will never bring your past junk back up.

Lord, thank you for forgiving and forgetting.

# צָרַעַת—*Tzahrahaht*

## "Leprosy"

A leper came to Jesus. He knelt down and begged him, "If you are willing, you can make me clean."
MARK 1:40 EHV

Leprosy. The first thing that flashes in your mind is probably *Ew, gross!* Lepers were riddled with pain—physical, emotional, psychological, spiritual, and social. They were cast out of every area of society. In that day, a temple sacrifice was the means of forgiveness, but a leper couldn't go anywhere near the temple. Lepers were essentially cut off from God's forgiveness. And other than the miraculous healing touch of God, leprosy was considered incurable. If a man appeared healed, he was forced to jump through several hoops for the high priest to declare him clean.

The fact that a leper dared to come to Jesus testified to his courage, humility, desperation, and huge faith. Words matter, and his words display a trust that Jesus could heal the incurable. But would he? Jesus can't say yes if the question is never asked. This man hit his knees and begged Christ to heal him because he knew that the temple's high priest had the ability to *declare* him clean but only Jesus had the ability to *make* him clean.

Jesus, thank you for healing sin's infection in my life.

# פּוּרִים—*Pooreem*

## "Lots"

[Peter] said, "Now I know for certain that the Lord has sent his angel and rescued me from the hand of Herod."
ACTS 12:11 NET

The book of Esther does not mention God's name, but the entire narrative is about his providential protection of his people. God uses Esther and her "foster father," Mordecai, to foil Haman's plot to slaughter the Jews. The word *Pooreem* (Purim) comes from Esther 3:7–13, where lots were cast to determine the day the Jews would be murdered.

The themes of deliverance and providence found in Esther also echo throughout the New Testament. In Acts 12:1–11, Herod had Peter arrested and intended to execute him. However, an angel of the Lord miraculously freed Peter from his shackles. Likewise, Paul escaped harm after being stoned in Lystra (Acts 14:19–20), was kept safe on his journey to Rome (Acts 27–28), and was protected from a plot to kill him (Acts 23:12–35). And just as God's protective hand choreographed events behind the scenes in Esther and protected Peter and Paul from certain death, we can trust that God is at work in our lives, even when we can't see him. Let this truth encourage you to have faith, patience, hope, and assurance that God is guiding your steps with purpose.

Lord, help me trust you when I can't feel you.

# גֶּפֶן—*Gehfehn*

## "Vine"

"I am the true vine.…Remain in Me."
John 15:1, 4 NASB

Throughout the Old Testament, Israel is depicted as a grapevine. In Isaiah 5:1–7, God, the Vinedresser, lovingly planted and cultivated Israel, the vine, but all it yielded was lousy fruit. Then in John 15, Jesus used a metaphor that resonated with his first-century audience: the grapevine. The image the Master painted in John 15 is one of the most majestic in all Scripture. Lying unsaid underneath John 15:1 is "You've been taught your whole lives that Israel is the vine." But then Jesus declared, "I am the true vine." The Father intended that Israel produce bushels of beautiful, sweet fruit, but it didn't. Enter Jesus, the true vine, who fulfilled where Israel flunked.

All believers for all time are connected to Jesus as branches are to the *gehfehn* (gefen). Jesus encourages us to abide (or remain) in him because life comes from the vine. Just as a branch that lands on the ground disconnected from the vine withers and dies, we wither spiritually if we disconnect from Jesus. Embrace your dependence on him and make it a habit to practice spiritual disciplines including prayer, fasting, Bible study, worship, service, fellowship, confession, and repentance.

Do you see evidence (fruit) in your life that you are abiding in Christ?

# כָּל—*Kahl*

## "All"

"'You shall love the Lord your God with all your heart, and with all your soul, and with all your mind.'"
MATTHEW 22:37 AMP

Woven throughout the Old Testament law is a laundry list of 613 mitzvot (rules and regulations) that even the very best person on the very best day could not keep perfectly. One day, a Pharisee asked Jesus which of the 613 was the most important. Jesus replied, "You shall love the Lord your God with all your heart, and with all your soul, and with all your mind." He immediately followed up with "You shall love your neighbor as yourself" (v. 39). He explained that these two mitzvot are the fulcrum from which all of God's Word hangs.

All means all. All heart, soul, and mind. It doesn't mean some, half, or nearly all. It means you love God with 1,000 percent of everything you are. It means total devotion to the Lord in every sphere of life. All means nothing is held back. It sounds too elementary, but it truly is as simple as this: Follow these two commands, and everything else will work itself out. When we love God and people like this, we entirely fulfill the spirit of all the law.

Lord, thank you for being my all in all.

MARCH 26

# דְּבַר—*D’vahr*

## “Word”

The word of God is living and powerful, and sharper than any two-edged sword.
HEBREWS 4:12 NKJV

In the New Testament, “the Word” refers to both Jesus and Scripture, but in Hebrews 4, it refers to the God-inspired written Word—the Bible. What does *inspired* mean? Where did the *D’vahr* (Davar) come from? Does it even matter?

The apostle Peter addressed the issue of inspiration: “Prophecy never came by the will of man, but holy men of God spoke as they were moved by the Holy Spirit” (2 Peter 1:21). The Bible is 100 percent God and 100 percent man. Everything that made Paul who he was permeated his writing. The same can be said for Moses, David, James, and the rest. We can no more remove Peter from 1 Peter than we can remove Ed from the devotional you’re reading. And everything that makes God who he is also permeates Scripture because he inspired every inerrant word. The Bible is not some tired collection of old books. It is the final source of truth, alive and applicable to all people, everywhere, for all time. Through the ministry of the Holy Spirit, it convicts, cuts like a sword, challenges, and will transform your life.

Connect with God’s Word daily and allow it to shape your worldview and actions.

# מִזְבֵּחַ—*Meez'bay'akh*

## "Altar"

On the fifteenth day of the eighth month, a day that he himself had designated, Jeroboam offered sacrifices on the altar at Bethel.
1 Kings 12:33 NLT

In 930 BC, Israel split into two kingdoms: Israel in the north, Judah in the south. Jeroboam, the first king of the Northern Kingdom, built golden calves as idols and placed them in temples in Dan and Bethel. Then he disregarded God's directions and appointed priests who were not Levites. As a counterfeit and rival of Yom Kippur (Day of Atonement), Jeroboam created a festival on that date for the people in the north and made idolatrous sacrifices. "He said to the people, '…Look, Israel, these are the gods who brought you out of Egypt!'" (v. 28).

In defiance of God's clear instructions, Jeroboam pridefully crafted his own system of worship. His altars led his people away from Yahweh and bore rotten fruit during the entire two-hundred-year life of the Northern Kingdom. Jeroboam's actions serve as a cautionary tale, reminding us to consider whether our words and actions move people closer to or further away from Jesus. True worship should be rooted in God's Word, not personal preferences. Are you following God's commands or personal preferences in your worship and daily life?

Lord, let my worship always be a pleasing aroma to you.

# מַלְאָךְ—*Mahl'akh*

## "Angel"

Bless the LORD, you His angels, you mighty ones who do His commandments, obeying the voice of His word!
PSALM 103:20 AMP

The Hebrew word *mahl'akh* (malak) can refer to both human and divine messengers (angels). Several Old Testament narratives paint an image of heavenly *mahl'akheem* (plural), the messengers God sends, providing his people assistance in times of trouble, offering military support, and even enforcing God's discipline.

The New Testament develops the role of angels all the more as "ministering spirits (servants) sent out in the service [of God for the assistance] of those who are to inherit salvation" (Hebrews 1:14 AMPC). They are constantly working from a thirty-five-thousand-foot perspective to move us toward the cross—providing purposeful, Jesus-focused nudges and support when called on. God dispatches helpful angels at the perfect time to come alongside and serve you. Trust that he is constantly watching over you and sending assistance, even in ways you will never see, perceive, or ever comprehend. This relentless heavenly support displays just how precious you are to your Creator and reaffirms your immense value in his eyes. Live every day with a profound sense of worth and purpose, knowing that he is your guardian.

How does knowing that God sends spiritual help through angels affect your perspective in the trials of life?

# קוּם—*Koom*

## "Arise"

He said to her, "Talitha koum!" which is translated, "Little girl, I say to you, arise."
MARK 5:41 MOUNCE

Jairus, a respected leader in the synagogue, approached Jesus with a plea to heal his daughter, who was clinging to life by a thread. Jesus agreed and went but got hung up by a bleeding woman who also needed his healing touch. By the time Jesus got back on the road to Jairus' house, news came of the daughter's untimely death. It was a waste of time for Jesus to even show up now, right? But Jesus told Jairus, "Do not be afraid; only believe" (v. 36), and they continued walking. When they arrived, the mourning process was in full swing. Jesus took the daughter's hand and said, "'Talitha koum!' which is translated, 'Little girl, I say to you, arise.'" Without delay, she got up.

This story serves as a powerful reminder that Jesus brings hope to the hopeless. In moments of despair, when everyone you know is screaming, "It's over; there's nothing you can do now," and when you feel hopeless and scared to death, remember that Jesus delivers light, healing, hope, promise, and life where death and darkness appear to have stolen the day.

Consider where in your life you need to respond to Jesus' call to *koom* (kum).

# הַר מְגִדּוֹ—*Hahr M'geedoe*

## "Armageddon"

The demonic spirits gathered all the rulers and their armies to a place with the Hebrew name *Armageddon*.
REVELATION 16:16 NLT

For years I held an apocalyptic image of the world's armies and Jesus' army throwing down at *Hahr M'geedoe* (Har Megiddo). In my mind's eye, it would be an epic hand-to-hand fight, with Satan leading millions of bad guys against millions of the redeemed led by Jesus on a white warhorse.

However, the Bible's account differs significantly from my imagination. In Revelation, the Beast, False Prophet, the kings of the earth, and their armies assemble at Armageddon to wage war, but Jesus singlehandedly deposits the Beast and the False Prophet into the lake of fire and quickly slays the rest. Soon, Satan, death, and hades will meet their ends as well. The "giant" battle is actually no battle at all because when it is God riding the warhorse, the fight is over before it starts. The war was won two thousand years ago when the warrior on the horse hung on a cross and died for you. This is one of the most powerful reminders in God's Word: No matter how powerful evil ever appears, it will absolutely, unconditionally be crushed and overthrown in the end.

Jesus, empower me to live with unwavering confidence, knowing that you've already won the war.

# הָרִאשׁוֹן יִהְיֶה אַחֲרוֹן—*Hah'reeshone Yeeyeh Ahkhahrone*

## "The First Will Be Last"

"Many who are first will be last, and the last, first."
MARK 10:31 AMP

The concept that those "who are first will be last, and the last, first" flies in the face of society's expectations regarding elevated social status, privilege, and reward. It is rooted in the belief that God's ways rarely line up with customs and attitudes dictated by culture. His choices often defy human logic, like when he chose Jacob over Esau and David over his brothers.

In Mark 10, Jesus reminded us that in the world to come, the tables will be turned. The things treasured by the world today will be of no value. Society's winners will become the kingdom's losers—and vice versa. Kingdom leaders serve rather than being served. The *least*—the starving, thirsty, outcast, naked, sick, and imprisoned—are prototype kingdom citizens (Matthew 25:40–45). Resist chasing after power, status, and recognition. While we live in a world that glorifies first place, Jesus reminds us that true greatness is displayed in humble service. Make it a priority to serve for the sake of Christ rather than for the sake of self, knowing that in God's kingdom, humility is exalted.

How can you better align your life with Jesus' standard of humility?

# כֵּפָא—*Kayfah*

## "Rock; Stone"

"You are Peter, a stone; and upon this rock
I will build my church."
MATTHEW 16:18 TLB

This is going to sound a bit like gobbledygook, so get ready. Jesus is doing a "word thing" here. In Greek, the name Peter is *Petros* (in Aramaic, *Kepha*), meaning "a smaller detached stone" while the word *petra* is a giant mass of immovable stone. In other words, "You are *Petros*, and on this *petra* I will build my church!" Debate has raged for two thousand years over what is the *petra* on which Jesus builds his church. Jesus is, well, God. Is it Jesus? Peter, as the spokesman for the Twelve, had just confessed Jesus as the Messiah. Is he the *petra*?

The church—the invisible body of Christ for all time—is unconditionally built on Peter's response to Jesus' question:

> "Who do *you* think I am?"
>
> Simon Peter answered, "The Christ, the Messiah, the Son of the living God." (vv. 15–16)

That is the massive, immovable *kayfah* (kefa)! All Christ followers are family, united together by faith alone in Christ alone. Because the *petra* is this confession of faith, you and I as believers are called, equipped, and empowered to play a critical role in the kingdom—that of making disciples.

How can you live out your role as a disciple maker today?

# שָׁלֶג—*Shahlehg*

## "Snow"

[Benaiah] once went down into a pit and killed a lion on a snowy day.
2 SAMUEL 23:20 CEB

Benaiah? Who is this dude? He wasn't a famous rabbi, king, priest, prophet, or rock-star worship pastor. Benaiah, whose name means "Yahweh has built up," was a regular guy turned warrior. He was ferociously loyal to King David and commanded a Delta Force–like unit of Cherethites and Pelethites. Benaiah supported Solomon's claim to the crown after David, and he killed Adonijah and Shimei. He was one of David's famous thirty mighty men and commanded a division of twenty-four thousand soldiers.

We're introduced to his valiance in 2 Samuel 23, when on a fateful day in Judah, he struck down two Moabite fighters, snatched a spear from the hand of a giant Egyptian, and killed the Egyptian with it. And listen to this: On this snowy day, Benaiah jumped into a pit with a lion, and he was the one who came out alive. What in the world is all that about? Fierce courage comes from fierce loyalty. Even in the worst circumstances ever, you can face your fears head-on. When the devil's assault comes, you can be strong and courageous, trusting that loyalty, bravery, and faithful stick-to-itiveness lead to spiritual growth.

Lord, thank you for turning my faith into strength and courage.

# אֵל רֳאִי—*Ayl Rah-ee*

## "The God Who Sees"

[Hagar] called the name of the LORD who spoke to her,
You-Are-the-God-Who-Sees.
GENESIS 16:13 NKJV

Hagar was an Egyptian slave of Abraham's wife, Sarah. When Sarah could not conceive, she gave Hagar to Abraham to bear a child. Hagar gave birth to a son named Ishmael, and Sarah dealt extremely harshly with her. Hagar fled, but God assured her that he would care for and bless her and Ishmael despite all her hardships. Therefore, she referred to him as the God who sees because he saw her plight and dealt kindly with her.

God comforted and encouraged Hagar when she felt abandoned, marginalized, and deep in a pit of despair. Have you ever felt disregarded or like an outcast? Alone? Forgotten? On the sidelines with nowhere to go? Turn to *Ayl Rah-ee* (El Roi) and trust that he sees you, cares deeply for you, and will never leave or forsake you. He does his most remarkable work when you are genuinely hurting and at the bottom of the pit. Hang your hat on Jesus' last words in Matthew: "I am with you always, even to the end of the age" (28:20).

Father, help me trust that you are with me, see me, care for me, and comfort me in every circumstance.

# מֹשֶׁה—*Mosheh*

## "Moses"

[Moses] had come to regard abuse suffered on behalf of the Messiah as greater riches than the treasures of Egypt, for he kept his eyes fixed on the reward.

HEBREWS 11:26 CJB

"Don't trade what you want most for what you want now." My dad must have told me this five hundred times as I was growing up. I added to it for my kids: "Sacrifice ain't sacrifice if there ain't no sacrifice!"

*Mosheh* (Moshe) made a conscious decision to sacrifice his standing in Pharaoh's palace along with all the pleasures that accompanied it. He didn't give it up for something equal or better. He traded royalty for oppression. Who would do that? How many Christians today would give up pleasure for pain? Would you? Moses, a charter member of the Hebrews 11 Hall of Faith, possessed an uncanny eternal perspective. This perspective is a fruit of faith, as it comes from seeing past the world's temporal values to the rewards in the kingdom of God. For the sake of Christ, we must choose integrity when tempted not to and stand up for what is right even when the world is screaming at us to sit down and be quiet.

Lord, let me align myself with your greater plan, even if it causes me to suffer.

# שְׁמִטָּה—*Sh'meetah*

## "Release"

"At the end of every seven years you shall grant a release (remission, pardon) from debt."
DEUTERONOMY 15:1 AMP

Deuteronomy 15:1 commands a radical form of generosity by pardoning debts every seventh year. By nurturing a spirit of mercy within the community, the poor were freed from the primary cause of poverty—debt—ensuring they did not become permanently shackled in financial bondage. For the lender, it was an act of absolute faith in Yahweh Jireh to provide.

This principle looked prophetically to the cross, where Jesus' sacrificial blood served as the pinnacle of debt release for all time, pardoning us from the wages of sin. He is the perfect model of forgiveness and taught us how to pray in this regard when he said, "Pray then like this: Our Father in heaven,… forgive us our debts, as we also have forgiven our debtors" (Matthew 6:9, 12 ESV). Is there someone you need to release, someone who needs your forgiveness or grace? What can you do to let go of the debilitating need for control? Find a way to strengthen your trust in Yahweh Jireh's provision and consider opening up your hands and heart to others.

Be a reflector of the grace God has poured into your life by finding someone who has wronged you and forgiving them.

# מָוֶת—*Mahveht*

## "Death"

To me, to live is Christ, and to die is gain.
PHILIPPIANS 1:21 NKJV

For the first thirty-five-ish years of my life, I was scared to death of death. Maybe you are too. When the Lord saved me in 2001, that fear vanished immediately. He's still working on most of the jacked-up things in my life, but he took that one away in a nanosecond. Paul wrote,

> To me, to live is Christ, and to die is gain. But if I live on in the flesh, this will mean fruit from my labor; yet what I shall choose I cannot tell. (vv. 21–22)

Paul knew that nothing could surpass walking into the loving arms of his Savior, but he also knew there was still a ton of crucial work to be done for the sake of Christ. He rhetorically asked, "Which one shall I choose?" Praise the Lord, for he chose well.

As a Jesus follower, your chief purpose in life is to boldly yet compassionately proclaim the gospel while there is still breath in your lungs. This is a difficult task if you are not becoming more like Jesus every day. Live with an eternal perspective, for sure, but don't neglect Jesus' present charge to be his witness (Acts 1:8).

What does fruit from your labor look like for you?

# גָּלִיל—*Gahleel*

## "Galilee"

"Follow me, and I will make you fishers of men."
MARK 1:17 EHV

Most of Jesus' disciples were from a region in northern Israel called *Gahleel* (Galil), particularly around the Sea of Galilee, which is, in fact, a sixty-four-square-mile freshwater lake. Walking along the shoreline, he called Simon (Peter) and Andrew and Zebedee's boys, James and John, to follow him and be his disciples.

Jesus didn't call into a life of discipleship men who were sitting around on the couch playing video games. He called hardworking, productive, industrious men—busy men who got things done. Most of them fed and clothed their families as commercial fishermen. This was not a call to go from netting fish to working some dead-end job. Jesus called them with authority, from catching tilapia to fishing for hearts, minds, souls, and eternities. They recognized his authority, and "they left their nets immediately and followed him" (v. 18 NET).

Are you ready to step out of your comfort zone and embrace the uncertainties of a life on mission? Just like those who left everything behind to follow Jesus, every day will be dedicated to fulfilling kingdom objectives—utilizing your gifts, skills, and abilities to lead people to Rabbi Jesus.

What is Jesus calling you to leave behind to follow him?

# אֵשֶׁת חַיִל—*Aysheht Khahyeel*

## "Woman of Valor"

I recall your sincere faith that first lived in your grandmother Lois and in your mother Eunice and now, I am convinced, is in you also.
2 Timothy 1:5 CSB

The *Aysheht Khahyeel* (Eshet Hayil) is a poem based on Proverbs 31:10–31. A Jewish woman's husband and children sing it in the home at the introduction of the Friday evening Sabbath meal. This passage describes a woman of valor—one with noble, excellent, or virtuous character. Verse 30 concludes, "Charm is deceptive and beauty is fleeting, but a woman who fears the Lord will be praised."

Two of the most noble and least discussed women in Scripture are Timothy's grandmother Lois and mother, Eunice. Paul probably led these two to Christ when he visited their hometown of Lystra on his first missionary journey, and subsequently, they won Timothy to the Lord between Paul's first and second journeys. Paul then called Timothy his "brother" (2 Corinthians 1:1), a "dearly loved and faithful child in the Lord" (1 Corinthians 4:17), and his "coworker in the gospel" (1 Thessalonians 3:2). Timothy was an important leader and the pastor at the church in Ephesus because he had a mama and grandmama who loved the Lord and poured Jesus into him.

Be intentional about passing on the faith deposit you've been given.

# לֵךְ אַחֲרָי—*Laykh Ahkharai*

## "Follow Me"

[Jesus] saw a man named Matthew sitting at the tax collector's booth. "Follow me," he told him, and Matthew got up and followed him.
MATTHEW 9:9 NIV

Matthew sat in his tax collector's booth day after day, hoarding money for Rome. He lined his pockets by charging more than Rome levied and inflating assessments. Most Jews considered tax collectors as shameful disgraces to their families and communities, and Matthew was no different.

Because of Matthew's location, he and Jesus would have seen each other often, but this time was different. This time, the Son of God looked into the traitorous tax collector's eyes and said, "Follow me." Matthew had probably long ago let go of any sliver of self-worth. *Why would this rabbi want me, a turncoat, on his team?* But Jesus saw something in Matthew that would benefit the kingdom. Matthew's call into discipleship was not a suggestion or even an invitation. It was a command. Matthew didn't respond with "Let me think, pray, and talk to my trusted advisers about it." He didn't flinch. He just got up and followed. Like Matthew, you are called to follow Jesus despite your past. The question is this: How will you respond?

Jesus, thank you for calling incredibly flawed people like me to be your disciples.

# קֶצֶף—*Kehtzehf*

## "Wrath"

"You don't know what you are asking! Are you able to drink from the bitter cup of suffering I am about to drink?"
MARK 10:38 NLT

James and John said to Jesus, "When you sit on your glorious throne, we want to sit in places of honor next to you, one on your right and the other on your left" (v. 37). Jesus responded, "Be careful what you ask for because you have no idea what's coming" (v. 38, author's paraphrase). In 1861, Charles Spurgeon described it as only he could:

> There was the cup; hell was in it; the Saviour drank it—not a sip and then a pause; not a draught and then a ceasing; but he drained it till there is not a dreg left for any of his people. The great ten-thonged whip of the law was worn out upon his back; there is no lash left with which to smite one for whom Jesus died. The great cannonade of God's justice has exhausted all its ammunition; there is nothing left to be hurled against a child of God.[5]

The magnitude of Jesus' sacrifice and its impact on humanity didn't fully resonate with his followers until Pentecost, when three thousand souls were saved from God's wrath. Has it hit you yet?

Jesus, please don't ever let me forget the enormity of your sacrifice.

---

5 Charles Haddon Spurgeon, "It is Finished!," December 1, 1861, The Spurgeon Center for Biblical Preaching at Midwestern Seminary, transcript, spurgeon.org.

# דָּבַק—*Dahvahk*

## "Cling"

Ruth clung to [Naomi].
RUTH 1:14 LSB

The word *dahvahk* (davak) means "to cling, cleave, hold fast, or stick to someone." Deuteronomy 10:20 says we are to "hold fast" to God (ESV). A man is to leave his parents and "cleave to his wife" (Genesis 2:24 LSB). Ruth's unwavering commitment to her mother-in-law, Naomi, in the book of Ruth exemplifies the beautiful meaning of *dahvahk* as it encompasses devotion, faithfulness, and steadfast love. Ruth held fast to Naomi physically, spiritually, and emotionally. She abandoned her Moabite roots and committed to Naomi's people and Naomi's God, Yahweh. Her decision to stick with Naomi not only changed her life but also impacted all of history since she is David's great-grandmother and is in Jesus' lineage (Matthew 1:5).

In the same way God is faithful to us, we are called to hold fast to those he has providentially placed in our lives. Who in your circle of friends needs steadfast loyalty and care from you? Just as Ruth gave up her old life for a new one, we are invited to abandon the old and faithfully cling to Jesus in love, trust, and devotion. Is there some old that you need to trade in for the best new ever—Jesus?

Lord, help me cling to you with unshakable Ruth-like faith.

# מַפְתֵּחַ—*Mahf'tayakh*

## "Key"

"I will give you the keys of the kingdom of heaven."
MATTHEW 16:19 LSB

Let's pretend the gospel is a Shelby Super Snake sports car with more than 830 horsepower. It has all the power it needs to fulfill its purpose. You can't do anything to increase its performance. Now imagine Jesus says to you, "Here are the keys, my child."

This is Matthew 16:19. The power to deliver freedom and break chains is found in the gospel. Jesus doesn't need us, but he places immeasurable value on us, and he wants me and you to be part of his work. So he tells us, "Here's the gospel. Here are the keys. Where are you going to take it?" We have been given the authority to bring the full power and truth of heaven to a broken, hurting, and sinful world—or we can park the gospel in the garage and just talk about how cool it is. I'm not about to pull the gospel out of the garage to give it a buff and shine, listen to the engine purr, and put it back so it doesn't get dirty. I hope you're with me. As the body of Christ, we need to grab the keys, come screaming out of the driveway, put the pedal down, and see what the gospel of Jesus Christ has under the hood.

What are you gonna do?

# טוּ בְּאָב—*Too b'Ahv*

## "15th of Av"

Above all things have intense and unfailing love for one another, for love covers a multitude of sins.
1 PETER 4:8 AMPC

The historical origin of the Jewish holiday of *Too b'Ahv* (Tu b'Av) is unclear. Yet we know it marked the end of internal division, restoration, and the beginning of a new chapter in Jewish history. Today, *Too b'Ahv* celebrations center around love, reconciliation, and fresh starts, all of which find their ultimate expression in the life, sacrificial death, and resurrection of Jesus.

Peter's letter to first-century persecuted Christians—those who had experienced salvation—encourages the value of loving one another and rallying together above everything. As stewards of God's incredible grace, we are not designed to live isolated in a vacuum. Authentic Christian fellowship results in support during intense distress and nurtures an ethos of forgiveness. Love, as exemplified by the sacrificial love of Jesus, has the power to heal, reconcile, and pave the way for a fresh, new start. It doesn't hide sin. It is the antivenom for sin's toxins. Love enables you to forgive much because you have been forgiven much. Therefore, where authentic Christian fellowship exists, molehills don't become mountains, and molehills are quickly and easily forgiven.

Father, thank you for perfectly modeling in Christ sacrificial love, reconciliation, and new beginnings.

APRIL 14

# עִמָּנוּ אֵל—*Eemahnoo Ayl*

## "Immanuel"

"A virgin will have a baby boy, and he will be called Immanuel," which means "God is with us."
MATTHEW 1:23 CEV

Adam and Eve had a perfect life in the garden—a perfect relationship with each other and a perfect relationship with God. Things were good—in fact, very good—until deception and sin shattered their idyllic paradise and created separation between them and God. This sin issue created a chasm between us and God that rendered us unable to come to him for repairs. But as God often does, he did something radical and came to us. Seven or eight hundred years before it happened, Isaiah prophesied that "the Lord Himself will give you a sign: The virgin will conceive, have a son, and name him Immanuel" (Isaiah 7:14 HCSB). Matthew added a huge explanatory note: *Immanuel* means "God is with us" (Matthew 1:23 CEV).

This is one of the most comforting nuggets in Scripture. Cancer diagnosis. God is with you! Wayward son. God is with you! Lost job. God is with you! Husband ran off. God is with you! Discouraged. God is with you! Experiencing homelessness. God is with you! Debilitating depression and loneliness. God is with you! When you can't, he can.

Jesus, thank you for being with me in the storm.

# יְהוָֹה אֱלֹהִים—*Yahweh Ehloheem*

## "LORD God"

The LORD God formed man of the dust of the ground, and breathed into his nostrils the breath of life; and man became a living soul.

GENESIS 2:7 KJV

As Genesis 2 recounts the intimate creation of man and woman, the divine name *Yahweh Ehloheem* (Yahweh Elohim) is used eleven times. It appears nearly six hundred additional times in the Old Testament. Here and throughout the Old Testament, "LORD God" highlights God's sovereignty, power, and authority. He has the right and the ability to do anything he wills, and his will is perfectly righteous.

The name *Yahweh Ehloheem* finds its fulfillment in the person and work of Jesus Christ, who embodies both God's sovereignty and his authority. The resurrected Jesus prefaced the Great Commission with "All authority in heaven and on earth has been given to me" (Matthew 28:18 EHV). Let this declaration remind us that he is sovereign over every sphere of our lives. Our response must be submission—surrendering our time, resources, decisions, relationships, and challenges to his lordship. Carve out time today to think through areas of your life where you may be fighting Jesus' authority.

Lord Jesus, today I give you all the areas in my life where I've resisted your lordship, and I ask you to direct my steps.

# פֶּסַח—*Pehsahkh*

## "Passover"

The next day he saw Jesus coming toward him, and said, "Behold, the Lamb of God, who takes away the sin of the world!"
JOHN 1:29 ESV

*Pehsahkh* (Pesach) is a holiday that celebrates freedom—particularly the liberation of the Israelite slaves from more than four hundred years of slavery in Egypt around 1500 BC. God encouraged Egypt, through a series of plagues, to free the Israelites. The tenth plague was the pinnacle: the death of every firstborn child. God instructed the Hebrews to slaughter a lamb and wipe the blood around their doorposts. He said, "The blood shall be a sign for you.…And when I see the blood, I will pass over you, and no plague will befall you to destroy you" (Exodus 12:13). God rescued them through the blood of the lamb.

Fifteen hundred years later, John the Baptist announced the inauguration of Jesus' public ministry with "Behold, the Lamb of God, who takes away the sin of the world!" Just as the blood splattered on the doorposts in Egypt rescued the Jews from certain death, Jesus' redeeming blood that was splattered on the cross at Calvary for the remission of sins can deliver you from eternal spiritual death.

Thank you for the blood applied. It washed me white as snow, and I will be forever grateful. I love you, Lord.

# דַּיֵּנוּ—*Dahyaynoo*

## "It Would Have Been Sufficient"

[Jesus] is the complete fullness of deity living in human form. And our own completeness is now found in him. We are completely filled with God as Christ's fullness overflows within us.
COLOSSIANS 2:9–10 TPT

*Dahyaynoo* (Dayeinu) is a traditional hymn sung on Passover that expresses thankfulness to God for his redemptive acts in the exodus story. Its point is that any one of them would have been sufficient for our lifelong gratitude and devotion. The Bible, cover to cover, is an epic tale—a redemptive history—of a holy God reeling wayward humanity back in. A complete list of his redeeming acts would be impossible.

In Colossians 2:9, Paul pointed out that Jesus is both completely God and the full expression of God in a human body. Those who are born again will find completeness in him. In fact, he is more than sufficient. His fullness floods the riverbanks of our lives. If you are in him, you lack nothing. He sufficiently provides for your salvation and sufficiently empowers you to live a God-honoring life. Undoubtedly, you have friends trying to fill the void in their lives with what doesn't work. Encourage them to allow Jesus to fill the emptiness completely. He always will.

How does Colossians 2:9–10 apply to you when you feel inadequate or incomplete?

APRIL 18

# כּוֹס הַגְּאֻלָּה—*Koce Hahg'oolah*

## "Cup of Redemption"

He also took the cup after supper and said, "This cup is the new covenant in my blood, which is poured out for you."
LUKE 22:20 CSB

The theme of redemption permeates Passover and, by default, the Passover Seder. At four different times during the night, a cup of wine is shared based on God's promised redemption in Exodus 6: "I am the LORD, and I will bring you out…and rescue you from slavery.…I will redeem you.…I will take you as my people" (vv. 6–7). The third cup, the cup of redemption, is raised at the end of the meal after the afikomen (a broken piece of matzah [unleavened bread]) is shared.

There had been more than fourteen hundred "third cups" since the exodus, but this one at the Last Supper was different. Was it still the cup of redemption? Yes, 1,000 percent, but it looked toward and represented redemption accomplished because of Jesus' precious blood. It inaugurated a new and different way—this new covenant "will not be like the covenant" God made with the wandering generation (Jeremiah 31:32). It provides permanent redemption from a curse far greater than anything Egypt could ever throw at us—the curse of sin.

Father God, I praise you and thank you for the redemption accomplished in Jesus, my Redeemer.

# סֵדֶר—*Saydehr*

## "Order"

"You shall tell your son on that day, saying, 'It is because of what the LORD did for me when I came out of Egypt.'"
EXODUS 13:8 NASB

The *Saydehr* (Seder) is the traditional meal of remembrance shared in the home on Passover. Only two biblical mandates must be observed: eating matzah (unleavened bread) and telling the story of God's rescue and redemption of Israel from bondage in Egypt. In practice, there is much, much more. It typically includes a fourteen- or fifteen-step order of events. The festivities include four cups of wine, songs, stories, and Passover-specific foods relating to the exodus story arranged on the *Saydehr* plate: A shank bone represents the sacrificial Passover lamb; a boiled egg represents mourning; a green vegetable represents renewal; horseradish represents the bitterness of bondage; and a sweet mixture of nuts, fruit, and wine represents the mixture that the slaves used to make bricks.

On the night of his arrest, Jesus, the ultimate Passover Lamb, celebrated the *Saydehr* with his disciples and instituted the Lord's Supper. He told them that the broken matzah represented his body, which would be sacrificed for them, and that the wine represented his blood, which would be spilled to inaugurate a new covenant (Matthew 26:26–28). His mandate was to do it in remembrance of him (Luke 22:19).

Jesus, please let me always remember the sacrifice you made for me.

# מְצָדָה—*M'tzahdah*

## "Stronghold"

The weapons we use to wage war are not worldly. On the contrary, they have God's power for demolishing strongholds.
2 Corinthians 10:4 cjb

Paul told us our weapons are not machine guns, tanks, and fighter jets. Our fighting gear is "the belt of truth," "breastplate of righteousness," "feet fitted with the readiness that comes from the gospel of peace," "shield of faith," "helmet of salvation," and "sword of the Spirit, which is the word of God" (Ephesians 6:14–17 NIV). The Holy Spirit is the armor-bearer, fully equipping believers for the combat that lies ahead.

In the spiritual battle, the strongholds of evil are false worldviews grounded in the lies the Adversary foists on society. Today's Armageddon is a clash of ideas, philosophies, and truth claims competing for your heart, mind, and devotion. And the bad guys are winning. Shockingly, only 4 percent of Americans hold a biblical worldview despite 66 percent professing to be Christian.[6] How can you defend yourself? Test competing worldviews against biblical truth and be careful not to let cultural trends or hollow philosophies distort your understanding of God's Word. Guard your mind by consistently studying Scripture in community and sitting under gospel-centric, doctrinally orthodox teaching.

Father, protect me from each *m'tzahdah* (masada) of the devil.

---

6 Dr. George Barna, *American Worldview Inventory 2024 (Release #2): Millions of Americans Embrace Common Unbiblical Perspectives, Survey Shows* (Cultural Research Center at Arizona Christian University, 2024), 3, PDF, arizonachristian.edu.

# קְרִיעָה—*K'ree'yah*

## "Tearing"

When the high priest heard this, he tore his clothes in anger.
MARK 14:63 ERV

*K'ree'yah* (keriah) is the name given to the traditional tearing of clothes in extreme anguish over someone's death. The Talmud instructs that it be done at the moment of death. It was also practiced every time a Jew laid eyes on the ruins of the temple. If a Jewish son commits to following Jesus, his parents often express their horror by *k'ree'yah*. Trust me, I've been there. My parents stared into my eyes and declared, "You're dead to us."

When Jesus was arrested, Caiaphas asked him if he was the Messiah. "Jesus said, 'I AM. And you will see the Son of Man seated in the place of power at God's right hand and coming on the clouds of heaven'" (Mark 14:62 NLT). Caiaphas and the entire council went berserk because this "I am" language was an unconditional claim of deity. Immediately, the high priest ripped his clothes in outrage over this brazen claim from the blaspheming hick from Nazareth, and they all agreed he deserved death. Jesus had boldly declared his identity as the Son of God despite knowing what lay ahead. Will you also boldly declare your faith even when it leads to opposition?

Lord, help me stand for truth no matter the cost.

# מַטֵּה מֹשֶׁה—*Mahtay Mosheh*

## "Moses' Staff"

"Take this staff in your hand so you can perform the signs with it."
Exodus 4:17 NIV

In Exodus 4, Moses was stressed out that the Israelites refused to believe God sent him to rescue them. God responded by giving Moses miraculous signs to prove his power. He turned Moses' staff into a snake and back into a staff. He made Moses' hand temporarily diseased and then healed it. Finally, he promised to turn the Nile waters into blood if needed. Moses still felt insecure about his speaking abilities, so God reassured him, saying Aaron, Moses' brother, would speak for him. Then he told him to hold on to the staff since it would be the tool the Lord used to perform signs and wonders.

Don't stress over your weaknesses. Moses was worried about his speaking ability, but God had a plan to help him. The next time you feel like you are not good enough or can't handle something, take a breath and know that God will provide you the skills, tools, or help to get through it. Moses' staff was just a stick, but God turned it into a divine instrument. God often turns each of the little, ordinary things in our lives into something extraordinary.

Lord, help me trust that you always have my back.

# תּוּן נוּרָא—*Toon Noorah*

## "Fiery Furnace"

"If you do not worship, you shall immediately be cast into a burning fiery furnace. And who is the god who will deliver you out of my hands?"
DANIEL 3:15 ESV

In Daniel 3, King Nebuchadnezzar built a huge gold idol and demanded that everyone worship it. Shadrach, Meshach, and Abednego refused, standing firm and trusting Yahweh. Livid at their disobedience, Nebuchadnezzar ordered them to be tossed into the furnace. But as he peered into the fire, the king saw an extra guy in there walking around with them and noted that "the form of the fourth is like the Son of God" (v. 25 NKJV). Shadrach, Meshach, and Abednego exited the fiery furnace completely unscathed—they didn't even smell like smoke. Nebuchadnezzar, shell-shocked, praised Yahweh, "Most High God" (v. 26 ESV), and even proclaimed to his subjects that no other god could save like our God.

Take special note that God didn't remove the three *from* the flames. No, no, no! He walked through the flames *with* them. When you're going through hard times, God doesn't leave you by yourself. He promises to never leave you or forsake you. He's smack in the middle of the fire, walking through it with you. His Word says that you may suffer persecution but will never be forsaken (2 Corinthians 4:9).

God, thank you for your eternal presence.

# נְתַתִּי—*N'tahtee*

## "Given"

"I have given you victory over them!"
JUDGES 7:9 NLT

In Judges, we see Gideon and his 32,000 men camped at the foot of Mount Gilboa. Meanwhile, 135,000 Midianites were just a few miles north and ready to wage war. God promised Israel victory, but he wanted to ensure they knew to whom the win would go. He basically told Gideon, "You have too many men. Send the scaredy-cats home." So 22,000 left. Still too many? Yup! Gideon dismissed 9,700 because of the way they drank water—down to 300. Would you fight with 300 against 135,000? No way! But "that night the LORD said, 'Get up! Go down into the Midianite camp, for I have given you victory over them!'" (v. 9).

The word *given* is in the perfect tense, which indicates a completed or past action. God didn't say, "Will give." The battle was won before it started because God said, "Have given." Just as Gideon and his men fought from a position of victory, you and I as Christ followers fight the battles of life from a position of victory. Because the win is a done deal, you don't have to sweat the small stuff or feel overwhelmed by trials. Despite the challenges, trust that God has already fought the battle for you and won.

How can you live more like the battle has already been won?

# מֹאזְנַיִם—*Moze'nahyeem*

## "Balances"

"When a stranger sojourns with you in your land, you shall not do him wrong."
LEVITICUS 19:33 ESV

As God prepared the Israelites to be his people, he called them to live a holy and just life, and he emphasized love for others, fairness, respect for God's Word, and ethics in everyday life. In their dealings with others, he summed up his thoughts with six simple words: "You shall not do him wrong." As part of this, he commanded that their business transactions be honest: "You shall have just balances, just weights, a just ephah, and a just hin: I am the LORD your God, who brought you out of the land of Egypt" (v. 36). A balance is an old-fashioned scale with a pan hanging on each end of a rod and a fulcrum in between.

Whether you're meeting with someone at work, selling a house, or buying a dresser on Facebook Marketplace, Leviticus 19 should remind you to be honest and fair with people. Don't cheat, cut corners, or take advantage of anyone. If you are a Christian, doing the right thing isn't optional. It is tied to loving and respecting God and his Word. A life of integrity honors both people and the Lord.

Lord, because you saved me, let me always have just balances with everyone.

# חוֹמָה—*Khomah*

## "Wall"

The rich think of their wealth as a strong defense; they imagine it to be a high wall of safety.
PROVERBS 18:11 NLT

The word *khomah* first appears in Exodus when the Israelites walked through the Red Sea on dry ground as "water stood up like a wall on both sides" (Exodus 14:29). The water walls protected the people as they marched between them. When they collapsed, drowning the Egyptians, the walls provided additional safety for God's people. God often erects walls to protect us from the dangers or to guide us to safety.

Although it can be fleshly, it's natural to count on money as security—to trust that it will protect you from the disasters of life. But money is not a guaranteed safeguard against problems. It often builds walls that cause even more significant problems. Without a biblical worldview, riches tend to deceptively lull us into complacency. Like a wall that looks strong but is a facade that collapses, relying on wealth can make you feel secure when you're actually vulnerable. Don't put your trust in something that can disappear in an instant. Your strong tower and tall wall of security is Jesus Christ and him alone. Trust him today.

Do you ever let your bank balance define your sense of security?

# קָרָא—*Kahrah*

## "To Call"

"Everyone who calls on the name of the Lord will be saved."
ACTS 2:21 CSB

God's Word means what it says, and in the first gospel sermon of the church age, Peter said, "Everyone." If he meant "some," he would have said, "Some." If he meant "one out of every three who cry out will be saved," he would have said that.

Across Christendom, believers argue about unconditional election versus libertarian free will, Calvinism versus Arminianism, blah, blah, blah. Granted, we cannot remove election from the pages of Scripture any more than we can remove free will from the garden. Yet the only definitive and dogmatic statement I believe an intellectually honest person can say is this: "If someone dies saved, then they were elect. If someone dies lost, they were not." The entirety of Scripture informs us that regardless of where you've been or what you've done, you can call on God and be saved. It is an exclusive club that is open to everyone without exception. Even in the middle of your junk, you can cry out to him. He stands ready to listen twenty-four hours a day, 365 days a year. You don't have to jump through hoops or be perfect to connect with God. Repent, believe, and ask.

Father God, thank you for being the only true constant in my life.

# עָקֹב—*Ahkove*

## "Deceitful; Crooked"

"The heart is deceitful above all things, and desperately wicked."
JEREMIAH 17:9 NKJV

I don't know about you, but I was raised under the philosophical banner of "People are basically good." I believed this for the first thirty-five years of my life despite two significant things: (1) the contrary evidence in every sphere of creation and (2) the testimony of Scripture. From Genesis 3 onward, the Bible depicts humanity as sinful—not necessarily meaning that every man or woman is a depraved serial killer but that every man and woman has an innate bent toward sin.

Feelings and emotions will often deceive us. Why? How? God declared through Jeremiah that the culprit is the heart. Your heart can trick you into thinking something is right and good when it is wrong and bad. Feeling good feels good, but good feelings don't make something right. Take a minute today to ask God to help you discern his desires for your life even when your feelings and emotions try to jerk you in the opposite direction. Trust that he sees the bigger picture and knows what is best for your heart and life even when it's still hidden from your eyes.

Lord, help me better recognize when my feelings are leading me away from what you have in store for my life.

# רָבָה—*Rahvah*

## "To Multiply"

The church throughout all Judea and Galilee and Samaria had peace and was being built up. And walking in the fear of the Lord and in the comfort of the Holy Spirit, it multiplied.
ACTS 9:31 ESV

The Western church has been in decline for many years despite being hyperfocused on church growth. Hmm—maybe that's the problem. For decades, churches have been obsessed with numbers. To be blunt, their church's numbers. *What's our average attendance? How many did we have for Easter? How many in Sunday school?* But the first Christ followers devoted themselves to four things: sound teaching, community, breaking bread together, and prayer (Acts 2:42). And the church experienced five results: It had peace, was strengthened, lived in awe of what God was doing, fully experienced the Holy Spirit, and multiplied.

It's super easy to get caught up in numbers: How many people are showing up on Sundays, how big is the church getting, or how many events do we have this month? But Jesus didn't call us to fill buildings; he called us to make disciples who make disciples by sharing the good news far beyond the walls of a church building. If you're not already in one, join a local, gospel-centric church that is hyperfocused on kingdom multiplication, not church growth.

God, teach me how to make disciples.

# פֶּה—*Peh*

## "Mouth"

Blessing and cursing come pouring out of the same mouth.
JAMES 3:10 NLT

Regarding the mouth, some of you heard, "If you don't have anything nice to say, don't say anything." My dad was a West Point graduate and a loving but hard man. I heard a thousand times, "Son, you better make sure the noise that's about to come out of the hole in your face is an improvement on the silence you're about to break." Hmm—maybe that's a little harsh. But James wrote that both sweet and sour "come pouring out of the same mouth." He declared the tongue "is sinful and…full of poison" (v. 8 NLV). Jesus said the mouth is the instrument that defiles us (Matthew 15:11), and its origin is our "desperately sick" (Jeremiah 17:9 LSB) and twisted hearts.

Your words will either tear people down or build them up. Your language, tone, and rhetoric paint a transparent image of the depth of your relationship with Christ. Don't praise God one minute and thirty seconds later gossip about the person in the cubicle next to you at work. Every word that comes out of your mouth either moves someone closer to Jesus or further away from him. Strive to be a fountain and not a drain.

Father, help me always speak words of kindness.

# מֶלֶךְ—*Mehlekh*

## "King"

"'Behold, your king is coming to you.'"
MATTHEW 21:5 LEB

Israel's history is full of other nations occupying it. In 722 BC, the Assyrians conquered the north. In 586 BC, the Babylonians ransacked Judah. In 539 BC, Persia took Babylonia and, in 538 BC, freed the Jews. In 332 BC, the Greeks seized Israel. They were independent from 165 BC to 63 BC, when Rome conquered the land. Jesus was born into a country consistently controlled by others but desperate for autonomy. The people fervently anticipated a *mehlekh* (melek) in David's line to kick Rome out and return Israel to its former glory. Shouts of "Hosanna to the Son of David" (v. 9) greeted Jesus when he triumphantly entered Jerusalem.

Even after more than three years of Jesus' teaching, his followers still thought, *Surely he's the one who will restore Israel? Surely he's the messianic warrior-king we've been waiting for? Political freedom and an earthly kingdom are just around the corner.* Right? Wrong! Jesus most assuredly is the King of kings descended from David's line, but his kingdom is not of this world—at least not yet. Throughout the last two millennia, his kingdom has grown every time someone repents and confesses him as their King, Lord, Savior, and Forgiver—one heart at a time.

Tell somebody today that the King wants to see them.

# אַף—*Ahf*

## "Anger"

He said to them, "Is it lawful to do good on the Sabbath, or evil, to save a life or destroy it?"
MARK 3:4 NET

*Ahf* is anger resulting from being genuinely wronged. Did Jesus ever experience or display anger? Of course. Did he ever display unjustified anger? Absolutely not. His anger was always a just response to unrighteousness, hypocrisy, or sin. One Sabbath, for example, Jesus was teaching in a synagogue and in walked a man with a defective hand. Knowing what he was about to do, Jesus looked at the religious leaders and essentially said, "Are y'all okay with this? Should we do good or bad on the Lord's Day?" They wouldn't even respond, but he knew what they were thinking.

> After looking around at them in anger, grieved by the hardness of their hearts, he said to the man, "Stretch out your hand." He stretched it out, and his hand was restored. (v. 5)

Yes, Jesus got angry but never over petty stuff. In this case, it was over cold and compassionless hearts. If you feel angry when you see unfairness or people being hurt, good! But don't get bitter and don't sin (Ephesians 4:26). The key is to let your anger move you toward righteousness.

Lord, help me recognize injustices and act on them with compassion.

# אֵל שַׁדַּי—*Ayl Shahdai*

## "God Almighty"

"I appeared to Abraham, to Isaac, and to Jacob, as God Almighty."
Exodus 6:3 web

In Exodus 4–5, the Lord told Moses that he would deliver Israel from the yoke of slavery in Egypt. Moses conveyed the "Let My People Go" message to Pharaoh, and Pharaoh essentially responded, "Not only no, but you're gonna have to find your own straw to make the bricks, and your brick quota ain't changing!" Israel had been enslaved for more than four hundred years with zero possibility of freedom, and now things were worse. Enter *Ayl Shahdai* (El Shaddai). It's his mighty hand that crushed Pharaoh and delivered Israel.

Years and years later, Jesus encountered a man in bondage to his money. Jesus told the crowd that it's superhard for a rich guy to enter the kingdom, but "the things that are impossible for people are possible for God" (Luke 18:27 ISV). Do you trust *Ayl Shahdai*'s power over your limitations? When you face impossible odds, remember that what's impossible for you is a "snap of the fingers" for God. Be encouraged to put complete trust in his power rather than relying on your abilities. Stop trying to control every nuance of your life and allow God to be God. Surrender to, submit to, and trust in his plan.

Lord, help me let go and trust that you can do what I can't.

# לָבַשׁ—*Lahvahsh*

## "To Clothe"

You were all baptized into Christ, and so you were all clothed with Christ.
GALATIANS 3:26–27 NCV

*Lahvahsh* means to clothe both literally and metaphorically. The author of the book of Judges beautifully used *lahvahsh*: "The Spirit of the LORD clothed Gideon" (Judges 6:34 AMP), empowering him to deliver his people. Deliverance is always in focus when the Holy Spirit "clothes" a person.

In the New Testament, Paul related being clothed to being wrapped in the righteous robe of Christ. He began with baptism language—the symbol of the death of the old you and the birth of the newly dressed you. You've been given the privilege of putting on Jesus. He totally envelops you with his Spirit, rescuing you from your old self. Along with your new clothes, you gain a new Father and a new family, the church. Show the church love, patience, and grace because just like you've been given new life, so have they. As soon as you put your Jesus on, your identity changes. Your new clothes provide you with renewed value that is fully funded by Jesus, not by other people's opinions or your past. Live life with confidence, knowing that you are clothed in his love and righteousness.

Jesus, let me always be aware that I am wearing you everywhere I go.

# אִמָּה—*Eemah*

## "Mother"

"I asked the Lord to give me this boy,
and he has granted my request."
1 Samuel 1:27 NLT

In the depths of the metanarrative of God's Word, Hannah surfaces as an exceptional example of an *eemah*. The Hebrew word *eemah* gently portrays a mother's faith, perseverance, and loving devotion—perfectly capturing the essence of Samuel's mother, Hannah.

Hannah's journey began with paralyzing grief because she was unable to bear children. With every one of the earth's trips around the sun, not only did the heartache grow, but the trash talk from her husband's other wife cut like a knife. But Hannah never gave in to the pain and bitterness; she completely surrendered to God through prayer, trusting in his sovereign plan for her life. Hannah promised that when God gave her a son, she would dedicate that son to serving God all the days of his life. When Samuel was born and weaned, Hannah told God, "I am giving him to the Lord, and he will belong to the Lord his whole life" (v. 28). Hannah's fervent faith, deep prayer life, and devotion are incredible examples of what godly motherhood is. And the Lord honored her, as Samuel went on to become one of Israel's greatest leaders.

Lord, thank you for the influence of godly mamas
and grandmamas.

# עֵד—*Ayd*

## "Witness"

"You will receive power when the Holy Spirit has come upon you; and you shall be My witnesses both in Jerusalem and in all Judea, and Samaria, and as far as the remotest part of the earth."
ACTS 1:8 NASB

The Hebrew word *ayd* primarily refers to a person present at the consummation of a legal transaction who could and would attest to the veracity of the event. As time progressed, the witness began signing a document verifying the transaction, much like a notary does today.

In Acts, Jesus instructed his disciples to be his witnesses by moving outward from their homes in concentric circles to ultimately reach the whole planet. He assured them that the Holy Spirit's presence in their lives would provide the necessary boldness, compassion, and clarity of message to complete the difficult task. An *ayd* testifies to the truth, which is precisely what they did and what we are to do.

Witnessing isn't about having the perfect words, answers, and speeches. It is about sharing what God has done in your life. People can argue theology all day, but they can't argue with your personal story. The world craves authenticity, so be real and leverage your Jesus story for someone else's forever.

Jesus, thank you for changing me and giving me a story to share.

# *Meshuggeneh*

## "Foolish Person; Foolish Behavior"

Claiming to be wise, they instead became utter fools.
ROMANS 1:22 NLT

*Meshuggeneh* is a Yiddish word that can be a noun or a verb referring to a foolish person or foolish behavior. My dad used to laugh and say, "He thinks he's a genius, but trust me, he's just a *meshuggeneh* with a vocabulary. I wouldn't trust him to boil water!"

In Romans 1, Paul wrote about those who deny Yahweh—you know, the ones who struggle to boil water. A thousand years earlier, David wrote, "The fool says in his heart, 'There is no God'" (Psalm 14:1 ESV). But Paul was writing into a polytheistic world with multiple religions and countless gods. Shouldn't he have been tolerant of their belief systems? They had religion. They had faith. They believed in something. Isn't that all that really matters? No! Faith is not itself a virtue. Faith for the sake of faith is nonsense. The object of one's faith matters, and the triune God is the object of our faith. Truth matters, and Jesus is the truth. Many believe that faith in God and intelligence are mutually exclusive, but these people miss the bigger picture—the meaning, purpose, and deeper truths about life that only make sense when we acknowledge the Creator.

Lord, I praise you for being exactly who you say you are.

# פֶּתַח—*Pehtahkh*

## "Door"

"Here I am! I stand at the door and knock. If you hear my voice and open the door, I will come in and eat with you, and you will eat with me."
REVELATION 3:20 NCV

The Hebrew word *pehtahkh* nearly always refers to a physical door, but its first use is metaphorical. God warned Cain that "sin is crouching at the door" (Genesis 4:7). Meanwhile, there's another metaphorical door at the other end of the Bible. In Revelation 3:14–22, Jesus addressed a church that had gotten fat and happy. They'd satisfied themselves with all the pleasures and material wealth the world had to offer and saw no need for Jesus. They filled the voids in their lives with boats, cars, and beach condos. And a person with no clue that they're drowning sees no need for a buoy.

Yet Jesus kept knocking, looking to transform them. He's not going to kick the door down and kidnap you into eternity. He's waiting for you to open the door. God honors our free will, but he's always there knocking, ready to come in and hang out. There's no need to clean up before you let him in; open the door just as you are and watch what he does.

Lord, forgive me for taking so long to open the door.

# מַה טֹבוּ—*Mah Tovoo*

## "How Good; How Lovely"

"How lovely are your tents, O Jacob! Your dwellings, O Israel!"
NUMBERS 24:5 NKJV

*Mah Tovoo* (Mah Tovu) is a prayer said as a Jew enters a synagogue in preparation for worship. The words in the first line are from Balaam, the pagan prophet, when he was sent to curse Israel (Numbers 24:5). Instead, he was overwhelmed with awe at the Lord. The rest of the *Mah Tovoo* is from the Psalms. In my family, it went something like this:

> How good and lovely are your tents, O Jacob, your dwelling places, O Israel! Only through your abundant grace, I enter your house to worship with awe in your sacred place. O LORD, I love the house where you dwell and the place where your glory resides. I shall prostrate myself, bow, and kneel before the LORD, my Creator. To you, Eternal One, goes my prayer: Let this be a time of your favor. In your abounding love, O God, answer me with the truth of your salvation.

Jesus called the temple and, by extension, churches, "my house," "a house of prayer" (Matthew 21:13 ESV), and "my Father's house" (Luke 2:49). Do you recognize your place of worship as holy ground? Do you approach worship with a sense of awe for the one you're worshiping?

Thank you, Lord, for the privilege of worshiping you.

# אוֹר—*Ore*

## "Light"

The light shines in the darkness.
John 1:5 ESV

Before God created the heavens and the earth, there was darkness. In creation, the first words out of God's mouth were "Let there be light" (Genesis 1:3). The light exploded onto the scene, piercing the darkness. The light marked the beginning of the beauty of God's creative activity. The God of heaven would speak again, and order and life would quickly appear. Many years later, "when the fullness of time had come" (Galatians 4:4), "the Word became flesh" (John 1:14). The Light of life dwelled among us. "The light shines in the darkness, and the darkness has not overcome it" (v. 5). Jesus exploded onto the scene, piercing the darkness of a broken world.

In the same way God's light brought life to creation in the beginning, Jesus' light brings the hope of eternal life to humankind. This light is not simply an ingredient in the cosmic formula of creation; it is the magnificent shekinah (divine presence), illuminating everything. If you are in a season of darkness or pain, the Lord wants you to know that he is the one who spoke light into existence from nothing and the one who shines brightest in your life today.

How can you trust God to lead you from darkness into his glorious light?

# עָנָה—*Ahnah*

## "To Respond"

"Come to me all you who are weary and burdened, and I will give you rest."
MATTHEW 11:28 EHV

Throughout the Old Testament, God reveals himself as a God who responds when his people cry out. He did not create everything and then head out on a vacation. He is a God who hears, responds, and answers us when we call on his name. Not only does God faithfully respond to us, but he also bids us to respond to him.

In Matthew 11, Jesus invited people who were drowning in the rules and regulations of first-century Judaism to come to him for rest. This invitation extends across time to those drowning in the legalism of twenty-first-century religiosity. Do you feel tired, weary, and flat worn-out? Are you struggling to shoulder the weight of life's challenges on your own? You may have stress at work, relational junk, or battles with addiction, but don't buy the lie that you simply need to be stronger. Jesus tells us that we don't have to. He invites you and me to bring it all to him. When the baggage is too much to bear, stop, take a breath, and surrender it to Jesus. He has big shoulders. Let him carry the load for you.

Jesus, thank you for bearing all my burdens.

# אָהוּב—*Ah'hoov*

## "Beloved"

"Among many nations there was no king like [Solomon], who was beloved of his God; and God made him king over all Israel. Nevertheless pagan women caused even him to sin."
NEHEMIAH 13:26 NKJV

The beginning of 2 Chronicles sets the stage for King Solomon's rule by saying, "God was with him and made him exceedingly great" (1:1 LEB). Solomon was beloved by God; crowned as king by God; blessed by God; and given wisdom, knowledge, riches, and influence by God. However, Solomon, like all of us, had a broken, sinful, and fallen nature. Even with God's love and blessings, he was not somehow divinely immune to sin. In total defiance and disobedience to the Lord, Solomon took hundreds of pagan wives. His story reminds us that we are all vulnerable to deception and struggle with our corrupt nature regardless of the incredible favor, grace, mercy, and blessings God pours into our lives.

Your walk requires vigilance, so stand firm in humility and obedience to God's Word. It is crucial to ensure that your relationships support and strengthen your faith, values, and connection with the Lord. Resist compromising biblical principles, even in the small stuff, as it will inevitably wreck God's purpose for your life.

Lord, let me resist temptation and live like your beloved child.

# בֹּקֶר—*Bokehr*

## "Morning"

Tears may flow in the night, but joy comes in the morning.
Psalm 30:5 GNT

All of us have had them—sleepless nights that seem to last for an eternity. The nights when everything seems devastatingly heavy. Nights when you lie down and stare at the ceiling while feeling like the entire weight of the world is pressing down and crushing your chest. The good news is that the feelings fade. They will not last forever. Psalm 30:5 says, "Tears may flow in the night, but joy comes in the morning." This is a truth God's Word says that you can hang your hat on. Undeniably, there are nights when tears flow uncontrollably, fear is consuming, and frustration is nearly paralyzing. But God promises that joy rises with the sun. It is as if he is saying, *[Your name], I know your pain is real, but hold on just a sec. I have something better coming.*

*Bokehr* is a symbol of hope. No matter how long your night seems, the joy-filled sunrise is imminent. So if you're mired in a season of darkness, hang tough. The Lord loves you, sees you, and knows exactly what you need. Cling to his promises because his joy is on the way.

Father, I praise you that you are the God of new beginnings.

# יָד—*Yahd*

## "Hand"

All the heads, and the mighty men, and also all the sons of king David have given a hand under Solomon the king.
1 Chronicles 29:24 YLT

First Chronicles 29 captures the coronation of Solomon as the king of Israel. "He prospered, and all Israel obeyed him" (v. 23 ESV). Solomon gathered all the leaders, mighty men, tribal heads, and his brothers, and they unanimously gave "a hand under Solomon the king" (v. 24 YLT). "Placing one's hands underneath a man" is an ancient Jewish idiom that signifies submission to that person's leadership and authority. God is the one who installs and deposes leaders. Paul wrote, "There is no authority except from God, and those that exist have been instituted by God" (Romans 13:1 ESV).

Just as Israel's leaders pledged their loyalty to Solomon, we are called to submit our lives to God's leadership. We are drawn every day to pursue our own agenda because we are pridefully convinced we know better, but true freedom and growth happen when we surrender to God's authority. Give your *yahd* under the Lord and trust that he is a benevolent king who only wants the best for you. Follow him wherever he leads you, even when the road is rocky.

How are you supporting the spiritual leaders in your life?

# לַג בָּעֹמֶר—*Lahg bah-Omehr*

## "Thirty-Three of the Omer"

After that, he was seen by more than 500 of his followers at one time, most of whom are still alive, though some have died.
1 CORINTHIANS 15:6 NLT

An *omehr* (omer) is a biblical unit of measure, particularly used for barley. The festival of *Lahg bah-Omehr* (Lag b'Omer) falls during the period of counting *Omehr*, which is between Passover and Pentecost. The counting of *Omehr* symbolizes the trek from slavery to freedom. *Lahg bah-Omehr*, celebrated on the thirty-third day of the counting, is not a biblical holiday. Rather, it commemorates the death of second-century Rabbi Shimon bar Yochai, the author of the Jewish mystical text the Zohar.

It was during the counting of the *omehr* that Jesus appeared to Peter, to the rest of the disciples, and then to more than five hundred of his followers. In 1 Corinthians 15, Paul made a point to state that Jesus also appeared to him and James (the Lord's brother), leading to both their salvations (vv. 7–8). Many deniers have nonsensically argued that the five hundred people who saw the resurrected Christ suffered a mass hallucination. Paul addressed this very issue in his letter to the folks in Corinth. He pointed out that most of the five hundred witnesses were alive and available for interviews. Is the resurrection real to you? Are you sold on the fact that a dead man walked out of a grave alive?

Lord, thank you for conquering the grave.

# אֱלָהָא עִלָּיָא—*Ehlahah Ee-lah'yah*

## "Most High God"

Nebuchadnezzar went near the opening of the furnace of flaming fire and said, "Shadrach, Meshach, and Abednego, servants of the Most High God, come out!"
DANIEL 3:26 CEB

On March 8, you learned God's name as Elohim. In other ancient Middle Eastern cultures, there was no equivalent word for *Elohim*. Therefore, a reasonable way for people to describe the Hebrews' God was in comparison to their false gods. Meet *Ehlahah Ee-lah'yah*, the Most High God.

In Daniel 3, King Nebuchadnezzar of Babylon had Shadrach, Meshach, and Abednego thrown into a roaring fire because they would not worship his god. God protected them through the flames and delivered them completely unharmed. Nebuchadnezzar acknowledged that only the one true God, the Most High God, could have rescued the three young men. He even blessed God and decreed that anybody who "speaks anything against the God of [these three] shall be torn limb from limb,…for there is no other god who is able to rescue in this way" (v. 29 ESV). The actions of these three men caused a pagan king to acknowledge God's greatness. Your life can be a powerful testimony to those around you, leading them to recognize the Most High God. Is it?

How can your response to life's challenges reveal God's Most High nature to your friends who don't believe?

# מִצְוָה—*Meetz'vah*

## "Commandment"

Faith is dead without good works.
James 2:26 NLT

Moses wrote, "Obey the commands of the Lord your God by walking in his ways and fearing him" (Deuteronomy 8:6). Although *meetz'vah* (mitzvah) literally translates to "commandment," it also means "good deed." God gave Moses 248 dos and 365 don'ts, totaling 613 *meetz'vote* (mitzvot, plural), that are recorded in the Torah as the basis of Israel's covenant with God. The people agreed to the terms. Pragmatically, we perform a good deed when we observe one of the 248 dos or refrain from one of the 365 don'ts.

Our whys matter! For Christ followers, obedience, kindness, and good works do not revolve around checking the boxes on a list of 613 laws. Instead, they are expressions of our love and devotion to the Lawgiver. When you perform good deeds, your faith becomes tangible, a reflection of the hands and feet of Christ. Jesus' brother James asked, "What good is it, my brothers, if someone says he has faith but does not have works? Can that faith save him?" (James 2:14 ESV). Are you crossing things off a to-do list, or are your actions an indication of the transforming power of the Holy Spirit living inside you?

Father, help me live out my faith through sacrificial acts that display your love and glorify your name.

# הִשְׁלַכְתָּ—*Heesh'lakh'tah*

## "You Have Cast"

It was for my peace that I had intense bitterness; but You have loved back my life from the pit of corruption and nothingness, for You have cast all my sins behind Your back.
Isaiah 38:17 AMPC

Different forms of the Hebrew verb *sh'lakh* appear 125 times in the Bible and mean "throw," "fling," or "cast." Moses *cast* a tree into the water (Exodus 15:25); on the day of the Lord, humankind will *cast away* idols (Isaiah 2:20); and the rebellious Israelites "*cast* [God's] law behind their backs" (Nehemiah 9:26 NKJV, emphasis added).

These are noteworthy uses of the word, but the deepest, most impactful of all is in Isaiah 38. The words in Isaiah 38:10–20 are from Hezekiah after the Lord healed him. He said, "You have cast all my sins behind Your back" (v. 17 AMPC), which means God has provided complete and total removal of sin's guilt—the sin is thrown away, never to be heard from again. The Lord does the same with your sin when you turn to him. Once God forgives you, it is permanent. He's not holding on to your past mistakes, nor will he ever drag them back up. You can finally stop beating yourself up over your past failures. If God has moved on, you should too.

Lord, thank you for never reminding me of my past.

# שָׁרֵת—*Shahreht*

## "To Serve"

Joseph pleased Potiphar and found favor in his sight and he served him.
GENESIS 39:4 AMP

The words *shahreht* and *ahvahd* are translated as "to serve" or "to minister to" in English. However, *shahreht* conveys the feeling of being privileged to serve rather than the feeling of enslavement that is associated with *ahvahd*. *Shahreht* is a higher level of service that includes trust, much like the role of a personal assistant today.

I once had a boss who told me, "If you want everything God has in store for your life, help enough other people get what he has in store for them." Joseph's life is a testament to this truth. Joseph didn't move up the ranks by chance; he was promoted through God's sovereign hand, hard work, a servant's heart, and honesty. In the face of difficulty, maintaining a heart of service, having a positive attitude, and acting with integrity will set you apart. God will honor—and people will notice—trustworthiness and reliability. Very often, these are the qualities that lead to opportunities and open doors you never expected. When you feel like life makes no sense, remember that every season has a purpose and that God will use them for his kingdom, his glory, and your good.

How can you build a reputation of integrity in your life?

# עֹבֵד—*Ohvayd*

## "Work"

The one who works his land will have plenty of food, but whoever chases fantasies lacks sense.
PROVERBS 12:11 CSB

A mentor once told me, "Proverbs is a how-to manual for teenage boys," and Proverbs 12:11 is a perfect example. Chapter 28 records almost the exact same advice: "The one who works his land will have plenty of food, but whoever chases fantasies will have his fill of poverty" (v. 19). Proverbs consistently portrays hard work as a characteristic of the wise while laziness and lack of focus are portrayed as the folly of the fool. Proverbs 12:11 identifies the character of people who don't work hard, and Proverbs 28:19 tells us what happens when we don't work hard. Fools end up starving.

These two proverbs remind us that if we work hard at something legit and important, like taking care of our families, the odds that we will have what we need dramatically increase. But wait. The flip side is also true. If we spend our time chasing magic bullets, fantasies, or get-rich-quick schemes, we'll likely end up with *bupkis* (Yiddish for "nothing"). Focus on investing your brain space and effort in things with high returns rather than wasting time by chasing squirrels.

Lord God, help me be a judicious steward of my time and resources.

# יוֹם—*Yome*

## "Day"

On the day of judgment many will call me their Lord.
MATTHEW 7:22 CEV

The Hebrew word *yome* (yom) has several different meanings: daylight versus darkness (Genesis 1:5), a twenty-four-hour period (Exodus 20:11), a period of unspecified rest (Genesis 2:3), or a point in time (Genesis 2:17). It is this last meaning that Jesus spoke about in one of the most frightening passages in the Bible—the description of the day of judgment in Matthew 7:21–23. Jesus warned that a day is coming when people will profess to be Christian.

> They will say, "We preached in your name, and in your name we forced out demons and worked many miracles." But I will tell them, "I will have nothing to do with you! Get out of my sight, you evil people!" (vv. 22–23)

Jesus exposed religious people with religious language who were doing religious things for religious reasons. He basically responded, "This is not about religion. It is about a relationship, and we don't have one. Get out of my face!"

Are you feeding the homeless, serving in the student ministry, or preaching the gospel because you are deeply entrenched in a saving relationship with the King of kings? Or are those things just a means to a cool social media post?

If you were on trial for being a Christian, what evidence would exist for a conviction?

# לָלֶכֶת—*Lahlehkheht*

## "To Go"

Go and preach the good news to everyone in the world.
MARK 16:15 CEV

In our fallen nature, we tend to complicate the simple.

Ed: Please grab me a cup of coffee on your way to church.

Susan: Cold brew or hot? Latte, macchiato, cappuccino, americano, or coffee? Dark, medium, or blonde? Tall, grande, or venti? Soy, oat, whole, or low-fat milk? Heavy cream? Sugar-free vanilla, hazelnut, or pecan syrup? How many pumps? Splenda, stevia, or sugar? How much?

Ed: I'll just have a bottle of water.

The gospel according to Mark, targeted at a fast-paced Roman audience, is like sixteen chapters of bullet points. Bam, bam, bam. Compared to the Jewishness of Matthew, the eloquence of Luke, and the richness of John, Mark is the no-frills Jesus story. Mark concluded his book with one straightforward charge to the reader: Go! Where? Anywhere! Whether to the folks next door or to China, just go somewhere. What do you need to take with you? All you need is the simple gospel message—the death, burial, and resurrection of Jesus of Nazareth. No PhD needed, only your Jesus story. Don't complicate something that's not complicated. While you may not vocationally be an evangelist, you have a simple story that people need to hear. Go!

Father, thank you for the simple message of Jesus.

# מָרַת—*Mahraht*

## "Bitterness"

The heart knows its own bitterness,
and no stranger can share its joy.
Proverbs 14:10 cjb

Proverbs 14 presents us with the sometimes-painful truth that feelings are internal and personal, residing in the heart of an individual, and cannot be fully communicated or shared with another person. The human heart is a funny thing, often harming or even destroying itself entirely in denial of logic. Seventeenth-century mathematician and theologian Blaise Pascal is credited with saying, "The heart has its reasons that reason does not know."

Arguably, bitterness is the worst of all human emotions because it is the birthplace of vengeance, hate, and murder. Knowing its cancerous nature, the author of Hebrews wrote, "Make sure that no root of bitterness grows up that might cause trouble and pollute many people" (Hebrews 12:15 CEB). Bitterness is a stealthy emotion, usually sneaking in through the back door unnoticed. When we're hurt, it's easy to cling to a grudge, but before we know it, the grudge has morphed into deep-seated bitterness. Make it a habit to consistently look in the mirror and ask, "Am I holding fast to any bitterness toward someone?" If your reflection answers yes, make sure to deal with it before it ravages you and pollutes the people around you.

Lord, today I choose to exchange my anger and resentment for your peace.

# נָסַע—*Nahsah*

## "Journey"

They journeyed, every one according to their families, according to their fathers' houses.
NUMBERS 2:34 DARBY

The Hebrew name for the book of Numbers is *B'meedbahr* (Bamidbar), which means "in the wilderness" and is a much more appropriate title. The book describes God's people journeying from Mount Sinai to the promised land. It's no surprise, then, that some form of the word *nahsah* (nasa) is used in the book of Numbers over ninety times and is variously translated "journey," "depart," or "to set out."

All of us are born on a journey searching for meaning, purpose, and truth. For some, this journey leads to destinations filled with disappointment and pain rather than the promised land that God intends. The Lord has a destination in mind for you, and it's a life found exclusively in Jesus—a life full of peace, purpose, meaning, truth, and joy. But you need to ditch your past, just as the Israelites had to leave Egypt behind. They couldn't look back. Destination Jesus means letting go of your Egypt—bitterness, fear, unforgiveness, or your past. The promised land is not some fairyland; in Jesus, you can experience it today. It's time to drop the baggage and set out in the freedom and new life God has in store for you.

Lord, let me remain focused on you as I journey through life.

# מָאַס—*Mah'ahs*

## "Reject"

The Lord told [Samuel], "Listen to the people and everything they say to you. They have not rejected you; they have rejected me as their king."
1 Samuel 8:7 csb

"We want to be like everybody else. We want a king. We want a king." Israel's incessant whining must have gotten all over God's last nerve. They failed to realize that they were turning their backs on the very king who had been leading them for nearly a thousand years—Yahweh himself.

Before you throw darts, remember that this is exactly how we sometimes treat God. We can get so hyperfocused on coveting what our neighbors have or chasing what looks good in the world's eyes that we forget God has already rolled out the very best plan for us. Israel believed a human king would magically solve all their problems, but they missed the forest for the trees—they were already being showered with God's perfect leadership. In our own lives, we often do the same thing by being deceived by the world's promises of success, status, or security, and in that pursuit, we unknowingly throw God's guidance to the curb. Yet he is the only true king and always leads us to what's best.

Father, help me trust in your perfect rule rather than always looking to other things.

# חָשַׁב—*Khahshahvah*

## "Planned; Meant; Devised"

"You planned evil against me; God planned it for good."
GENESIS 50:20 CSB

If any Old Testament saint ever had cause for an unforgiving spirit, it would be Joseph. Despite being betrayed by his own brothers and sold into slavery, Joseph ultimately rose to a position of power in Egypt. When he encountered his brothers years later, he chose to forgive them, demonstrating remarkable faith, trust, and love. Before the time of Jesus, Joseph was an inspiring example of Christlikeness. He left justice entirely in God's hands, trusting the Lord to manage righting the wrongs of his brothers. While he acknowledged his brothers' wickedness ("You planned evil against me"), he fervently trusted that God's sovereign hand would prevail ("God planned it for good"). To cap it off, Joseph responded to their evil with forgiveness and affection: "Do not fear; I will provide for you and your little ones" (v. 21 ESV).

When you are knocked down, beaten up, and stranded in the throes of hopelessness, know that you can place your life in the hands of the greatest, most powerful, and most "situation-flipping" God ever. He will spin all the junk around to mold and strengthen you—all for his glorious kingdom.

Whom do you need to forgive like Joseph forgave his brothers?

# אִשָּׁה—*Eeshah*

## "Woman"

"I will make him a helper suitable for him."
GENESIS 2:18 MEV

God created light good; the waters good; vegetation good; fish, birds, animals good. The capstone of God's creation came on day six when he breathed life into man. When God saw the totality of his creation, the Bible declares that "it was very good" (Genesis 1:31). In a ninety-second read from Genesis 1:31, though, we find something that is not good: "It is not good that the man should be alone" (2:18). Adam was busy exercising the dominion he was given over creation and thinking of names like *lion*, *tiger*, *shark*, and *flea*. But being alone stinks. We know it, the Bible confirms it, and God acts to handle it. He put Adam to sleep, took a rib, and made it into an *eeshah* (ishah) (vv. 21–22).

When God created Eve for Adam, she was not just a random companion. Eve was crafted as the perfect partner to complement Adam in every way. Sometimes we freak out about finding the right person—whether we're looking for a spouse, friend, or mentor in that season of life—but Genesis 2 reminds us that God already knows what and who is best for us. Trust that he will cross your path with the right person at the perfect time.

Lord, thank you for knowing exactly who is best for me.

# שַׁח—*Shahkh*

## "To Be Humbled"

The proud look of man will be degraded and the arrogance of men will be humbled, and the LORD alone will be exalted in that day.
ISAIAH 2:11 AMP

The Assyrian and Babylonian exiles fulfilled several of the predictions in Isaiah 2, but the passage primarily looks forward to the coming day of the Lord, when the whole world will be judged. It's a stark reminder that pride and arrogance have no place in front of a holy God.

It's too easy to get wrapped around the axle of self-importance, as if our achievements or successes are worthy of a throne. We have an unquestionable tendency to push "me" into the spotlight, to run after fame, and to long for recognition. However, all human pride will be humbled before God. Despite the mountains you believe you've scaled, God is higher still, and your "glory" is a flicker next to his million-watt bulb. Keep your ego in check, remembering that he is the source of everything.

Twenty-eight hundred years ago, Isaiah wrote, "The LORD alone will be exalted." Rather than living for pats on the back, impressing others, and making your name known, focus on bringing God glory and making his name known through the testimony of your life.

What can I do today to exalt Jesus?

# זְרֹעוֹתֶיהָ—*Z'roh-ohteh*

## "Arms"

She wraps herself in strength, carries herself with confidence, and works hard, strengthening her arms for the task at hand.
PROVERBS 31:17 VOICE

The last section of Proverbs is a portrait of wifely excellence. She is trustworthy, loyal, creative, business savvy, charitable, funny, and blessed. Stir all that up, and you get a life of strength and purpose. The Proverbs 31 woman is a physical, spiritual, and emotional powerhouse. She is ready to wrestle with whatever comes her way with muscle and gusto. You are also called to be strong in every part of your life—not just physically but also in your faith walk.

Strength isn't about being perfect or having it all together. Authentic strength emanates from surrendering to and relying on Jesus' strength. We all face challenges and get tired. Sometimes life is downright overwhelming. However, like the Proverbs 31 woman, you can prepare yourself by acknowledging that you can only thrive by depending on God's strength. He provides perfectly what you need to push through even when you feel weak. So be a person who wraps yourself in strength today. Hit the floor and ask God to give you the strength you need to face a tough day, to be patient with loved ones, or to trust him more.

Lord, make my arms strong for whatever's next.

# אָח—*Ahkhee*

## "Brother"

It is good not to eat meat or drink wine or do anything that causes your brother to stumble.
ROMANS 14:21 ESV

The Hebrew word *ahkhee* primarily refers to a male sibling. However, it also referred to a fellow Israelite or comrade. In our culture, we would say, "I love you, bro." The apostle Paul had this use in mind when he penned his letters. In 1 Corinthians 8, he essentially told the church at Corinth, "Eat whatever meat you want (temple sacrificed or not). Drink what you want. You're free. But keep in mind that it's not always beneficial to flaunt the freedom." He encouraged the Romans not to do anything that would trip up a brother.

The principle is to love your brother enough to willfully suppress your freedom. Always be mindful of how your actions can affect or influence others. If your friend is a recovering alcoholic, care enough about them not to serve wine when they visit for dinner. Are you free to have a glass of wine? Of course, but do you love your friend more than your freedom to have a chardonnay? Don't ever be the cause of a brother or sister falling or failing. Ask yourself, *Did dinner with me reel them in or push them away from the Lord?*

Father, help me always choose love over personal freedom.

## MAY 31

# יַיִן—*Yahyeen*

### "Wine"

In Cana of Galilee Jesus did his first miracle. There he showed his glory, and his followers believed in him.
John 2:11 NCV

Jesus performed thirty-six miracles in the Bible—seven in John's gospel. Why miracles? Why heal the blind man or the official's ailing son? Why raise Lazarus? Was it simply to restore the man's sight, cure the boy, and extend Lazarus' life? Was it solely because of compassion for human suffering? No, it was not!

Of course, Jesus had enormous compassion for those in pain, but his signs and miracles contained layers of purpose, the most vital being "that you may believe that Jesus is the Christ, the Son of God" (John 20:31). His first miracle was turning water into wine at a wedding celebration in Cana. It had nothing to do with human suffering. Was he merely keeping the celebration from running aground? By no means. It was a sign intended to point people to the truth of his divinity so they would recognize his glory and subsequently place saving belief in him. It worked because immediately "his followers believed in him" (2:11).

When God does something mind-blowing in your life, make it a memorial stone of his awesome power and goodness. Let those precious moments boost the fervency of your trust in him.

Jot down a list of times when God miraculously intervened in your life.

# חֻפָּה—*Khoopah*

## "Canopy"

Husbands, love your wives, just as Christ loved the church and gave himself up for her.
EPHESIANS 5:25 NIV

The *khoopah* (chuppah) is the traditional canopy the bride and groom stand under during a Jewish wedding ceremony. Typically, the *khoopah* is ornately decorated, and a tallit (prayer shawl) is often simply hung on its four corners. In Isaiah 4, the Lord paints a future image of Mount Zion, when his protective presence will envelop it and "over everything the glory will be a canopy [*khoopah*]" (v. 5). The *khoopah* represents both the groom's protection of the bride and the Lord's protection of the couple.

Of the several Greek words for "love" at Paul's disposal, he chose *agapaō* to express Christ's covenantal, protective, sacrificial love toward his church. Husbands are to model that same love for their wives. *Agapaō* is not only an "I'll jump in front of the train for you" love, but a husband demonstrates it by willingly and joyfully denying himself for the benefit of his wife. This means putting her needs and well-being far ahead of his—loving her unconditionally and regardless of circumstances.

Lord, teach husbands to be a *khoopah*—to love and protect their wives with the selfless, sacrificial love of Jesus. Inspire wives to respect their husbands so that every marriage glorifies you.

# עָנָן—*Ahnahn*

## "Cloud"

The LORD went ahead of them in a pillar of cloud to lead them on their way during the day.
EXODUS 13:21 HCSB

Enough! It was time for God's people to be freed from bondage in Egypt and move into the promised land—the land of milk and honey. They needed to know that they were loved, they would be his people, he would be their God, and they must follow him.

The Judean wilderness was the perfect classroom for God to teach the children of Israel how to trust and follow him. A single-day supply of manna fell from heaven each day. If they tried to hoard it, it spoiled overnight. *Trust me*, God was saying. *I will sustain you*. Then he inspired them to trust his guidance. "The pillar of cloud by day and the pillar of fire by night never left its place in front of the people" (v. 22). They didn't need to figure out the way. They just had to follow God's lead. He knows the way, even when you don't. When you feel lost or unsure about your next step, trust in God's leadership. He sees the whole journey when you can only see one step at a time.

Lord, when I feel like I'm wandering aimlessly, help me simply follow you.

# אֵל עוֹלָם—*Ayl Olahm*

## "Everlasting God"

I am Alpha and Omega, the beginning and the end, the first and the last.
REVELATION 22:13 KJV

In Genesis 21, Abraham made an everlasting covenant with Abimelech to possess a place called Beersheba. Abraham's mind was flooded with memories of God's unwavering, promise-keeping faithfulness—promises for land, descendants, a great name, and, most importantly, blessings to the world through him. The Lord said his promises would be "an everlasting covenant, to be God to you [Abraham] and to your offspring after you" (Genesis 17:7 ESV). It was at Beersheba that Abraham called the Lord "the Everlasting God" (21:33).

In Revelation 22:13, Jesus said, "I am the Alpha and the Omega, the first and the last, the beginning and the end." He is all that is, ever was, or ever will be. He is *Ayl Olahm* (El Olam), the everlasting cornerstone of your life. Let this truth remind you to anchor your faith in him alone. Despite your circumstances, you can trust his sovereignty and authority over everything from creation to Jesus' second coming. Live with assurance in his care and control over your life. You can confidently dump all your worries and anxiety on him and trust his perfect game plan.

Lord, let me live all my days with purpose, knowing that my life is part of your greater, eternal story.

# חִנָּם—*Heenahm*

## "For Nothing"

"Under no circumstances will I offer up to the Lord, my God, burnt offerings that cost me nothing."
2 Samuel 24:24 NCB

We often deceive ourselves by labeling things we give or do as "sacrificial" when they cost us nothing—when we don't have to give up something we care about to provide the gift or service. Araunah offered to provide oxen and wood for David's sacrifice. David responded, "I insist on paying you for this. Under no circumstances will I offer up to the Lord, my God, burnt offerings that cost me nothing" (v. 24). This would be a complete denial of what it means to sacrifice.

Your giving—whether money, time, or resources—should be from a joyful heart of gratitude and trust. The poor widow in Mark 12:41–44 sacrificed "everything she possessed" (v. 44) in absolute surrender, trusting God to provide what she needed. How can you give in a way that stretches your faith and forces you to rely completely on God's provision? Look out because he might lead you to bump up your giving to your local church—from nothing to 5 percent, from 5 percent to 10 percent, or even from 10 percent to 25 percent. Trust him, test him, and watch what he does.

Father, help me embrace a lifestyle of sacrifice.

JUNE 5

# נְאֻם—*N'oom*

## "Utterance; Declaration"

"Behold, I am against the prophets, declares the LORD, who use their tongues and declare, 'declares the LORD.'"
JEREMIAH 23:31 ESV

Over 98 percent of the nearly four hundred times *n'oom* is used in the Old Testament, it is used in a prophetic context. A prophet is one who speaks for God, so in prophecy after prophecy, we read, "Declares the LORD." Conversely, one who claims that God said something when he didn't say it is a liar, a false prophet, and condemned by God. In fact, God speaks a little sarcastically about them through the prophet Ezekiel: "They claim, 'This is the LORD's declaration,' when the LORD did not send them, yet they wait for the fulfillment of their message" (Ezekiel 13:6 HCSB).

False prophets existed three thousand years ago and are still present with us in the twenty-first century. Therefore, everything tagged "Christian" is not necessarily Christian. Take notice and be discerning when someone claims, "God spoke to me and said…" because sometimes people say things they think are from God but are not. Be sure to always measure what you hear against the Word of God. Have a vibrant relationship with Jesus, a strong prayer life, and a good understanding of his Word.

Lord Jesus, open my heart and mind to understand your Word exactly as you want it to be understood.

# יִשְׂבָּע—*Yees'bah*

## "Satisfied; Content"

"Wealth is treacherous, and the arrogant are never at rest. They open their mouths as wide as the grave, and like death, they are never satisfied."
HABAKKUK 2:5 NLT

Habakkuk 2:2–20 reveals God's response to the prophet's second complaint (1:12–2:1), in which Habakkuk questioned how God could use a wicked, prideful, arrogant, and greedy nation—the Babylonians—to judge his chosen people. But it also contains an incredible, timeless truth for us: An insatiable appetite for riches never delivers on its promise of peace. It continuously and treacherously deceives, leading you to believe you are secure when you aren't. You should build your life on the firm foundation of the gospel rather than the roller-coaster ride of material wealth.

Greed always leaves you empty and wanting more. It is cancerous, relentless, and unceasing. No matter how much you amass, it will never be sufficient. Habakkuk reckons it to the ravenous hunger of the grave; it ceaselessly claims lives, is "never satisfied," is never content, and always longs for more bodies to consume. True and lasting contentment grows out of gratitude and satisfaction in the Lord for what he has accomplished. Have you allowed money or success to control your joy? Do you constantly want more, or are you content with what God has provided?

Father, allow me to live solely in the joy of the salvation you've provided me.

# כִּסֵּא—*Keesay*

## "Throne"

God rules the nations. He sits upon his holy throne.
PSALM 47:8 GW

Psalm 47 is a plea to all people to celebrate the kingship of Yahweh, the merciful, sovereign Lord of all. He is worthy of praise because he is who he says he is and can do everything he says he can do. He "rules the nations" from his "holy throne" with justice and grace.

Something or someone is going to sit on the throne of your life. Will it be self? Kids? Spouse? Career? Wealth? Or will it be the creator of everything, who loves you more than you could ever imagine and wants your heart and mind? Keeping God in his proper place encourages you to approach him in prayer and worship, trusting his matchless authority. Surprisingly, genuine freedom is only found in letting go and submitting to the Lord's authority. Just as he is the sovereign ruler of nations, he desperately wants to be the leader and forgiver of your life. Accept the challenge to willingly surrender control and allow God and his Word to influence the choices you make every day. While it is exceptionally tough to loosen your grip, the rewards are life-changing.

What have you allowed to creep onto the throne of your life?

# הִפְרֵתִי—*Heef'raytee*

## "To Be Fruitful"

"I will make you exceedingly fruitful."
GENESIS 17:6 RSV

God's covenant with Abraham, as revealed in Genesis 17, is not just a promise of fruitfulness but a promise of over-the-top fruitfulness—a great name, people, land, blessings, and the Messiah. There is no Hebrew word that translates as "exceedingly." *M'ode* (it appears twice in Genesis 17:6) is typically used two or more times to emphasize the idea of a large quantity, much like we would say, "She is very, very smart."

Just as Abraham's trust in the Lord marked the beginning of faith in the one true God, forever changing the spiritual landscape for humankind, the church's birth at Pentecost was equally a game changer. Jesus said, "Whoever lives in Me and I in him bears much (abundant) fruit" (John 15:5 AMPC). Christians are called to bear abundant fruit in a world that is not just in need but urgently in need of Jesus. The only way we can fulfill this calling is by remaining connected to him as our source of spiritual nourishment. Intentionally spend time in prayer, Bible study, and fellowship with other believers. The more you walk with Jesus, the more "exceedingly fruitful" your life will be, and the more impact you will have for the gospel.

Jesus, let my life be a testimony of bearing fruit for your kingdom.

# יֹאכְלוּ—*Yohkh'loo*

## "Devour; Eat"

The Syrians from the east and the Philistines from the west will bare their fangs and devour Israel.
Isaiah 9:12 NLT

After painting a majestic image of the coming Messiah in Isaiah 9, the prophet characteristically returned his pen to his nation in jeopardy. With the Philistines already lying in wait on the eastern side, Isaiah wrote of the Israelites falsely thinking they were creating a strategic alliance with the Syrians when, in reality, both foes "will bare their fangs and devour" them. Sin and evil always look to ravage and devour.

The apostle Peter wrote, "Stay alert! Watch out for your great enemy, the devil. He prowls around like a roaring lion, looking for someone to devour" (1 Peter 5:8). Be reminded that dark spiritual forces are working tirelessly to ensnare and eat everything in their path, including you, your friends, and your family. The devil knows precisely which of your buttons to push. Whether it is temptation, doubt, depression, anxiety, or fear, the Deceiver looks for tiny cracks in your armor—even nanoseconds of temporary weakness. Remain watchful and recognize the Enemy when he bares his fangs so you can fight back with prayer, faith, and God's Word.

Father, help me recognize the Serpent for the slimy dirtbag he has always been.

# פָּנַי—*Pahnai*

## "Face"

Cain became very angry, and his face fell.
GENESIS 4:5 LEB

In biblical and extrabiblical writings, a fallen face refers to a countenance that displays a negative emotional state—one that reflects sadness, anger, or distress. It is typically the result of terrible news, rejection, or a dramatic change in circumstances.

Why did Cain's face fall? Let me quickly tell you a story. When Cain had some free time, he brought God the equivalent of a few carrots. His brother, Abel, brought the Lord "the firstborn of his flock and of their fat portions" (v. 4 ESV). God accepted Abel's offering but rejected Cain's. Cain didn't attempt to make it right with God. Instead, he got seething mad and murdered his brother. Cain's "fallen face" was the result of a fallen heart. God was an afterthought for Cain. When Cain finally got around to it, he brought God leftovers. On the other hand, Abel offered the Lord the first and best of his flock. Y'all, we don't serve a leftovers God. He should always be life's highest priority. Of utmost importance is not what you do for the Lord but the attitude and heart behind it. He is much more interested in our love and devotion than our external efforts.

What steps can you take to ensure you always give your best and first to God?

# יְתוֹמִים וְאַלְמָנוֹת—

# *Y'tomeem V'ahl'mahnote*

## "Orphans and Widows"

He cares for the orphans and widows.
PSALM 146:9 NLT

Psalm 146 is a psalm of praise to the Lord, who holds a special place in his heart for the least of society—orphans, widows, the hungry, the blind, and the strangers. Showering them with his justice and grace, he is a father to the fatherless, a husband to the widow, a chef to the hungry, an ophthalmologist to the blind, and a shelter to the stranger.

Our charge as believers is to have the same heart for those society has cast out and forgotten. When you feed the hungry, you're feeding Jesus. Welcome a stranger; you're welcoming the King of kings. Put a winter coat on a freezing man; you're clothing the Lord of lords. Visit the prisoner; you're having fellowship with the Savior of the world. Jesus said, "Whatever you did for one of the least of these brothers and sisters of mine, you did for me" (Matthew 25:40 NIV). Matthew 25:40 reminds us that how we treat people, particularly those marginalized by society, reflects Christ in us. Whether it is the homeless person on the street or a struggling coworker, serve them as you would Jesus.

What can you do in the next week to serve the "least" of Jesus' brothers and sisters?

# מִשְׁפָּט—*Meesh'paht*

## "Justice"

He has shown you, O man, what is good; and what does the LORD require of you but to do justly, to love mercy, and to walk humbly with your God?
MICAH 6:8 NKJV

Micah 6 metaphorically takes up the courtroom scene that began with God's accusations in chapter 1. The prophet implored the people to "hear now what the LORD says" (6:1). God, as a prosecutor, asked what fault the people have with him. The people responded, through Micah, by essentially saying, "We'd just like to know what you want. What sacrifices will please you? More calves? Rams? How about our firstborn?" Micah responded for an exasperated God: "You already know. You've been told what's good, noble, and right" (v. 8, author's paraphrase). Then he explained goodness with three incredibly simple requirements: "To do justly, to love mercy, and to walk humbly with your God."

Life cannot revolve around exploiting others and only looking out for yourself. Treat people fairly at home, at church, or in the marketplace. Stand up for the oppressed even when it's unpopular and hard. The Christian life is messy, and people are imperfect and can be nasty and unforgiving. Show mercy and grace anyway. Keep your feet on the ground by eliminating pride and taking one humble step after the next.

Lord, help me keep the uncomplicated, uncomplicated.

JUNE 13

# עֵת מוֹעֵד—*Ayt Mo'ayd*

## "Appointed Time"

At the right time he will bring everything together under the authority of Christ—everything in heaven and on earth.
EPHESIANS 1:10 NLT

Throughout the Old Testament, God, under the umbrella of his perfect plan, appointed times for various unique events. The infertile Sarah had a son at the appointed time. God instructed Israel to keep the Passover every year at its appointed time. Daily offerings occurred at appointed times. In his wondrous sovereignty, God providentially selects moments across the tapestry of time to intervene like a skilled weaver fabricating a beautiful cloth.

And then Jesus came in "the fullness of time" (Galatians 4:4 ESV). Of Jesus' return, Paul wrote, "This is [God's] plan: At the right time he will bring everything together under the authority of Christ—everything in heaven and on earth" (Ephesians 1:10 NLT). Though sometimes mysterious, God's timing is always impeccable.

As a Christian, despite the chaos of life, you can bank on God's bigger, better plan for you unfolding in his perfect timing. Don't freak out when things are moving like a turtle crossing the road. Worship in the wait. Mature and trust that he knows the perfect millisecond to step in on your behalf.

Father, help me trust that you are constantly working everything together for my good. I love you!

# חֶרֶב—*Khahrehv*

## “Sword”

Simon Peter, who had a sword, drew it, struck the high priest’s servant, and cut off his right ear.
John 18:10 csb

With Peter, what you see is what you get—good, bad, and ugly. He could be irresponsible. On the night of Jesus’ arrest, Jesus asked Peter to stand watch while he went and prayed, and Peter fell asleep…three times. He could be disloyal. When Jesus was arrested, Peter denied even knowing him…three times. Peter could be obstinate. After fishing all night and catching nothing, Jesus told him to lower the nets one more time. He sarcastically responded with something like, “Been there, done that, but if I gotta prove to you that there’s no fish out here, I will.”

Peter could also be fiercely bold, courageous, and loyal. Some people step up while others step back. Peter nearly always stepped up. Who else got out of the boat and walked on the water toward Jesus? In the olive groves of Gethsemane, Peter, the fisherman wielding a sword, jumped to Jesus’ defense. Swinging the blade to sever Malchus’ head, he missed and took off an ear. Peter came to Jesus just as he was. Jesus wants you just as you are: the good, the bad, and the ugly.

Jesus, take me like I am but don’t leave me the same.

# שָׁבוּעוֹת—*Shahvoo'ote*

## "Feast of Weeks; Pentecost"

When the day of Pentecost arrived, they were all together in one place.
ACTS 2:1 ESV

Deuteronomy 16:9 establishes *Shahvoo'ote* (Shavuot): "You shall count seven weeks. Begin to count the seven weeks from the time the sickle is first put to the standing grain." It is a holiday celebrating the firstfruits that occurs fifty days after the first night of Passover. Since the destruction of the temple in AD 70 and despite God's instruction, *Shahvoo'ote* has morphed into a celebration of God's giving of the Torah.

On the first *Shahvoo'ote* following Jesus' death, burial, and resurrection, Jews from all over the Roman Empire were in Jerusalem to celebrate the firstfruits. Peter—impetuous, bold, Jesus-denying, falling-asleep-on-guard-duty Peter—preached the first gospel message of the church age (Acts 2:14–40) during the celebration of the harvesting of firstfruits. How'd that message turn out? Was it effective? Was the Holy Spirit working through Peter? "Those who received his word were baptized, and there were added that day about three thousand souls" (v. 41). The firstfruits of the sacrificial death of the Lamb of God were three thousand Jews who woke up Pentecost morning lost but went to bed Pentecost evening found.

Jesus, thank you for using everything that was in Peter to harvest the firstfruits of the church age.

# הֶאָח—*Heh'akh*

## "Aha"

He burns half of it in the fire; over this half he eats meat; he roasts it and is satisfied. Also he warms himself and says, "Aha, I am warm."

Isaiah 44:16 MEV

God's prophets consistently warned Israel to stay away from worshiping idols. Isaiah addressed the lunacy of it in Isaiah 44. He told of an idolatrous craftsman who took half a tree and used it for firewood to grill a T-bone and then snuggled up to the campfire declaring, "Aha, I am warm." All good? Maybe not. He took the other half of the tree and crafted it "into a god....He falls down to it, and worships it, and prays to it, and says, 'Deliver me, for you are my god'" (v. 17). Dude, really? Who believes this craziness? We do!

Today's idols might not be made of wood, yet we continue to value things like social media, constantly seeking validation and deliverance through likes and followers. Stop worshiping the approval of others; they don't define your worth. Worshiping your career is another dead end. Like wooden idols, a job can only do so much for you. Belief that your job will complete you will inevitably leave you empty and unsatisfied. The only one who completes and satisfies is Jesus.

Lord, I worship you and only you.

# מִקְוֵה יִשְׂרָאֵל—*Meek'vay Yees'rah'ayl*

## "The Hope of Israel"

"O Hope of Israel, our Savior in times of trouble, why are you like a stranger to us?"
JEREMIAH 14:8 NLT

In a time of intense drought and famine in Judah, Jeremiah cried out to the Lord:

> Our wickedness has caught up with us, LORD,
> but help us for the sake of your own reputation.
> We have turned away from you
> and sinned against you again and again.
> O Hope of Israel, our Savior in times of trouble,
> why are you like a stranger to us?…
> Please don't abandon us now! (vv. 7–9)

Biblical hope is not wishful thinking. It looks confidently and expectantly "forward to a city with eternal foundations, a city designed and built by God" (Hebrews 11:10). We can look forward to this city because Jesus is *Meek'vay Yees'rah'ayl*, our Savior, Deliverer, and Forgiver. When we have complete confidence in God and fully trust in his promise-keeping character, our hearts, minds, and lives will be transformed. The Hope of Israel fills us to the brim with confident expectation—hope! Do you genuinely rely on Jesus as your hope, or do you tend to look for security elsewhere? Are you walking through life confident in God's ability to deliver and save, or are you quietly, maybe even defiantly, self-reliant?

Father, let my hope in you be an encouragement and strength for the people in my world.

# רֵעַ—*Ray'ay*

## "Friend"

The LORD spoke to Moses face to face as a man speaks with his friend.
EXODUS 33:11 NCV

It is mind-blowing that the phrase "The LORD spoke to Moses" is recorded in the Torah seventy times, and Exodus 33:11 tells us that the two of them spoke as friends. Yes, God is holy, and yes, Moses was a sinner, yet somehow God's holiness remained intact even though he and a sinful man were friends and hung out together.

The image of Moses on Mount Sinai, engulfed in a conversation with the creator of the universe, inaugurates a fifteen-hundred-year process of divine revelation that culminates in Yahweh revealing himself in the person of Jesus of Nazareth, God in the flesh, who hung out with tax collectors and sinners (Matthew 9:10). The religious elite wouldn't dare have friends in such low places, but to capture their hearts and win their eternities, Jesus did. And they became his friends. He loved them all—tax collectors, prostitutes, divorcées, lepers, Samaritans, criminals, Pharisees, the unclean, the homeless, and the poor. He loves you, too, and he wants to be your friend. He said, "Greater love has no one than this, that someone lay down his life for his friends" (John 15:13 ESV). And that is exactly what he did.

Lord Jesus, let me love who you love.

# כֶּרֶם—*Kehrehm*

## “Vineyard”

“When evening came, the owner of the vineyard said to his foreman, ‘Call the laborers and pay them their wages, beginning with the last, up to the first.’”
MATTHEW 20:8 ESV

Vineyards were a primary agricultural industry in ancient Israel. Because of the fertility of the soil, they were typically located in hill country and required massive work to yield results. As the greatest rabbi ever, Jesus consistently used everyday things like vineyards, sheep, coins, and trees to convey spiritual truths.

In Matthew 20:1–16, he did this in a parable about a vineyard owner who hired workers at different times of the day. Imagine some started at 6 a.m., others later, and a few just before 5 p.m. When it was time to pay the workers, the owner gave everyone the same amount, regardless of how long they worked. The workers who started at dawn whined about it, but the vineyard owner reminded them that they agreed to their wage when hired. And he further explained that he owned the vineyard and could do what he wanted to with his money.

Comparison is a joy stealer. Resist comparing God’s provision for others with his provision for you. Understand that God’s generosity will never conform to your image of fairness. Exalt him for his generosity toward you and ignore what others get.

Lord, I praise you for your tailor-made generosity.

# טֹוב—*Tove*

## "Better"

It is better to trust in the LORD than to depend on people.
PSALM 118:8 GNT

It's not hard to choose between something good and something demonstrably bad. But the line between good and better may be a little gray. If you're living in the good, it may feel comfortable and familiar. However, better is better. Psalm 118:8 is incredibly simple yet conveys a giant spiritual truth: God is better. The writer of Hebrews likely had this verse in the forefront of his mind as he penned his first-century letter. The Jews to whom Hebrews was written had the covenants, the law, the patriarchs, religious traditions, sacrifices, and priests. And for a thousand years, prophets spoke to them on God's behalf. God was on their side, and it was good.

But Jesus showed up and fulfilled the law, inaugurating a new, better covenant. He was a better prophet, priest, and sacrifice. He was better than the angels; better than Moses, David, and Solomon; and better than all the Old Testament people of faith combined. I encourage you to dive into Hebrews, where "a better hope is introduced" (Hebrews 7:19 ESV). The message is that Jesus is infinitely better and that placing saving faith and trust in him is better than any other way because he is the only way to God.

Jesus, thank you for being better than everything.

# שַׁאֲלוּ—*Shah'ahloo*

## "To Ask"

Ask ye the peace of Jerusalem.
Psalm 122:6 YLT

You've probably heard this verse many times and seen the T-shirts and memes, but it always begins with the word *pray*. In Psalm 122, "ask" is a better translation of *shah'ahloo* since it conveys the petitioning of the psalmist. *Ask* is simple but powerful. Here, God invites us to ask for peace—not just to wish for it or hope it happens but to come to him and ask. Our asking is an acknowledgment that he is the very source and provider of everything.

*Shah'ahloo* means our prayer life should be active rather than a simple waiting for things to magically work themselves out. Asking God to intervene reminds us that we're not in control but know the one who is. Are you ever reluctant to ask? Do you ever feel like your mess is too petty for God to fool with because he's extremely busy running the entire universe? Maybe you think your problems are too big. Do you struggle to find the right words? Know this: God's not about a bunch of *thee*s, *thou*s, and *unto*s. He's about you approaching him sincerely and asking.

What's on your heart and mind today? Don't hold back. Ask him. He hears you.

Lord, thank you for always being just one ask away.

# יֵחָלֵק—*Yay'khahlayk*

## "To Divide"

The people of Israel were divided into two factions. Half of the people followed Tibni son of Ginath, to make him king, and half followed Omri.
1 Kings 16:21 AMPC

The context for today's verse involves a civil war in the Northern Kingdom of Israel following King Zimri's death. God's people chose sides like kids playing stickball in the cul-de-sac on a warm spring afternoon—the "shirts" versus the "skins." Very little upsets the Lord as much as the godlessness of division and the leaders who cause it (Titus 3:10–11). God calls children of strife an abomination (Proverbs 6:19). Jesus' brother Jude added, "They stir up arguments; they love the evil things of the world; they do not have the Holy Spirit living in them" (Jude v. 19 TLB). Tibni and Omri sowed division by drawing people to themselves rather than the Lord.

Unfortunately, today's church life can be much the same. While church people are busy fighting over the carpet's color, sanctuary's temperature, or worship service's order, lost people are dying on the streets of their cities, headed for eternities in hell. The entirety of Scripture tells us that a significant proof of the Holy Spirit's influence in our lives is a gospel-centric passion for unity in the body of Christ.

What can you do today to sow unity rather than division?

JUNE 23

# יֵדְעוּ—*Yayd'oo*

## "To Know"

They will no longer need to teach each other to say, "Know the Lord!" because they will all know me, from the least of them to the greatest, declares the Lord.
Jeremiah 31:34 CEB

The root of the word *yayd'oo* carries a range of meanings. However, they all fall under essentially two camps: to know by observation and to know through personal experience. Jeremiah 31:34 is part of his prophecy of a coming day when Yahweh would institute a new covenant, the hallmark of which is the internal presence of his Spirit in believers' hearts. They will *yayd'oo* him because they will personally experience his presence twenty-four hours a day, 365 days a year.

The apostle Paul wrote, "I think that all things are worth nothing compared with the greatness of knowing Christ Jesus my Lord" (Philippians 3:8 ICB). Effectively, Paul said, "Take my MDiv and PhD from Pharisee University, along with all my leadership trophies, and burn them in a dumpster fire because I know the Savior of the world." For you to know him better, listen for his voice in your life. You might ask how. Hold on tight; it's complicated: (1) Open up your Bible; (2) flip to Matthew, Mark, Luke, or John; and (3) read Jesus' words out loud.

Do you value your relationship with Jesus more than anything else?

# עֲנָוִים—*Ahnahveem*

## "The Meek"

The Lord lifts up the meek;
He casts the wicked down to the ground.
Psalm 147:6 MEV

The Old Testament uses the word for "meek" variously as a noun or adjective about twenty-five times—always reflected positively. For example, "Moses was very meek" (Numbers 12:3 KJV); "The meek shall eat and be satisfied" (Psalm 22:26); God guides and teaches the meek (25:9); "The meek shall inherit the earth; and shall delight themselves in…peace" (37:11); God "will beautify the meek with salvation" (149:4); and Isaiah foresaw the Messiah preaching "the Gospel of good tidings to the meek" (Isaiah 61:1 AMPC).

Jesus echoed the psalmist when he declared, "Blessed are the meek: for they shall inherit the earth" (Matthew 5:5 KJV). If the Bible paints a picturesque image of the special place the meek have in God's economy and Jesus elevated meekness as a worthy character trait, we should take notice. *Ahnahveem* are humble and fully dependent on God rather than self. The meek are not weak. They are strong yet self-controlled, and they respond to persecution with a calm and gentle spirit. Therefore, walking in meekness is a contagious display of Jesus in you.

How can your calm responses in trying circumstances help others see the difference that Jesus makes in your life?

# נַחֲמוּ—*Nahkhahmoo*

## "Comfort"

Comfort, comfort my people, says your God.
Isaiah 40:1 RSV

Comfort is a significant theme of Isaiah 40–66. There, God addressed a group of future exiles and wanted them to be comforted and assured that they were still his covenant people. They had betrayed him, but he would never abandon them.

Paul surely thought back to Isaiah's words when he described the Lord as "the Father of mercies and God of all comfort, who comforts us in all our affliction, so that we may be able to comfort those who are in any affliction" (2 Corinthians 1:3–4). Many people have a twisted view of our heavenly Father as a grumpy old man looking to punish us, but that is not the God of the Bible. When we hurt, he is merciful, gracious, and eager to put his loving arms around us. The hard times you experience are not all about you. Surrender these past trials to the Lord. He often draws on your struggles to build empathy into your DNA and uses these experiences to equip you to be his loving arms for the people in your world. When you work through sufferings, you inevitably develop more compassion toward people in similar boats.

Father, cross my path today with someone who needs a hug from you and let me give it to them.

# גֵיא—*Gay*

## "Valley"

Even when I go through the darkest valley, I fear no danger, for You are with me; Your rod and Your staff—they comfort me.
Psalm 23:4 HCSB

Standing on Mount Carmel in 2023, looking over the Jezreel Valley, and knowing the massive scope of darkness and death that would occur there in the last days, I found myself engulfed in Psalm 23. Strangely, I did not feel sadness but joy—joy not just because we win in the end but because we can live triumphantly in this life as well.

Psalm 23 takes us on a faith-filled journey that begins with David's declaration that "the Lord is my shepherd" (v. 1). The path leads to the beauty and serenity of "green pastures" and "quiet waters" (v. 2), the stability found in "right paths" (v. 3), and finally, the challenges of "the darkest valley" (v. 4). Our lives typically mirror these same twists and turns. Is there a pot of gold at the end of this meandering trail? Yes—the courage, confidence, and comfort that flow from the Good Shepherd's intimate, faithful, watchful, and protective presence in your life.

Lord, I praise you today for promising that "goodness and mercy shall follow me all the days of my life, and I shall dwell in [your] house…forever" (v. 6 ESV).

# בִּכּוּרֵי—*Beekooray*

## "Firstfruit"

Christ has been raised from the dead, the first fruits of those who have died.
1 CORINTHIANS 15:20 NRSVUE

The theology of firstfruit comes from the Old Testament concept that the first of everything is the most treasured and is to be brought to the Lord (Leviticus 23:10). The very nature of the word *first* in 1 Corinthians 15:20 implies that there will be more fruit to come, and by delivering the first and best to the Lord, the whole harvest is consecrated.

First Corinthians 15 is focused on resurrection but is laser focused on Jesus' resurrection, which embodies and wholly fulfills every aspect of *beekooray*. He was not the first one to be resurrected (he previously raised Lazarus and Jairus' daughter), but he was the first to rise and never taste death again. Praise the Lord that his resurrection serves as a promise and guarantee of more to come—billions more, including ours as Christians. Seeing Jesus as the firstfruit is like getting a sneak peek of what's coming. Just as the *beekooray* signaled a full harvest, his resurrection is a promise of what's around the corner for you. You can live confidently knowing that your eternal future is secure, solid, and guaranteed because he lives.

Jesus, thank you for the assurance I have because you were the firstfruit.

JUNE 28

# חֵן—*Khayn*

## “Favor; Grace”

Noah found grace in the eyes of the LORD.
GENESIS 6:8 KJV

Years ago, I had a friend who declared, “I like the God of the New Testament better.” I looked at him like he was crazy and asked, “Wait, what?” He explained, “The Old Testament God is angry, but the New Testament God is merciful and loving.” Yet just six chapters into the Old Testament, “Noah found grace in the eyes of the LORD.”

God is immutable—the same yesterday, today, and tomorrow. While this is not an exhaustive list of his attributes, he is also loving, good, just, merciful, omnipresent, omnipotent, omniscient, holy, perfect, self-existent, transcendent, sovereign, eternally present, and, yes, full of grace—always has been and always will be.

Grace is the gift of the unearned, undeserved favor of God toward humanity. It defies logic and violates the principle of cause and effect because though we deserve death, we receive life by God’s grace. As a Christian, you’ve been showered with and have experienced his grace. Therefore, divine grace should flood every relationship you have. Let my friend’s foolish statement remind you to be patient, forgiving, kind, and merciful and to filter all life through the lens of grace, even when it’s exceptionally difficult.

Lord God, I praise you today because my mistakes don’t define me. Your grace does.

# שָׂנֵא—*Sahnay*

## "To Hate; to Set Against"

Whoever does not discipline his son hates him, but whoever loves him is diligent to correct him.
PROVERBS 13:24 ISV

The Hebrew word *sahnay* covers a range of negative emotions, from hate as hyperbole (Proverbs 13:24) all the way to intense, murderous rage, much like Joseph's brothers' hatred of him. In the Old Testament, the primary meaning leans more intense.

With that understanding of hate, Jesus taught a crowd about the cost of discipleship: "If anyone comes to me and does not hate his father, mother, wife, children, brothers, and sisters, as well as his own life, he can't be my disciple" (Luke 14:26). Who would say such a thing? Was Jesus instructing the crowd to violate honoring Mom and Dad? Was he recanting his many teachings on love? Of course not. His point was this: Our love and devotion for him must be so life altering, all-encompassing, and undivided that our love for anyone else, as passionate as it may be, would seem like hate in comparison. Additionally, the price of your love for him may be your mom, dad, brother, and sister. That was the price I paid as a Jew who surrendered his life to Christ. I love my family, but I love Jesus more. Do you?

Jesus, let me always love you the most.

# גְּאוֹן—*G'own*

## "Pride"

The Lord, the God of hosts, says: I abhor, reject, and despise the pride and false, futile glory of Jacob (Israel), and I hate his palaces and strongholds; and I will deliver up the city [idol-worshiping Samaria] with all that is in it.
AMOS 6:8 AMPC

Amos 6:8 records the most scathing indictment of pride in the Bible. The Northern and Southern Kingdoms were in the crosshairs of the God of hosts (armies) because he'd had enough of their pride, arrogance, and extravagance. They were on top of the world in every imaginable way and indeed believed they'd put themselves there. Their palaces were packed with the results of oppressing the poor. God despised all of it: the money, gold, buildings, fake glory, and *pride*.

Amos 6 makes it plain as day that the path of pride ends in utter destruction. When you buy the lie that your strength has made you invincible, you have blinded yourself to your weaknesses, have become vulnerable, and are set up for a mighty fall. God clearly loathes pride but loves a humble servant. Honor the King of kings by heeding Amos' warning against self-congratulatory pats on the back. Live with the humility that comes from dethroning yourself and recognize that every good thing in life is a gift from him.

Lord, help me consistently suppress my prideful tendencies.

# Kvetch

## "Relentless Whining"

This I declare about the LORD: He alone is my refuge, my place of safety; he is my God, and I trust him.
PSALM 91:2 NLT

As a middle schooler, I whined about wanting Adidas shoes like my friends. Mom said, "Stop kvetching!" Izod shirts? "Stop kvetching!" Levi's jeans? "Enough with the kvetching!" *Kvetch* is a Yiddish verb that means "relentless whining."

As Moses led more than two million miraculously freed slaves out of Egypt, they started kvetching from the get-go. At the shore of the Red Sea, when the Egyptian army was approaching, the Israelites asked, "Why did you bring us out here to die in the wilderness?" (Exodus 14:11). Then more kvetching: "It's better to be a slave in Egypt than a corpse in the wilderness!" (v. 12). "You have brought us into this wilderness to starve us all to death" (16:3). "Are you trying to kill us… with thirst?" (17:3). Just three weeks had passed between freedom and the Red Sea. Just like the kvetching Israelites, the speed at which we forget is shocking. Why? Because we get scared. Fear has the amazing ability to wreak havoc on our memory. Fear is a liar. It is a deceiver. When you feel fear creeping in, remember God's mighty acts throughout history and trust him.

Lord, help me never forget who you are and what you've done.

# יְהוָה רֹפְאֶ—*Yahweh Rofeh*

## "The Lord Who Heals"

He touched his ear and healed him.
Luke 22:51 RSV

When the Israelites were wandering in the desert, the Lord promised them that if they would listen to him, "I will put none of the diseases on you that I put on the Egyptians, for I am the Lord, your healer" (Exodus 15:26 ESV). He heals physically, emotionally, mentally, and spiritually.

There are fifty-one healings recorded in the New Testament, but one truly stands out to me. On the night of Jesus' arrest, Judas betrayed Jesus with a kiss. Peter whipped out a blade, chopping off the ear of Malchus, the high priest's servant or guard. I imagine Jesus picking the dude's ear off the ground, wiping it off, and sticking it back on. Really? Yes, really! Can you imagine the conversation around the dinner table when Malchus got home from work that day? "Honey, you're not going to believe it, but a crazy Jewish fisherman cut my ear off today, and a poor Galilean carpenter put it back on." I'm certain I will see Malchus in heaven. As huge as all the Bible's physical healings are, they are nothing compared to the merciful touch of the Son of God as he softens a sinner's heart and saves a man's or woman's soul.

What effect has the Healer's touch had on you?

# הוֹי—*Hoy*

## "Woe"

Woe to those who call evil good and good evil!
ISAIAH 5:20 CJB

When was the last time you used the word *woe* in a conversation? It's just not a word we use anymore, but Isaiah used it twenty-two times as a warning that God was about to pop someone. Because of Israel's rotten fruit, in Isaiah 5, God delivered six woes to us…oops, I meant Israel.

Do you ever wake up and think, *What the heck's going on?* When did left become right, up become down, and evil become good? And did our declaring it so make it so? Today's culture has normalized and even celebrated ideas that are clearly prohibited in God's Word. We've made truth subjective, turned honest disagreement into hate, and embraced the philosophy that might makes right. Does wrong become right because 51 percent of people say so, or do good and evil exist independently of our opinions? Isaiah reminds us of the real danger of getting too comfortable in this environment. It is easy to become discouraged when so much around us seems backward, but God's Word delivers truth with clarity. God's people are to measure culture's fallible word against what God infallibly says is true, good, and right.

Lord, give me the discernment to always distinguish truth from lies.

# בַּמֶּרְחָב—*Vahmehr 'khahv*

## "Set Me Free"

In my distress I called to the Lord;
he answered me and set me free.
Psalm 118:5 GNT

Psalm 118 is a song praising God for his covenantal, freedom-inducing love. The psalmist repeated "His steadfast love endures forever" four times (Psalm 118:1, 2, 3, 4 ESV). Based on God's faithful love, the psalmist quickly concluded that he'd been rescued, delivered, and set free. What a beautiful, timeless truth this is—that true freedom is a gift our gracious and merciful Lord of lords gives. The psalm ends the way it began: God's "steadfast love endures forever!" (v. 29).

Today is Independence Day in the United States—a day we celebrate freedom's triumph over the chains of tyranny. As you think about authentic freedom today, consider Paul's words about truly being set free: "We have freedom now, because Christ made us free. So stand strong. Do not change and go back into the slavery of the law" (Galatians 5:1 NCV). The apostle's words are a compelling reminder that you weren't set free just to return to the garbage that previously held you captive. No! You've been unleashed for a life without the shackles of sin, guilt, and shame—a life of real freedom and forgiveness that flows from the liberating blood of Christ.

How is your life a testimony of your blood-bought freedom?

# דְּאָגָה—*D'ahgah*

## "Anxiety; Worry"

Anxiety in a person's heart weighs him down,
but an encouraging word brings him joy.
PROVERBS 12:25 NET

Approximately 40 million adults in the United States have an anxiety disorder.[7] In 2022, at least 10 percent of prescriptions filled in nearly all US states were for anxiety and depression medications.[8] Anxiety is not a new phenomenon. Nearly three thousand years ago, King Solomon penned Proverbs 12, which says that God's wisdom, not modern medicine, informed him that worry and anxiety weigh crushingly and heavily on a person's heart. And it was most likely through observing the seemingly medicinal effects of empathy, encouragement, and kindness that he concluded verse 25 with "an encouraging word brings him joy."

Even if it is invisible to you, the paralyzing effects of anxiety and depression may be silently suffocating and destroying many of your friends and family members. A quick call or text message with a caring and kind word can sometimes mean the difference between life and death. When your peeps know you have their back, the heaviness lightens, even if only for a moment. Rest assured that minutes of relief can morph into days, months, and years of joy, which may be traced back to a few kindhearted words in a simple text message.

Lord, help me to simply be kind.

---

7 "Anxiety Disorders—Facts & Statistics," Anxiety & Depression Association of America, accessed May 8, 2025, adaa.org.

8 Dr. Trinidad Cisneros, "Fills for Mental Health Prescription Drugs Rose During COVID and Remain High," GoodRx, February 21, 2023, goodrx.com.

# יִשְׁתַּחוּ—*Yeesh'tahkhoo*

## "Worship"

Moses immediately threw himself to the ground and worshiped.
EXODUS 34:8 NLT

As much as I love contemporary Christian music, it doesn't define *yeesh'tahkhoo*. Exodus 34 finds Moses on Mount Sinai with two fresh tablets, having earlier smashed the originals in anger. The omnipotent creator of the heavens and earth passed in front of Moses and proclaimed,

> Yahweh! The LORD! The God of compassion and mercy! I am slow to anger and filled with unfailing love and faithfulness. I lavish unfailing love to a thousand generations. I forgive iniquity, rebellion, and sin. But I do not excuse the guilty. I lay the sins of the parents upon their children and grandchildren; the entire family is affected—even children in the third and fourth generations. (vv. 6–7)

Considering Moses' current events and Yahweh's words, the only possible response for any reasonable human being would be to collapse to the ground in awe and complete surrender, reverence, love, devotion, praise, and gratitude. When you walk into your church's sanctuary next Sunday, bring Moses' philosophy of worship with you. Glance up and reread Exodus 34:6–7 and reflect on God's character. The God who revealed himself on Sinai is the same one who "so loved the world that he gave his one and only Son, that whoever believes in him shall not perish but have eternal life" (John 3:16 NIV). Yeah, worship is not just music.

All I can say, Lord, is wow.

# יִלוֹד—*Yeelode*

## "To Be Born"

"I tell you the truth, unless you are born again, you cannot be in God's kingdom."
JOHN 3:3 NCV

There's a lot of *begetting* in the Old Testament. In fact, the word appears 498 times. We know the biology: We're born once from our mother's womb, we live, and then we die, right? Whoa, not so fast. Jesus turned all that biology stuff inside out.

Thinking back to the first time I heard the phrase *born again*, I threw the nonsense flag just like Nicodemus, who asked, "If a person is already old, how can he be born again? He cannot enter his mother's womb again" (v. 4).

Jesus got real…real fast. He responded, "No one, and I mean no one, enters the eternal dominion of God's authority—on earth and in heaven—without experiencing the blood-bought spiritual transformation of extraction from the domain of darkness and placement into the domain of light—commonly known as being 'born again'" (from the new Ed Grifenhagen paraphrase. LOL). Upon said rebirth, you are presented with a new passport as a citizen of heaven, which comes with the added benefit of eternal life. Best news ever! Tell everyone you see about it.

Father, thank you for my mother who birthed me but thank you also for Jesus, who rebirthed me.

# חָדָשׁ—*Khahdahsh*

## "New"

Sing to the LORD a new song.
PSALM 96:1 NASB

Newness is a significant theme throughout Scripture. The psalmist praised the Lord through new songs in six psalms (Psalms 33, 40, 96, 98, 144, and 149). Old versus new wineskins are mentioned several times in the Old Testament. Celebrating the new moon, called *Rosh Khodehsh* (Rosh Hodesh; literally, "head of the new moon"), is referred to dozens of times. Isaiah spoke about God doing "something new" (Isaiah 43:19). God did an incredible new thing on day six of creation when he breathed life into the nostrils of Adam, and he does a mind-blowing new thing every time a man, woman, or child surrenders their life to Jesus and becomes a new creation.

The indwelling Holy Spirit empowers your *new* to crush your *old*. Now you can cast away the old and spiritually dead you, end the messed-up behavior, abandon the rebellious and lustful cravings (Ephesians 4:22), and you can "let the Spirit renew your thoughts and attitudes. Put on your new nature, created to be like God—truly righteous and holy" (Ephesians 4:23–24 NLT). Because you are "a new creation; [and] the old has passed away" (2 Corinthians 5:17 CSB), you are free to let go of your past mistakes, regrets, or anything that holds you back. So whatcha waiting for?

What are some of the old things that need to go?

JULY 9

# בָּחַר—*Bahkhahr*

## "To Choose; Chosen"

"The Lord did not set his heart on you and choose you because you were more numerous than other nations, for you were the smallest of all nations! Rather, it was simply that the Lord loves you."
Deuteronomy 7:7–8 NLT

This passage gives us a peek under the hood at the heart of God's choice or election. He wanted a nation to fill the available position in his "Missions Department," but why would he ever choose Israel? They weren't anything special—not all that impressive, not the best looking, and certainly not the biggest. God chose them because he loved them and had made a promise to Abraham. Pure and simple, he chose Israel because of his grace. They did not deserve it, did not earn it, nor could they ever earn it. It was a gift, not a reward.

Praise the Lord that this is also true for us. God's love has nothing to do with our goodness, strength, or spirituality. It is based on him—his character, his sovereignty, his steadfast love, and his commitment to his word. We're not chosen because of our impressive résumé but because he loves us, and he gets to love whom he wants because he's God. His choice rests in his grace, not our greatness.

Father, thank you for choosing little old unimpressive me.

# דֶּשֶׁן—*Dehshehn*

## "Fullness"

They are abundantly satisfied with the fullness of Your house, and You give them drink from the river of Your pleasures.
PSALM 36:8 NKJV

God doesn't just want us to have *some* of himself. He wants us to have *all* of him—in abundance. David's snapshot of abundant satisfaction and guzzling from "the rivers of [God's] pleasures" is an invitation into a life of experiencing the Lord's fullness, a life of complete satisfaction fully funded by his overwhelming, never-ending presence.

The apostle Paul added to this image by expressing his heartfelt desire for you to "know the love of Christ that is beyond knowledge so that you will be filled entirely with the fullness of God" (Ephesians 3:19 CEB). Jesus is the trail that culminates in this fullness, and the more you experience his love, the more God fills you, overflowing your heart, mind, and soul with his loving-kindness. When you feel tapped out, empty, and exhausted, he is there with his living water to fill you with peace, joy, strength, and hope that will undoubtedly flow into every area of your life. His faithful love is more than enough to fill any thirst you have. He's calling you to gently inch closer and drink from his grace.

Jesus, overflow my life with your precious love.

# תְּמוּרָת—*T'mooraht*

## "Substitute"

He was punished to make us whole again. His wounds have healed us.
ISAIAH 53:5 NIRV

Although the word *substitute* is not in today's verse, Isaiah 53 perfectly demonstrates the substitutionary nature of the sacrificial system of Isaiah's time. In the Old Testament, God laid out the way that people were to be forgiven: "They must place their hand on the head of the burnt offering. Then the LORD will accept it in place of them. It will pay for their sin" (Leviticus 1:4). The worshiper placed their hands on the goat's head, symbolizing the transfer of sin to the goat as a substitute. The animal was then killed, shouldering the consequences of the worshiper's sin. This act made the worshiper right with God.

Isaiah 53:5 animates that image through Jesus' crucifixion. Christ became our substitute. He was punished for every sin, every mistake, every regret, and every nasty thought. He bore our sin willingly, making us permanently whole, healed, and forgiven. He bore as our substitute the punishment we deserved, giving us peace with God. Remember that Jesus didn't come to simply lend us a hand and help. He came to stand in our place and bear what we couldn't.

How does knowing Jesus bore your sins affect how you see yourself and your relationship with the Lord?

# דּוּמִיָּה—*Doomeeyah*

## "Silence"

God alone my soul waits in silence; from Him comes my salvation.
PSALM 62:1 AMPC

In the nonstop twenty-first-century world we live in, silence can feel awkward. We've become accustomed to incessant noise—music, phone calls, mindless scrolling, IMs, DMs, and probably a bunch of other *M*'s. But David tapped into something special in Psalm 62: the value of waiting silently before God. When you are still and quiet, you create margin and grant God permission to speak into your life, calm your restlessness, and remind you that he does, in fact, contain the whole world in the palm of his hand.

Silence helps us let go of the obsessive struggle to defend, explain, or justify ourselves. It is really an act of trust to let God be the one to move, save, and lead. This quiet space isn't about being lazy. Its focus is patient expectation, knowing that God is in the background at work while we're still. Take a few minutes now and wait silently at the foot of the Master. Quiet the noise, lay aside distractions, and just hang out with Jesus. Watch him calm your worries and recognize that he alone is your salvation.

Thank you, Jesus, for your presence, strength, and peace. You give me hope in the quiet stillness of the morning.

# עֲפַר הָאָרֶץ—*Ahfahr Hah'ahrehtz*

## "Superabundant"

I will make your offspring like the dust of the earth.
GENESIS 13:16 HCSB

"Dust of the earth" is an idiom that sometimes means complete annihilation (2 Samuel 22:43). Other times, the phrase refers to "superabundance," as it does here in Genesis 13:16, where God promised to make Abraham's offspring superabundant. God has been in the superabundance-making business for a long time, and he's really good at it!

In Paul's doxology in Ephesians 3, he had a "dust of the earth" view of the Lord:

> Now to Him Who, by (in consequence of) the [action of His] power that is at work within us, is able to [carry out His purpose and] do superabundantly, far over and above all that we [dare] ask or think [infinitely beyond our highest prayers, desires, thoughts, hopes, or dreams]. (Ephesians 3:20 AMPC)

This is a mind-blowing truth: God can and does overwhelm us with his goodness, going "far over and above all that we [dare] ask or think." Sadly, our prayers often lack faith and fall short. And we tend to ask for what we've determined is possible. Both are huge mistakes. God doesn't work within our boundaries or, for that matter, any boundaries.

Lord, I trust you today and every day to intervene and blow me away with your superabundant blessings and provision.

# קִנְאָה—*Keenah*

## "Envy"

A heart at peace gives life to the body, but envy rots the bones.
PROVERBS 14:30 NIV

I once saw today's verse in a meme with the simple heading "TRUTH!" Proverbs 14:30 gets real about just how much envy, jealousy, and covetousness can jack us up spiritually, of course, but also, the writer was really talking about the horrid effects on our bodies.

When you obsess over the other guy's Ferrari or that the Smiths next door go on their private jet to have dinner in Paris every weekend (at least according to their social media accounts), it's not just a joy thief. It can dramatically affect your health. Envy creates tension, stress, and anxiety, which all weigh heavily on your body, causing fatigue, sleeplessness, headaches, gastrointestinal problems, weight gain, depression, and so on. Jealousy is like pouring cyanide into your soul, and it somehow finds a way into every fiber in your body. Rather than ingesting envy's poison, God's Word calls for a peaceful heart. A heart that is at peace isn't constantly trying to measure up to someone else's yardstick of success. It's secure, content, and filled with Jesus. It needs nothing else. When you're fully nourished with Jesus, you can live joyfully without shouldering the burden of covetousness.

When you're feeling envious, how does it affect your energy, mood, or even your relationships?

# צֶלֶם—*Tzehlehm*

## "Image"

God created mankind in his own image; in his own image God created them; he created them male and female.
GENESIS 1:27 ISV

Consider the impact of God's declaration concerning humankind as the crown of his creation: He created humans in his own image. Think about what's packed into the word *image*: representation, likeness, reflection, and impression. You are one of a kind. The creator of all uniquely handcrafted you with incredible meaning, worth, and purpose.

Beyond that, Paul reminded us, "We are God's masterpiece, created in the Messiah Jesus to perform good actions that God prepared long ago to be our way of life" (Ephesians 2:10). Our identity isn't grounded solely in being created by God but also in being re-created in Jesus. Have you allowed the world to define who you are—your value, your success, or how you stack up? Don't! God's Word says your identity is found only in Christ. Because of Jesus' sacrificial work on the cross and his resurrection, you are not defined by your failures, your past, or even your accomplishments. You are defined by who God says you are: his masterpiece, image bearer, and reflection, designed with purpose.

Lord, help me see myself as your work of art created purposely for kingdom impact.

# מִגְדַּל־עֹז—*Meeg'dahl Oze*

## "Strong Tower"

You have been a shelter and a refuge for me, a strong tower against the enemy.
PSALM 61:3 AMP

Hung with one thousand shields (Song of Solomon 4:4), the Tower of David near the Jaffa Gate in Jerusalem was initially built by King David. It has been wrecked and rebuilt several times over the last three thousand years, but it is still a breathtaking reminder that the God of Abraham, Isaac, and Jacob is a strong tower, a fortress, and a refuge.

Longing for the Lord, David composed Psalm 61 from a foreign land. He wrote,

> You have been a shelter and a refuge for me,
> a strong tower against the enemy.
> Let me dwell in Your tent forever;
> let me take refuge in the shelter of Your wings. (vv. 3–4)

Rest in the truth that when life throws you a curveball and you feel overwhelmed, you can trust the *Meeg'dahl Oze* to provide protection and strength. Stop, fix your eyes on Jesus, and ask him to be your fortress. Trust that you can always take refuge under his compassionate and loving wings. Take a minute and jot down five ways you can more intentionally spend time in God's presence.

Thank you, Jesus, for protecting and leading me in the past. Let those memories strengthen my trust in your faithfulness.

# Schmooze

## "To Chat Casually"

"Behold, the virgin shall conceive and bear a Son."
ISAIAH 7:14 NKJV

Think of the ladies shopping and schmoozing down at the Bethlehem produce market. Dvora said, "A virgin's going to have a baby. Yeah, right." Milka jumped in with "And camels can fly." Then Yael declared, "That Mary. Good gracious. Either she's not pregnant, or she's not a virgin." Wrong on all three counts: Mary was pregnant, she was a virgin, and camels can't fly.

An angel came to young Mary and said several astonishing things: "You have found favor with God" (Luke 1:30), "You will conceive" (v. 31), "The Holy Spirit will come upon you" (v. 35), and "You…shall call His name JESUS" (v. 31). But perhaps the most life-changing thing the angel told her was "With God nothing will be impossible" (v. 37). God consistently does things beyond our understanding. If he could create everything from nothing and then bring Jesus into the world in such a miraculous way, the odds are pretty high that he can handle whatever seems impossible in your life. May you humbly reply like Mary: "I am the servant of the Lord; may it be done to me according to your word" (v. 38 AMP).

Lord, when my situation seems hopeless, let me remember how wrong the schmoozing women at the produce market were.

# יִשְׁבֹּת—*Yeesh'bote*

## "To Cease; to Rest"

On the seventh day God had finished his work of creation, so he rested from all his work.
GENESIS 2:2 NLT

God didn't rest on the seventh day because he was just plumb worn out. He possesses all the power that could ever exist, so it wasn't weariness that sparked the rest. It was a rest of completion, celebrating the end of a perfectly created everything. He backed up, checked it all out, and stopped because it was awesome and enough. It was a rest of satisfaction, not exhaustion. This same idea shows up in Hebrews: "When Christ had offered for all time a single sacrifice for sins, he sat down at the right hand of God" (Hebrews 10:12 RSV). He sat down because it was done (John 19:30), it was perfect, and it was enough.

God invites you into a rest born out of knowing that your salvation is complete. God rested after creation week, and Jesus sat down at God's right hand after his death, burial, resurrection, and ascension. You, too, get to rest in the more-than-enoughness of what Jesus did for you.

Jesus, thank you for making provision for me to be able to take a seat, knowing that I am 1,000 percent accepted, loved, and saved by you.

# עֵת—*Eet*

## "Time"

People don't know when their time will come.
ECCLESIASTES 9:12 CJB

Nothing is as unpredictable as the meandering ebbs and flows of life. King Solomon—the "Preacher" in Ecclesiastes—reminded us that we have no idea when the jig will be up for us. James, the Lord's brother, echoed this truth: "You don't even know if you will be alive tomorrow! For all you are is a mist that appears for a little while and then disappears" (James 4:14). It doesn't take four PhDs and a cup of coffee to figure out that we don't have an endless supply of time. Then why do we live like we do?

How often do you kick the can of the important things down the road? You convince yourself, *I'll pray tomorrow, talk to Linda about Jesus later, take my grandson fishing next month, and write the book next year*. Tomorrow ain't guaranteed. Every day you wake up on this side of the ground is an opportunity to impact the people around you for Jesus. So rather than scrolling mindlessly on your phone, what if you lived for the Lord with urgency—investing in people, seeking God's will, and serving? Love, pray, witness, fish, write, apologize, and forgive. Choose purpose over procrastination.

Life is short; do stuff that matters.

# כָּתַבְתִּי—*Khatahv'tee*

## "Inscribe"

When he finished speaking with Moses on Mount Sinai, he gave him the two tablets of the testimony, stone tablets inscribed by the finger of God.
Exodus 31:18 CSB

When God inaugurated the old covenant, an inscription revealed the loving and eternal written Word—the Ten Commandments. Israel was given "stone tablets inscribed by the finger of God." Ironically, there was also an inscription at the inauguration of God's new covenant. It revealed the loving, eternal, and incarnate Word—Jesus. "Pilate wrote an inscription and fastened it to the cross. It read, 'Jesus of Nazareth, the King of the Jews'" (John 19:19 MOUNCE). Pilate then posted the sign as a warning for passersby that this was the humiliated, naked, beaten, crucified "King of the Jews." It communicated that any claim of kingship outside of Caesar would be crushed.

In another twist of irony, God rewrote the sign: "Jesus of Nazareth, the King of Jews and gentiles, of the rich and poor, of everyone who is Black or White or Brown, and of you." Through the death of the King of kings, God redeems all creation. The God-man hanging below the sign would soon die and rise in three days, thereby destroying the Deceiver's dominion and establishing God's kingdom.

Jesus, you are the King of kings. Today I confess you as my Lord of lords. Help me walk with you forever.

# יִשְׂגֶּה—*Yees'geh*

## "Grow"

"Can the papyrus grow up without a marsh? Can the reed grow without water?"
JOB 8:11 MEV

A long, long time ago, Bildad the Shuhite asked Job these two questions. They should make us think about our own growth. Just like plants depend on the right conditions to thrive, God wants us to have what we need to grow spiritually. Papyrus withers and dies without a swamp, and reeds will not grow without water. We also cannot grow without a deep, intimate connection with God and without knowing his direction.

Spiritual growth does not just magically happen. It takes effort and intention and requires you to strategically put yourself into environments where God can shape and mold you. This means spending more time in prayer, studying God's Word, serving, and being in community with other people who love Jesus. Without these things, you're just a papyrus without a marsh. You will not grow strong, and you're going to wither away when life gets tough. God wants us to be rooted in him so we can grow, stand tall and firm, and flourish. He is not suggesting that we try to succeed in our own strength but that we keep ourselves in places where he can pour into and feed us.

Lord, keep me in your presence and grow me like a California redwood.

# הֲדֹם רַגְלָי—*Hahdome Rahg'lay*

## "Footstool"

God never said to any of the angels, "Sit at my right side until I make your enemies into a footstool for you!"
HEBREWS 1:13 CEV

Hebrews 1:13 is part of a larger argument in Hebrews that Jesus is greater than anyone or anything else—in this case, angels. The right side was the place of honor, power, and authority, and it was never given to angels but to Christ alone.

Sometimes we may get wrapped up in life's daily struggles or distractions and start seeing Jesus as just another part of the story. This verse reminds us that he's not part of the story; he *is* the story. He's not just a good teacher, prophet, or some kind of magic man. As the focus of every teaching, prophecy, and miracle, he has all authority over all things. He has already won all the battles for you. Whatever you may be facing today, rest in the truth that you've already won because Jesus is on the throne with his feet on the stool. Every trial, challenge, fear, worry, or struggle has been made subject to him, and his feet rest comfortably on top of them.

How can you better rest in Jesus' authority and power when you're constantly tempted to rely on your own strength?

# יָנִיעוּ—*Yahnee'oo*

## "Wag"

All who see me mock at me, they make mouths at me,
they wag their heads.
Psalm 22:7 RSV

Psalm 22, written a thousand years before Jesus, shockingly describes his crucifixion. "Those who passed by derided him, wagging their heads" in scorn (Mark 15:29). In ancient Jewish culture, this gesture displayed intense contempt. Coincidence? I think not. It was prophecy coming to life.

As Jesus hung affixed to the cross by nails, offering himself sacrificially, people shouted things like, "If you're God's Son, get yourself down." And "Call God. Maybe he can help." Psalm 22 reminds us that Jesus willingly bore not just physical pain but also deep emotional wounds for us. The people around him were so clueless and nasty. They stood right in front of the Savior of the world, yet rather than shedding tears of love and compassion, they responded with ridicule and disdain.

Though we don't physically wag our heads at Jesus, we surely may be wagging away in our hearts. When you doubt his promises, question his plans for your life, or ignore the guidance of his Holy Spirit, you may be doing precisely the same thing those mockers did on that first Good Friday.

Lord, don't let me be a head wagger. Let me love, revere, honor, and share Christ.

# הֵיכָל—*Haykhahl*

## "Temple"

Solomon determined to build a temple for the name of the LORD.
2 CHRONICLES 2:1 NKJV

God promised David that his son Solomon would build God's house. Second Chronicles 2–5 records a synopsis of the massive building project that took seven and a half years and tens of thousands of workers to complete. For the temple to function as God intended, the only thing left was to deliver the ark of the covenant from its home on Mount Zion and to install it in its new home.

From the time of Moses, the ark represented God's presence, so it was placed in the Most Holy Place, the holy of holies, at the center of the temple (2 Chronicles 5:7). The position symbolized God's central place in Israelite life. It is too easy to get wrapped up in your own little fish tank, obsessing over your own stuff. God's proper place is as the focal point of every sphere of your life, directing it all—not as some afterthought benched on the sidelines. Despite the gold and grandeur of Solomon's Temple, it would have been woefully incomplete and meaningless if the ark had been missing. The same is true for us. If we can manage to keep the Lord in the center, life's purpose, direction, and meaning come beautifully into focus.

What have you placed in your holy of holies?

# שָׁבָה—*Shahvah*

## "Restore"

It was restored like the rest of his flesh.
EXODUS 4:7 NASB

When God called Moses to lead the charge in liberating his people from slavery, Moses was nearly paralyzed with feelings of inadequacy. To let him know that his task was not based on his strengths but on God's, the Lord gave him two signs. First, he turned Moses' staff into a snake and then back again. And second, he made Moses' hand leprous.

> [God] said, "Put your hand inside the fold of your robe again." So [Moses] put his hand into the fold again, and when he took it out of the fold, behold, it was restored like the rest of his flesh. (v. 7)

God can also heal the "leprous" areas of your life. In his grace and strength, God can bring restoration to your busted relationships, lost opportunities, or horrific addictions. Cling to hope and bring the issues faithfully to him, trusting that he can make things whole again. After all, Moses saw his hand go from healthy to diseased and back to healthy again. Do-overs are real. No matter how far you've fallen, Jesus offers you a do-over. Amid the mess, remember that God is all about second chances and restoration.

Jesus, thank you for second, third, and hundredth chances.

# חָזוֹן—*Khahzone*

## "Vision"

"They speak visions from their own minds, not from the mouth of the Lord."
Jeremiah 23:16 niv

Has your day ever been interrupted by someone declaring, "God told me to tell you…," and you felt a little icky? Jeremiah, a legit prophet, gave us a warning about false prophets. He painfully revealed that not everything people say is from God actually is and that not everyone claiming to speak for God actually speaks for him.

False prophets make big promises that never pan out and only provide false hope because their words all come from their minds, not God's. God warned, "Do not listen to what the prophets are prophesying to you; they fill you with false hopes. They speak visions from their own minds, not from the mouth of the Lord" (v. 16). Be careful, then, which voices you allow into your ears. Just because somebody speaks in King James English, sounds spiritual, or stands in a church pulpit doesn't mean their message is Holy Spirit driven. Measure their words against God's. My grandpa told me long ago, "If it doesn't sound quite right, the odds are pretty high that it's wrong." So let's practice:

Me: Hey, dude, God gave me a word for you.

You: Thanks. Let's make sure it 100 percent aligns with Scripture.

God, please help me always recognize truth from lies.

# שָׁמוֹעַ תִּשְׁמְעוּ—*Shahmoah Teesh'm'oo*

## "Obey!"

"If you will indeed obey My voice…, then you shall be a special treasure."
Exodus 19:5 NKJV

Seventy-five days after the Lord unshackled the Israelites from Egypt, he instructed Moses to deliver this message: "If you will indeed obey My voice and keep My covenant, then you shall be a special treasure to Me above all people" (v. 5). Because Hebrew has no punctuation, we lose something in the translation of *shahmoah teesh'm'oo* to "obey." It seems like a lot of Hebrew to land on the little word *obey*, right? The root of the two words *shahmoah* and *teesh'm'oo* is the same, so it really translates to "obey, obey." In our culture, we would add five exclamation points or write *OBEY*.

Here are two more little nuggets. First, the root of *shahmoah* and *teesh'm'oo* also often translates as "hear." Second, the verse here begins with *if*, making God's covenant conditional. Israel would have heard the booming voice of God saying this: "If you hear, hear and obey, obey…" God is like a divine GPS, with obedience as the preferred route. Obedience means abiding in his guidance. How? Through knowing his Word, consistently connecting with him in prayer, and asking for his strength, you can arrive at the destination he has perfectly prepared for you.

Father, help me hear you and obey your Word.

JULY 28

# סְגֻלָּה—*S'goolah*

## "Special Treasure"

"If you will indeed obey…, then you shall be a special treasure to Me above all people."
EXODUS 19:5 NKJV

Today is the *then* of yesterday's *if.* God said, "If you will indeed obey My voice and keep My covenant, then you shall be a special treasure to Me above all people" (v. 5). To better understand *s'goolah* in Exodus 19:5, consider some different translations: "precious possession" (CEB), "you will belong to Me" (NLV), and "my own little flock" (TLB). *S'goolah* implies a treasure like that of diamonds and gold, a treasure of immense value owned privately and individually by a king. Choice is also part of the equation since a king chooses the diamonds and gold that he wants because he is the king. If Israel accepted and obeyed the terms of God's proposition, Israel would be his own priceless treasure.

When you choose to listen to God and walk in his ways (though imperfectly), you become his unique treasure. Feeling insignificant? Remember that to him, you're more precious than the Hope Diamond. Knowing that you're God's foremost treasure will transform how you view yourself. When you get it, you'll begin making better life decisions, let go of shame, embrace grace, pursue purpose, and treat others with love.

Lord, help me see myself and others as you do.

# שְׁאֵרִית—*Sh'ayreet*

## "Remnant"

Who is a God like you, forgiving sin and passing over rebellion for the remnant of his inheritance?
MICAH 7:18 LEB

Micah 7:18 looks back to the exodus, when God liberated Israel, and forward to the eventual supreme freedom and pardon available in the cross. In Exodus 34:6–7, God declared to Moses that he would shower Israel with grace and forgiveness even after the people built an idol when Moses was on Sinai, but the book of Micah focuses on God's dealing with the faithful few—the remnant. It seems like God has always dealt with remnants. Even when most are rebellious, God remains merciful to those who persevere to the end, and those who persevere to the end do so because of his saving grace. In Micah's time, despite widespread unfaithfulness, God pardoned the sins of the remnant. Despite how wicked the world gets, when we remain in him, he remains in us. Jesus promised, "I am with you always, to the end of the age" (Matthew 28:20 CSB).

Paul reminded us, "It's the same way in the present age: there is a remnant, chosen by grace" (Romans 11:5 CJB). You can take tremendous comfort in knowing that even today, God's mercy and grace "removes guilt and pardons sin for the remnant of his inheritance."

Jesus, let me live boldly for you because you live boldly for me.

JULY 30

# אֶשְׁכַּח—*Ehsh'kahkh*

## "Forget"

I will delight in Your statutes; I will not forget Your word.
PSALM 119:16 HCSB

Psalm 119 is a beautiful collection of twenty-two prayers and meditations, arranged alphabetically, that reflect on the nature of God's Word. The psalmist encouraged us to revel in Scripture. It is God's love letter to humankind—a personal message full of promises, wisdom, and truth. When the psalmist wrote, "I will delight in Your statutes," he testified to an intentional choice to rejoice in God's Word, effectively declaring, "This matters to me. It's not just a list of dos and don'ts; it is my source of life, peace, and direction."

In the busyness of life, it's easy to forget to spend time every day with God in his Word. This verse challenges us to dive in headfirst and delight in it every day. It reminds us that Scripture isn't white noise in the background of life; it is the very heartbeat of our faith. Choose to make his testimony a priority in your life. Use this devotional to meditate on one of God's words daily or copy Billy Graham's habit of reading five psalms every day. Whatever method you choose, be intentional and joyful and allow God's Word to shape your heart and renew your mind.

Lord, help me hear from you in the pages of your Word.

# נַחֲלָת—*Nahkhahlaht*

## "Inheritance"

He is the Maker of all things, including Israel,
the people of his inheritance.
Jeremiah 10:16 NIV

The word *nahkhahlaht* generally refers to a possession someone has a legal right to. Jeremiah was written in the context of Israel's continual plunges into idol worship. In this verse, God essentially argued, "No! You are my possession. I'm the one who created everything, and you are my special people."

This idea of inheritance really goes both ways. We are his, and he is ours. Paul carried the thought forward in Ephesians when he wrote about the exceptional blessings of Christ. He proclaimed that when we heard the gospel and placed saving faith in Jesus, we "were sealed with the promised Holy Spirit, who is the guarantee of our inheritance until we acquire possession of it" (Ephesians 1:13–14 ESV). When you surrender your life to Jesus, the Holy Spirit takes up residence inside you as a seal—a mark of ownership, protection, and inheritance with a guaranteed future. His presence in your life is like holding a winning lottery ticket until you finally take possession of the prize. Therefore, live confidently and boldly through difficulties or victories, knowing that he will lead you, guide you, and hold your spot at the Lord's table.

How can you better lean into the Holy Spirit's guidance?

# מָשִׁיחַ—*Mahsheeyakh*

## "Messiah; Anointed"

"It is finished."
JOHN 19:30 ESV

In the King James Version, *Mahsheeyakh* is translated "Messiah" twice and "anointed" thirty-seven times. One who is anointed is set apart for something special—for a unique mission. Have no doubt that Jesus of Nazareth was born for a mission, one that would forever quench the flames of our greatest troubles. He was born to destroy pain, tears, disease, rebellion, and sin and to finally right humanity's failure in the garden through his death and resurrection. This was a mission only the *Mahsheeyakh* could accomplish.

First-century Jewish expectation was that God's Anointed One would enter Jerusalem in an M1A2 Abrams tank and blow the Romans back to Rome. But to their surprise, he was beaten mercilessly and physically died a criminal's death. In the seconds before he took his last breath, he uttered the Aramaic word *mashelem* (in Greek, *tetelestai*; in English, "It is finished"). What was finished? His task and very reason for being were finished, completed. Redemption was accomplished, once-for-all forgiveness became available, and Christ followers now have unfettered access to God because "it is finished." In that nanosecond, Satan became a defeated foe, and humankind entered the winner's circle.

How does the finished work of Christ on the cross impact the way you handle feelings of guilt, shame, or unworthiness?

# יְהוָה נִסִּי—*Yahweh Neesee*

## "The Lord Is My Banner"

Thank God! He gives us victory over sin and death through our Lord Jesus Christ.
1 Corinthians 15:57 NLT

The Amalekites were the first to attack the Israelites after they came out of slavery in Egypt. Flying the "banner" of the power of *Yahweh Neesee* (Yahweh Nissi) and led into battle by Joshua, Israel whipped Amalek and his warriors at a place called Rephidim. "Moses built an altar and named it The Lord Is My Banner" (Exodus 17:15 AMP). Ancient armies carried banners that evoked passionate feelings of devotion to their cause. This altar became a rallying point of worship, a place of recognizing that Yahweh himself was the banner of Israel who ensured victory.

MercyMe captured two mighty words in the title of their 2017 hit song "We Win." As Christ followers, we fight from a position of triumph because God "gives us victory over sin and death through our Lord Jesus Christ." Sin and death no longer wield power over us because we fly the flag of Christ. Does your walk reflect an understanding that you've already won, Satan has already lost, and Jesus reigns victoriously from the right hand of the Father as your advocate?

Jesus, I praise you today for winning the battle on my behalf.

# בְּקָדְשׁוֹ —*B'kahd'sho*

## "His Sanctuary"

Praise God in his sanctuary.
Psalm 150:1 KJV

The Hebrew root for "sanctuary" (קדש) is the same as the words for "holy," "hallowed," "sacred," and "consecrated." If that doesn't paint a picture of what should occur in every church on the planet, I don't know what does. The word *praise* is repeated thirteen times in Psalm 150's six verses. Over and over, the psalmist declared, "Praise God! Praise him! Praise the Lord!"

Walking through church doors into a sanctuary should be an incredibly unique experience, with the worshiper feeling an overwhelming sense of holiness, peace, unity, and belonging. In the sanctuary, you morph from an isolated individual to a critical part of a community united by Jesus. Singing, raising hands, praying together, hearing God's Word—it's all worship. Praising and worshiping him pave the way for deep connections with the Lord and lead to meaningful relationships with each other. So praise him in his house. It is where anxieties, fears, and doubts can be brought in and left permanently at the foot of his cross. Praise God for his "mighty acts" and "excellent greatness" (v. 2). The next time you breach the doors of a sanctuary, shout hallelujah and dance like David danced (tell them I said it's okay).

Lord, I praise you that I can praise you all the days of my life.

# מִדְבָּר—*Meed'bahr*

## "Wilderness"

"I will make a way in the wilderness."
Isaiah 43:19 LEB

Isaiah 43 looks back to the exodus events in Egypt and possibly toward the deliverance of thousands of Jews from captivity in Babylon. God said, "I am about to do a new thing!…I will make a way in the wilderness" (v. 19). However, in much grander fashion, it looks forward to the deliverance from sin offered to humanity through Jesus' sacrificial work and the hope he provides. As monumental as God's many Old Testament acts of redemption are, they are all but a shadow or type of the Son's delivery of billions from long seasons in the wilderness to the Father's loving arms.

Do you feel stuck in the mire of isolation? Or maybe you're in a prolonged season of spiritual drought, feeling empty, lifeless, and directionless as if you were in a desert. Smack in the face of your feelings, God declares he will make a way in *your* wilderness. He will blaze a path where you never dreamed a path was "blazable." When you're frustrated and feeling thoroughly dehydrated, rest in the hope of God's promise of new things, new paths, new joy, new purpose, new meaning, and new life.

Yahweh, I trust you're working in the barrenness for my good and your glory.

# נָחָשׁ—*Nahkhahsh*

## "Serpent"

The serpent was more crafty than any other wild animal.
GENESIS 3:1 LEB

Over the years, Bible scholars have used many different words to describe the snake that slithered here and there in Eden—*crafty*, *cunning*, *shrewd*, *subtle*, *clever*, and *sneaky*. My personal descriptor is *slimy dirtbag*. They all provide a glimpse into the nature of evil, sin, temptation, and deception.

God gave Adam and Eve complete dominion over creation with one exception: Don't eat from that one tree over there. And the first words that spewed out of the serpent's mouth were "Did God really say, 'You must not eat from any tree in the garden'?" (Genesis 3:1 NIV). And humankind plunged into a lifetime of struggling with sin and temptation. Every sin begins with the same question: "Did God really say [fill in your greatest temptation]?" *Did he really say I should keep forgiving my sister when she keeps hurting me? Well, he must not know her.* When you're tempted to reinterpret God's Word to suit your own desires, don't. It's a short trip down that road to completely rationalizing your sin, embracing the snake, and ignoring the one who died for you. Remember, the serpent is a lying scumbag and wants to wreck your life.

Lord, guard my heart from the devil's deception.

AUGUST 6

# שָׁוְא—*Shahv*

## "In Vain"

Unless the Lord builds the house,
they labor in vain who build it.
Psalm 127:1 NKJV

Psalm 127, typically credited to Solomon, is about the huge blessing of a fruitful family life, specifically the heritage of children. We have no idea how many children Solomon had, but with three hundred wives and seven hundred concubines, it must have been a bucketful. So he knew at least something about kids. Solomon was telling us that "unless the Lord builds the house," everything is meaningless. The word *shahv* is best understood as "nothingness." The big picture truth is this: Unless the Lord builds your work life, marriage, family, kids, church, and relationships, the labor is in vain.

How can you build a great "house"—career, family, or church life? Work diligently and efficiently, as if it completely depends on you. Pour into your kids, serve in your church, and nurture your relationships as if all the successes rely on you. But pray as if it all depends on God, which of course it does. Live life knowing that if you build anything on your own, then you're on your own. But if anything is built with God's strength, then you're under his blessing.

What houses in your life do you need to give God to build?

# מִלְחָמָה—*Meel'khahmah*

## "Battle"

"He may have a great army, but they are merely men. We have the LORD our God to help us and to fight our battles for us!"
2 CHRONICLES 32:8 NLT

In about 701 BC, Sennacherib, the king of Assyria, invaded Judah and headed toward Jerusalem. Hezekiah, Judah's king, encouraged the people to "be strong and courageous" (v. 7), an exhortation that appears eleven times in the Old Testament to encourage people and their leaders when facing challenges. Hezekiah told his people that Sennacherib "may have a great army, but they are merely men. We have the LORD our God to help us and to fight our battles for us!" His reassurance that God had their backs instilled confidence that they could face the daunting task of opposing the frightening Assyrian military. It didn't matter if Sennacherib had a hundred million Apache attack helicopters; God could flick them into oblivion with his pinky finger.

When there is a seemingly unconquerable mountain in front of you, remember that God's power is greater than ten thousand mountains or valleys. Rather than depending on your solutions or strength, let your courage and confidence rest in the truth that the battle belongs to the Lord because his ability to defend you knows no limits.

What battles do you need to give God today?

# מְהַדֵּר—*M'hahdahr*

## "To Honor"

I, Nebuchadnezzar, looked up toward heaven, and I was in my right mind again. Then I gave praise to God Most High. I gave honor and glory to him who lives forever.
Daniel 4:34 ERV

Nebuchadnezzar was a prime-time success story—powerful and wealthy beyond belief. He believed he was in control, was invincible, and was eaten up with pride. Then life turned upside down. God humbled Nebuchadnezzar big-time. The king lost his mind and lived like an animal in the wild. Unfortunately, he didn't look up until he was deep in the pit. That's when humility struck, his mind was restored, and he recognized that all honor belongs to the God of Israel, not the man in his mirror.

This story reminds us to refrain from pridefully chasing our own ambitions, working for recognition and praise, or forgetting where our gifts, skills, and abilities came from in the first place. Nebuchadnezzar's transformation is proof that honor doesn't come from elevating self but from embracing the Lord's sovereignty in our lives. Learn from Nebuchadnezzar's experiences and look up long before you find yourself in a pit. Praise and honor God in your successes and in your failures, and you'll find peace and purpose like you never have before.

How can you better give credit where credit is due?

## AUGUST 9

# שְׂפָתַי—*S'fahtah*

## "Lips"

I will sing of your forgiveness, for my lips will be unsealed.
PSALM 51:14–15 TLB

Imagine this pivotal moment in David's life. He felt the heavy weight of his mistakes and cried out for God's mercy and forgiveness. If the Lord could find the grace to forgive him, David promised, "I will sing of your forgiveness, for my lips will be unsealed—oh, how I will praise you" (vv. 14–15).

Think about a time when you messed up—I mean really messed up. For me, the feelings of guilt, shame, and unworthiness shut me down. I didn't want to talk to God or anyone else. I wanted to crawl under a rock like Adam trying to hide from God in Eden. But David wasn't hiding here, nor was he looking for a free pass. Instead, he was longing to reconnect with the God who controlled his slingshot when Goliath fell. He knew that if God forgave him, the unburdening would be so overwhelming that his lips would proclaim God's goodness from the mountaintops.

Therefore, when you fail or falter, turn to God in transparency rather than running and hiding in silence. He longs for the reconnection more than you do. And when you experience his forgiveness, unseal your lips and share the story with everyone you know.

Lord Jesus, thank you for always being there with open arms.

# בָּרָא—*Bahrah*

## "Create"

By faith we understand that the universe was created by the word of God, so that what is seen came into being from the invisible.
HEBREWS 11:3 NCB

From the Bible's first words, we're introduced to the God who loved us before the foundation of the world and chose to masterfully create—spontaneously, intentionally, orderly, purposefully, and out of nothing. From the beauty of a snowcapped mountain standing tall and unwavering to the sun emerging from the horizon to provide divine light across the sky to the rhythmic waves in the Pacific, God speaks. Just look at the endless palette of stars in the night sky, each flickering like a diamond on the finger of a bride-to-be and positioned exactly where the Sovereign decided it should be.

Yahweh's hand is clear in the quiver of a hummingbird's wings, the elaborate pattern on a snowflake, and the symphony of robins and blackbirds at first light. And now for the pinnacle of his creation—man and woman. The Creator's wisdom is woven into the very tapestry of life, and his imprint is stamped on the intricate design of a human cell, where tiny little machines work together in perfect harmony. Yeah, I'm thinking creation wasn't random chance.

Lord, when I think of the work of your hands, I stand in awe and worship.

# יְהוָה יִרְאֶה—*Yahweh Yeereh*

## "The Lord Will Provide; the Lord Will See to It"

God will be faithful to you. He will screen and filter the severity, nature, and timing of every test or trial you face so that you can bear it. And each test is an opportunity to trust him more, for along with every trial God has provided for you a way of escape that will bring you out of it victoriously.
1 Corinthians 10:13 TPT

In Genesis 22, as Abraham was heading up the mountain to sacrifice his son, *Yahweh Yeereh* (Yahweh Jireh) was proactively providing the substitute: A ram was hiking up the other side. I have no doubt that Abraham was tempted, over and over, to turn around, look up, and say, "C'mon, Lord! I ain't doing it." But he trusted and pressed on.

Everyone experiences times of temptation. Sometimes the periods seem unending, and sometimes they're fleeting. I love the image The Passion Translation paints in 1 Corinthians 10:13. It emphasizes that God is faithful and goes above and beyond to provide a way out of every temptation. Our role is to trust him and actively search for and recognize his provision, whether through prayer, Bible study, or accountability partners.

When temptation hits, Lord, help me trust you, believing you will provide an escape route.

# דַּיָּן הָאֱמֶת—*Dahyahn Hah'ehmeht*

## "The Righteous Judge"

We know that God causes everything to work together for the good of those who love God and are called in accordance with his purpose.
ROMANS 8:28 CJB

The *Dahyahn Hah'ehmeht* (Dayan Ha'emet) is a prayer said at Jewish funerals declaring that God is a sovereign and righteous judge. He is the one who holds the keys to life and death, and we don't have the luxury to question him.

Consider the experience of second-century Rabbi Akiva ben Yosef, who couldn't find a place to stay. Instead of getting angry, he thought, *Everything God does is for the best*. He camped under the stars with his donkey, his rooster, and a lamp for Torah study. During the night, his lamp blew out, a snake killed his rooster, and a lion ate the donkey. In the morning, he found out thieves had attacked the nearby village. But he realized that if his lamp had been lit or the animals had made noise, the thieves would have found him too. All this trouble actually saved his life.

In the middle of the fire, as a Christ follower, you can trust that God is working all things for good despite your inability to see the complete picture. His will is to conform you to the image of Jesus, which provides hope beyond the junk of life.

Jot down a few ways you've seen God turn lemons into lemonade.

## AUGUST 13

# תִּשְׁעָה בְּאָב—*Teesh'ah-b'Ahv*

### "9th of Av"

Jesus was born in Bethlehem in Judea, during the time of King Herod.
MATTHEW 2:1 NIV

*Teesh'ah-b'Ahv* (Tishah-b'Av) is a day of mourning that commemorates the date when the First Temple fell to Babylon, the Second Temple fell to Rome, and the Jews were thrown out of England in 1290 and Spain in 1492. It is a fast day similar to Yom Kippur. Jews refrain from eating, bathing, wearing perfume, listening to music, having sex, wearing leather, and doing anything pleasurable. Other than the book of Job and the parts of Jeremiah that deal with destruction, the study of Torah on *Teesh'ah-b'Ahv* is forbidden. Jewish tradition provides hope by saying that the Messiah will be born on *Teesh'ah-b'Ahv* and will eventually lead the building of a third temple.

As a Christian, the birth pangs of my hope began when *Y'hoshooah Mahsheeyakh* (Jesus the Messiah) was born around 5 BC. Months earlier, an angel came to Jesus' earthly father, Joseph, and said that Mary "will give birth to a son, and you are to give him the name Jesus, because he will save his people from their sins" (Matthew 1:21). He came not to lead a building project but to lead people into a saving relationship with Yahweh via his sacrificial blood.

Thank you, Jesus, that you turn mourning into dancing.

# תְּאֵנָה—*T'aynah*

## "Fig"

"There was a man who planted a fig tree in his orchard. But every time he came to gather fruit from his tree he found none, for it was barren."
LUKE 13:6 TPT

Figs were the first fruit mentioned in the Bible when Adam and Eve covered themselves with fig leaves (Genesis 3:7). In Jewish literature, fig trees often represent prosperity, security, or the nation of Israel—particularly its spiritual state.

In Luke 13:6–9, Jesus used an illustration about a fruitless fig tree to teach about repentance and God's patience with us. Finding a fig tree barren, the owner said, "Cut it down!" (v. 7). But the gardener pleaded for his tree, asking the owner to give it another year to bear fruit.

Praise God that he's long-suffering with us. If there is breath in our lungs, we can turn to him, accept his forgiveness, and bear fruit. Do you consistently recognize his patience in your life? The fig tree's lack of fruit resulted in a warning of judgment. In the same way, our lives ought to display evidence of repentance and transformation because a fruitless Christian is an oxymoron.

Lord, show me the areas in my life where I need to repent and help me bear fruit for your kingdom.

# צֹאן שַׁעַר—*Tzone Shah'ahr*

## "Sheep Gate"

"Do you truly long to be well?"
JOHN 5:6 TPT

In 586 BC, the Babylonians destroyed the wall around Jerusalem. About 150 years later, Nehemiah took on the task of rebuilding it. As part of that project, the high priest Eliashib and other priests rebuilt the Sheep Gate (Nehemiah 3:1).

Five hundred years later, in the pool of Bethesda, just 150 feet from the Sheep Gate, Jesus encountered a man on the Sabbath who had been an invalid for thirty-eight years. It seemed like an odd question, but Jesus asked the man if he honestly yearned to be well. This man explained that he agonized daily, trying to pull himself into the pool's waters, which many people believed had healing power when they stirred. But every time he got close as it was churning, someone jumped in first. For years and years, he believed this water had magical healing power. Jesus' original question was really a statement: *If you genuinely desire healing, stop wasting your time obsessing over that useless water and focus on me!* Into the sick man's misplaced faith, Jesus spoke, "Get up…and walk" (John 5:8 ESV). If you really want to be whole and healed, stop looking in all the wrong places. Focus on the only one who has the power, authority, and ability to do it—Jesus.

Jesus, let me keep my eyes laser focused on you.

# עַיִן טוֹבָה/עַיִן רָעַע—

## *Ahyeen Tovah/Ahyeen Rah'ah*

### "Good Eye/Evil Eye"

"'Is it not permitted for me to do whatever I want with what is mine? Or is your eye evil because I am generous?'"
MATTHEW 20:15 LEB

In ancient Jewish culture, the evil eye was tied to jealousy, greed, and a nasty attitude. The good eye referred to a person who was generous, was kind, and looked at others with a positive, compassionate attitude. For example, "He who is generous [*ahyeen tovah*] will be blessed" (Proverbs 22:9).

In Matthew 20:1–16, Jesus told a parable about a master who hired workers at different times of the day. Each agreed to his wage when hired. But at the end of the day, the ones who worked the longest were enraged because the ones who worked the fewest hours were paid the same amount. The master essentially responded, "Who died and left you in charge? Can't I do what I want with my money? Or do you begrudge my generosity?" Like that master, God is merciful to whomever he decides to be merciful. We don't have the privilege to question. My dad was saved at age eighty-nine, about thirty hours before he died. Trust me that there is no remedial section in heaven for those "hired" late in the day. My father is in the arms of the Savior.

Father, I praise you that your ways are not my ways.

# אֲדוֹן עוֹלָם—*Ahdone Olahm*

## "Lord of the World"

When I consider your heavens, the work of your fingers, the moon and the stars, which you have set in place, what is mankind that you are mindful of them, human beings that you care for them?
Psalm 8:3–4 NIV

*Ahdone Olahm* (Adon Olam) is a five-stanza prayer sung in synagogues everywhere at the end of every Sabbath service. It praises God for his transcendence and immanence. The first three stanzas reflect on his transcendence—the fact that he created everything, his sovereignty, rulership, glory, uniqueness, power, dominion, and eternal presence. The final two stanzas ask the worshiper to consider that despite God's transcendence, God is also near; he is your Rock, Redeemer, Refuge, Portion, and Protector.

In Psalm 8, David posed an obvious question: Why in the world would the sovereign creator of everything that will ever exist care one iota about us? While we cannot know God's mind, we can trust in his love and providential care for us. The crescendo of God's love and care for us came in the form of his Son's birth, death, burial, resurrection, and ascension, all of which paved the way for an eternity with him.

Lord, when I'm in a season of doubt or feeling insignificant, let me rest in the truth that I am a child of the one true King.

# אַבָּא—*Ahbah*

## "Father"

You received a Spirit that shows you are adopted as [God's] children. With this Spirit, we cry, "Abba, Father."
ROMANS 8:15 CEB

The term *ahbah* (abba) is not used in the Old Testament, but it appears three times in the New Testament. It is a term of endearment that conveys a sense of personal intimacy. Ancient Jews never addressed God using *Ahbah* because it is much too familiar. However, on the night of Jesus' arrest, he prayed in Gethsemane: "'*Abba*!' (that is, 'Dear Father!')" (Mark 14:36 CJB). This is a striking image of an intimate Father-Son relationship.

In Romans 8:15, Paul used adoption as a metaphor for the relationship between Christ followers and God. Adopted children often feel deeply wanted by their adoptive parents due to the extensive efforts made during the adoption process. When we are indwelled with the Holy Spirit, we're infused with the undeniable reality that we are wanted by God and have the privilege of calling him *Ahbah*. As a Christian, you can wake up daily knowing that you belong to God and are loved by him as a father. He yearns for you. What a remarkable thought! You can crawl up in his lap every day and share your deepest needs with him.

What practical steps can you take today to embrace the freedom of being an adopted child of God?

## AUGUST 19

# רָעָה—*Rah-ah*

## “To Feed”

“Feed my sheep.”
John 21:17 esv

On the heels of Peter’s three denials of even knowing this Jesus guy, he and Jesus had a heart-to-heart conversation. Jesus asked Peter three times if he loved him, and Jesus commanded Peter three times to “feed my sheep.” In this passage, *feed* moves far beyond Purina sheep chow. It’s all about spiritual development—making disciples who make disciples. Peter was commissioned to care for those who follow Jesus and ensure they were intentionally and strategically nurtured in faith, truth, and love. Consider shepherds. They don’t just randomly chuck food at the sheep and leave; they lead the sheep to good pastures, protect them from anything that would bring harm, and keep a watchful eye on them.

In much the same way, you are called not only to surrender to Jesus’ lordship but to actively care for those around you who are his, share his truth, offer encouragement, and be a compassionate guide when someone strays from the fold. You can’t work remotely and be a good shepherd. You must walk alongside your sheep in their journeys, strengthening their faith and being an ever-present reminder of God’s steadfast love for them. Deep investment into people’s lives is what every day demands.

Who around you needs to be fed today?

AUGUST 20

# מְדָּה—*Meedah*

## “Measure”

“Wisdom began when God gave power to the wind. It was when he measured the water and put limits on it.”
Job 28:25 ICB

Job 28:25 reminds us that God isn’t some faraway entity who set the world in the sky, spun it, and went to the Bahamas till the end times. He is actively involved, carefully designing, crafting, and sustaining everything we see and don’t see. Every wind gust and raindrop are part of his plan—ordered and intentional.

The God who powers the wind and measures the rain is also the God who powers your faith and measures your tears. If he is paying meticulous attention to the minutiae of the physical world, can you even imagine the level of attention he pays to the crown of his creation—you? You are not the result of a cosmic mud-puddle experiment gone luckily haywire; you are the beautiful creation of a lovingly intentional and detailed God. Despite the feelings of chaos the world may evoke, God is anything but arbitrary. He’s a strategic planner who opens and closes doors, guides steps, and orchestrates events for the good of those who are his. Trust him to be just as precise with the details of your life as he is with the details of creation.

Thank you, Lord, for your purpose-driven hand.

# אֲבַקֵּשׁ—*Ahvahkaysh*

## "I Will Search"

"I will search for the lost. I will bring back those who have wandered away. I will bandage the ones who are hurt. I will make the weak ones stronger."
EZEKIEL 34:16 NIRV

Speaking about NFL Hall of Fame linebacker Dick Butkus, Deacon Jones said, "Butkus would follow a man up in the stands and hit him. He would follow him up in the tunnel in the coliseum. I've seen him do it."[9] That's an image, maybe a weird one, of God's relentless pursuit of men and women.

When we were far from God, he was patient with us because he doesn't want anyone to eternally perish (2 Peter 3:9). It is exceptionally comforting to know that regardless of where we are today or what we've done in the past, God's pursuit is constant. He is perpetually and actively searching for the lost to help them find their way back to him—to unshackle those in chains, heal the wounded, and strengthen the weak. So if you are feeling distant and disconnected from the Lord or have never entered into a personal relationship with him, remember that he has been hunting you down for years and will continue to do so as long as there's breath in your lungs. It would serve you well to consider allowing him to catch you.

How can you open yourself up to God's healing power?

9 Deacon Jones, "Sports Illustrated Presents NFL Crunch Course," produced by NFL Films, posted February 7, 2015, by Ian Ward, YouTube, 46 min., 16 sec., youtube.com.

# עִוְרִים—*Eev'reem*

## "The Blind"

The Lord opens the eyes of the blind.
Psalm 146:8 ESV

Psalm 146 kicks off the final five psalms, which all begin and end with "Praise the Lord!" In verses 7–9, the psalmist used eight metaphors for the praiseworthy salvation available in Yahweh. For those who feel like they're stumbling around in the dark, the psalmist declared, "The Lord opens the eyes of the blind," painting a picture of how God rescues us from the darkness.

On the "dark side" of the cross, we're like people walking through life in the pitch black, making self-serving decisions driven by pride. Salvation is like God flipping the switch and flooding life with light. Finally, we see who we are, who he is, and our desperate need for him. God's rescue mission is comprehensive; he doesn't simply give us twenty-twenty vision and hit the road. He lifts us up, dusts us off, and walks alongside us until he calls us home. Metaphorically, providing sight to the blind is about enlightenment, freedom, and a relationship with a loving Father who doesn't want us flailing away in darkness. If you feel stuck in blindness, remember that God has been in the business of providing light for a long time.

Lord, open my eyes to what you have for me.

# בֹּחֵן—*Bokhayn*

## "To Test"

"I know also, my God, that you test the heart and take pleasure in integrity."
1 Chronicles 29:17 cjb

Do you ever lay your head down at night feeling like life dumped a giant boulder on you just to see how you'll react? David would say, "Get in line." In 1 Chronicles 29:10–20, he was coming to the end of his life and delivered a beautiful prayer in front of the whole assembly of Israel. In verse 17, he acknowledged that Yahweh is a heart-testing God, but his tests aren't pass-fail tests. Instead, they're opportunities to discover the heart of the issue—what's really going on inside us.

It's easy to say, "I trust the Lord," when all is well. But when you're getting beat up in a season of testing, the true you is exposed. Do you turn to God or turn to yourself? Do you lean on his strength or act like you have it covered? This verse reminds you that God takes pleasure "in integrity"—a heart that's authentic and righteous. Therefore, turn every testing period into a growth period by allowing him to refine and shape you into who he wants you to be by conforming you into the image of his Son.

Jesus, please don't ever stop testing my heart.

AUGUST 24

# לֵץ—*Laytz*

## "Scoffer"

"Scoffer" is the name of the arrogant, haughty man who acts with arrogant pride.
Proverbs 21:24 ESV

If the book of Proverbs had a Gallery of Fools, the scoffer would be its centerpiece. He and his revolting attitude appear nearly twenty times in the book, hating correction (9:7), not heeding rebuke (13:1), failing to find wisdom (14:6), causing misery for parents (17:21), serving as an example to the naive (19:25), and causing division (22:10). The scoffer is the dude who always has something negative to say, rolls his eyes at everything, and thinks he knows better. Since Proverbs is wisdom literature, this verse is a warning against becoming a person who is so full of themself that they can't see past their arrogant pride.

God is calling you away from a scoffing mindset and into a lifestyle of humility—listening more and scoffing less. Scoffers don't just erect walls between themselves and others. No, no, no. They also build mountains between themselves and God. Pride blinds you to wisdom and discernment and stunts growth. Therefore, check yourself regularly and make sure arrogance is not sneaking into your life. Be coachable, kind, and humble. Rather than being a know-it-all, be an encourager, lifting people up for the sake of the gospel.

Lord, help me embrace correction, love wisdom, and champion unity.

# הִנְנִי שְׁלָחֵנִי—*Heen'nee Sh'lahkhaynee*

## "Here I Am. Send Me!"

"Here I am. Send me!"
Isaiah 6:8 NCV

Imagine Isaiah seeing himself in a vision. He was standing in the temple and hearing a thunderous voice like James Earl Jones reverberating everywhere: "Whom can I send? Who will go for us?" (v. 8). Isaiah immediately responded he was in. He didn't say, "I need to pray about it." He didn't say, "Let me write down the pros and the cons." He brazenly and unashamedly declared, "Here I am. Send me!"

The Lord's question in Isaiah 6:8 echoes throughout history to us today: *Who is willing to share the good news of the love, hope, and forgiveness found in my Son, Jesus? Who is willing to reach out around the globe to those who haven't heard?* The evangelical tone in today's verse is clear. God is looking for willing hearts to proclaim the gospel. But you are probably not a preacher or a missionary, so are you asked to go too? Yes! The charge is not for a select few. The mission is for every single Christ follower. If you feel unqualified, consider Isaiah's exhaustive list of credentials: (1) willingness. If you are willing to be sent, God will happily fill in all the gaps.

Jesus, I will go wherever you direct me to go.

# מְצוּלָה—*M'tzoolah*

## "Deep; Depth"

You, with all God's people, will be given strength to grasp the breadth, length, height and depth of the Messiah's love.
EPHESIANS 3:18 CJB

Ephesians 3:14–21 captures Paul's heartfelt prayer for the believers in Ephesus. He prayed that they—and by extension all Christ followers throughout history—would be strengthened in Christ, indwelled by his Spirit, and wholly immersed in his love. How wide is Jesus' love for you? How long? High? Deep? Forever in every direction. These four dimensions simply cannot contain the love of Christ.

I don't know how you were raised, nor do I know where you are today. Perhaps you were raised in a deeply dysfunctional family and never felt the love and devotion of godly parents. Maybe you are in a marriage devoid of sacrificial love. Maybe you've bought the lie that your past disqualifies you from love, period. God declares otherwise. His love is big enough for every person who yields in submission to him at the cross. There is no limit. It's deep enough for the abused and the abuser, the addict and the pusher, the woman who underwent an abortion and the abortionist. Corrie ten Boom once said, "There is no pit so deep that God's love is not deeper still."[10]

Lord, thank you that your love is bigger than my past.

10 Kaylena Radcliff, "A War Story: 'There Is No Pit So Deep God's Love Is Not Deeper Still,'" *Christian History*, 2017, 43, christianhistoryinstitute.org.

# בֶּגֶד—*Vehgehd*

## "Garment"

"'You must not wear a garment made of two different kinds of material.'"
LEVITICUS 19:19 NET

This verse begins with a prohibition against breeding different types of animals and different categories of plants and ends with the command against wearing garments of various fabrics. You can almost see the logic in the first two, but the don't-wear-a-polyester-and-cotton-T-shirt rule seems utterly absurd—until we realize that there's more to it than meets the eye. The Lord used these examples to teach his people about being distinct, unique, and set apart from the nations surrounding them. By obeying these commands, they were reminded every day of their special identity as God's people. He symbolically encouraged them not to assimilate their beliefs and practices with the cultures around them, particularly concerning idol worship and customs and traditions that were dishonoring to God.

The principle of Leviticus 19:19 lives on and should be honored. God calls us to think, speak, and live differently—not by being like a hermit but by making choices that reflect biblical values and point people to him. It may be choosing honesty when it's easier to bend the truth, feeding a homeless guy downtown when others choose indifference, or clinging to hope in a storm when negativity surrounds you.

Lord, help me be in the world without being of the world.

AUGUST 28

# אֶהְיֶה—*Eh'h'yeh*

## "I Am"

"Before Abraham was, I am."
John 8:58 LSB

Moses questioned God about what he should say if the Israelites asked who sent him (Exodus 3:13). God responded, "Tell the people of Israel: 'I Am has sent me to rescue you'" (v. 14 VOICE). Huh? "I Am"? I expected God to come back with something like "The creator of the universe. Who else?" A longer way of translating *Eh'h'yeh* (Ehyeh) is "I am being who I am being, and I will be who I will be, and no other anything or anyone could ever be like who I am."

Leap fifteen hundred years forward to a conversation between Jesus and several religious leaders. They claimed their Abrahamic ancestry afforded them unique standing before God. To this, Jesus boldly declared, "I say to you, before Abraham was, I am" (John 8:58 LSB). This was a direct reference to Exodus 3 and a claim of divinity. The leaders, understanding the gravity of his words, reacted immediately and violently by attempting to kill him.

Jesus made seven other "I am" statements of his Godness. He claimed to be the bread of life, light of the world, door of the sheep, good shepherd, resurrection and the life, way and the truth and the life, and true vine (John 6:35; 8:12; 10:7, 11; 11:25; 14:6; 15:1).

Who do you say that he is?

# חֲרָשׁ—*Khahrosh*

## "To Plow"

Jesus said, "Anyone who begins to plow a field but keeps looking back is of no use in the kingdom of God."
LUKE 9:62 ICB

"Of no use" is strong. Do you think Jesus really and literally meant such people are useless for the kingdom? Picture a farmer on his John Deere plowing a field while constantly looking behind him. His rows would be anything but straight. Likewise, constantly looking back at your past blunders or regrets will inevitably distract you from God's purpose for your life. When you wake up tomorrow, try driving your car down the street while focused on the rearview mirror—actually, my lawyer said not to do that. Jesus' point here is to encourage going all in for him and dumping anything that may impede your walk with him.

Moving forward means kicking old habits, fears, doubts, and distractions to the curb. Of course, you can't go back in time and change the past, but you sure can shape your tomorrow by filtering every future choice you make through the lens of the gospel. Are you clinging to anything that is keeping God from showering you with a life filled with meaning and purpose? If so, let it go and confidently press on.

Jesus, help me press ahead and keep my eyes fixed on you (Hebrews 12:1–2).

# Yenta

## "Gossipmonger"

The wrath of God is revealed from heaven against all ungodliness and unrighteousness of men who in their wickedness suppress and stifle the truth.
Romans 1:18 AMP

The Yiddish word *yenta* refers to a gossipmonger, like the sweet little lady in church who calls to let you know that "Betty Sue is struggling because her husband, Bill, is having an affair with Jenny Lee, and he moved in with her." But she's only letting you know "so that you can pray for Betty Sue. And make sure you keep it to yourself." Yeah, right.

Contrary to popular opinion, gossip is a grave sin. In one of the most frightening passages in Scripture, Romans 1, Paul addressed the ungodliness, the unrighteousness, and the "truth supressingness" of those who reject God. He said they should know better but instead barter away God's truth for a lie. Because of that, God "gave them up" (v. 28 ESV) to their foolish ways of thinking. The apostle capped off the passage with a horrifying list of twenty wicked characteristics of God rejecters. Halfway through the list, he wrote, "They are gossips" (v. 29). Never forget the destructive nature of gossip. It divides, obliterates trust, destroys relationships, and ruins your witness. As a believer, you are called to speak words that encourage and edify.

Lord, help me speak words that build up, not tear down.

## AUGUST 31

# קָטֹנְתִּי—*Kahtone'tee*

## "Am Not Worthy"

"I am not worthy of the kindness and continual goodness you have shown me."
GENESIS 32:10 NCV

Have you ever felt unworthy? Many of us have had parents, teachers, coaches, or spouses who venomously screamed, "You'll never amount to anything." Speaking about God's love and salvation, my friend Tom said, "You don't know what I've done. That ship's *done* sailed for me." Hmm, nah! When you feel like garbage, unworthy, not good enough, and insignificant, let Paul's words sink in: "God showed his great love for us by sending Christ to die for us while we were still sinners" (Romans 5:8 TLB). God doesn't wait for you to clean up your mess, get "good enough," or prove yourself deserving of his love. He loves you in the middle of your unlovableness. When you were spitting mad, shaking your fist at Jesus, and cussing him out, he willingly went to the cross and died for you.

When those "I'm worthless" feelings creep in, remember that his love for you was never about anything you bring to the table but always about his grace. He is fully aware of your flaws, fears, failures, and sin. And he still calls you beloved.

Jesus, thank you for loving me when I hated you.

# הֲלָכָה—*Hahlahkhah*

## "The Path or Way of Life"

Brothers and sisters,…we have boldness to enter the sanctuary through the blood of Jesus—he has inaugurated for us a new and living way through the curtain (that is, through his flesh).

Hebrews 10:19–20 csb

*Hahlahkhah* (Halaka) refers to the volumes of Jewish law drawn from the Written and Oral Torah. It incorporates laws, customs, and traditions that guide every aspect of the day-to-day life of a Jew. In Jewish life, *hahlahkhah* is the path or way of life that leads to righteousness.

But Jesus is far better than the old *hahlahkhah*. Summing up the chapters before it, Hebrews 10:20 describes "a new and living way" provided by Christ. Why is this new path better? Because the old path, which "should have" led to righteousness, led to failure and death. But the new one carved by the blood of Jesus leads us into the very presence of God. This new way gives believers his cell phone number, email address, and social media handle. Now you can confidently seek God's presence in prayer and worship, knowing there is no hurdle between you and him. Jesus' sacrifice replaced the old rituals and paved a path based on grace. Live in freedom, not shackled by legalism but spurred on by gratitude for what he's done. It's his righteousness you now possess.

Lord, help me boldly draw near to you.

# תַּכְרִכִים—*Takh'reekheem*

## "Shroud"

God shows no partiality.
ROMANS 2:11 ESV

In the first century, Jews began to be buried in simple muslin, linen, or cotton shrouds. It started with Paul's rabbi, Gamaliel, who insisted he be buried in a plain white shroud rather than expensive attire to show that both wealthy and poor stand as equals before a holy God.

People often live as if there is some cosmic dotted line with "those God approves" above it and "those God rejects" below. Lives are lived to do something that or be somebody who "earns" a spot in the area above the line. For hundreds and hundreds of years, Jews thought that being in Abraham's bloodline got you above the line. But it doesn't—never did, never will. Having Christian parents, giving to the church, leading a small group, and attending church every week don't get you special favor either. It is easy to slip into hoping God will play favorites and that you'll be one of them simply because "Grandpa was a pastor." But Romans 2:11 crushes this idea. Grandpa can't believe for you. We all stand equally guilty below the dotted line. However, as fatalistic as that sounds, we are all equally extended grace. Jesus offers us a piggyback ride across the line into an eternity with him. Hop on!

Father, help me treat everyone equally with respect, dignity, and love.

# אֵל קַנָּא—*Ayl Kahnah*

## "A Jealous God"

"Don't worship any other god. I am YAHWEH KANAH—the jealous LORD. That is my name. I hate for my people to worship other gods."
EXODUS 34:14 ERV

Why is it so hard for humans to keep the very first commandment? "No other gods, only me" (Exodus 20:3 MSG). Seems simple, right? Well, apparently it's not. Though very few people today are running around worshiping Baal, the Canaanite false god of fertility and rain, don't buy the lie that idols aren't worshiped in the twenty-first century. What have you allowed, intentionally or not, to become a priority over God? Anything that gets between you and him is an idol—money, drugs, sex, children, parents, a job, your spouse, golf, cars, or your pastor.

God is not a self-aggrandizing, egomaniacal, self-absorbed narcissist. He is a loving God who zealously desires to be in an exclusive relationship with you so he can shower you with mercy and grace. He is *Ayl Kahnah* (El Qanna), jealous for you—all of you—heart, mind, soul, spirit, time, resources, and actions. He wants you to go to bed thinking about him and wake up focused on him. He wants you when you're going in and when you're coming out (Psalm 121:8). Keep God in his rightful place—the first one!

Lord, thank you for being jealous for me.

# דֶּרֶךְ—*Dehrehkh*

## "The Way"

"I worship the God of our fathers according to the Way."
ACTS 24:14 EHV

In the pluralistic culture we live in, people believe there are multiple paths to God that all are equally true, valid, and effective. Truth is subjective, and what is true for you is true simply because it is true for you. Your belief determines truth—and mine does too. The problem with the previous three sentences is that they are utter nonsense. Regardless of what you or I believe, a claim cannot be both true and false at the same time in the same sense. Jesus either entered a tomb dead and exited alive, or he didn't. Neither my belief nor my friend's unbelief changes history.

The first-century Jesus movement was known as "the Way" (Acts 9:2; 19:9, 23; 24:14, 22). Acts records the birth and life of the early church—the way they walked, talked, and treated people. Jesus summed up how the Way should be: "Love the Lord your God with all your heart, with all your soul, and with all your mind" (Matthew 22:37). And "Love your neighbor as yourself" (v. 39). Love God and love people! The Way is the only way, and everyone has the opportunity, by grace alone through faith alone in Christ alone, to join the Way.

Lord, let me walk all the rest of my days in the Way.

# יִבְנֶה—*Yeev'neh*

## "Build"

"Those who don't put into practice what they hear are like a person who built a house without a foundation. The floodwater smashed against it and it collapsed instantly. It was completely destroyed."
LUKE 6:49 CEB

Jesus asks why we call him Lord but don't do what he says. If you choose to call him Lord, be prepared to obey him. Genuine Christ followers not only hear his words but also embrace and obey them, leading to real life change.

Luke 6:46–49 paints a word picture for us. A born-again believer who hears and obeys Jesus' teaching is like a person who builds a house on a foundation deeply embedded in rock. No matter what challenges come their way—tornado, hurricane, earthquake, or flood—their house stands firm. Conversely, those who hear and do nothing have built a foundationless house. It may look the same, but it's built on nothing. The slightest bit of weather comes, and it is completely wrecked. Jesus' imagery of a destroyed house stresses that storms are in the forecast. Your readiness for them is up to you. Building your life on the foundation of Christ's teachings will provide you the wherewithal to endure the rough patches. Is your spiritual foundation prepared for the inevitable hurricanes of life?

Lord, help me put Jesus' words into action every day of my life.

# סֵתֶר—*Saytehr*

## "Secret"

Joseph of Arimathea asked Pilate if he could take away the body of Jesus. Joseph was a disciple of Jesus, but a secret one because he feared the Jewish authorities.
JOHN 19:38 CEB

Like Nicodemus, Joseph of Arimathea believed in Jesus, but shhh, it's a secret. He kept it on the down-low until Jesus hung dead on the cross. Then enough was enough. He just couldn't keep it buried any longer. He had to stand up.

This wealthy and highly respected religious leader is a powerful example of the cost and courage of taking a stand for Jesus. By asking Pilate for the Lord's body, he publicly identified himself with Jesus. Stepping up and saying, "I'm with that guy," exposed him to ridicule, scorn, and potential danger at the hands of the Jewish leaders, but he did it anyway. Following Jesus often involves risk. Friendships are jeopardized, criticism is thrown in your face, and family relationships can be wrecked. Joseph's actions demonstrate that authentic faith calls you to take a stand even when there is significant cost. The gospel invites you to walk out your trust in Jesus with courage, which may mean swimming upstream a lot by speaking truth in the face of lies and taking risks you never saw yourself taking.

Jesus, let me never waver in the face of ridicule.

# אָמֵן—*Ahmahn*

## "Believe; Trust"

God so loved the world that he gave his one and only Son, that whoever believes in him shall not perish but have eternal life.
John 3:16 NIV

I remember learning as a child that Abraham was the first Jew and that I should revere him because he did what God told him to do. That was as far as my understanding went for the next twenty to twenty-five years. And then I crashed into Genesis 15:6 as a thirty-four-year-old, skeptical Jewish guy: "He believed in the Lord; and he counted it to him for righteousness" (KJV). I understood "he believed" but had no clue what "counted it to him for righteousness" meant. I found out, in terms that I could understand then, that it meant he went to heaven.

What? He didn't do anything. Yeah, he believed. Big deal. Don't you have to do stuff to get to heaven? I set it aside for several months until I read John 3:16. *Here we go again with the "believe" thing*, I thought. But in John 3:16, it's God's sacrificial giving of his Son that provides heaven for whoever believes. This was a radical paradigm shift for me. Four months later, realizing I could never do enough, I, too, believed in the Lord and was credited with righteousness.

Thank you, Jesus, for saving me.

SEPTEMBER 8

# צְדָקָה—*Tz'dahkah*

## "Righteousness"

"I tell you, unless your righteousness exceeds that of the scribes and Pharisees, you will never enter the kingdom of heaven."
Matthew 5:20 esv

It's easy to hammer the Pharisees for their hypocritical and manipulative behavior, but most first-century Jews highly regarded them as the truly holy ones. Over hundreds of years, they gradually added to God's law mountains of regulations, which eventually came to be seen as nearly as important as the Bible itself.

Standing on a hill overlooking the Sea of Galilee in spring 2023, I imagined myself sitting on a rock and hearing Jesus deliver the Sermon on the Mount. I could see him pointing to a group of Pharisees off in the distance and then effectively saying to the crowd around him, "Unless your righteousness exceeds the righteousness of those guys over there, you're not getting in." Their obvious response would be "No way. They're the perfect people. If they're the yardstick, I'm out." But Jesus' entire point in Matthew 5:20 is that the only righteousness that provides entry into the kingdom is his, which is freely given to you. The righteousness of the religious leaders was external. Jesus spoke of the internal change that occurs when God invades a person's heart.

Who in your circle of friends and family needs the righteousness Jesus provides?

# מַעֲשֵׂה יָדָיו—*Mah'ahsay Yahdai*

## "Handiwork"

The heavens declare the glory of God; the sky displays his handiwork.
PSALM 19:1 NET

Have you ever driven US 287 between Rawlins and Willow Creek, Wyoming, and looked up at the night sky unobstructed by the light of civilization? It is a stunning sight to behold. The countless stars, planets, meteors, and galaxies aren't just beautiful lights but a grand masterpiece revealing God's glory. Creation itself is a way to hear the very voice of the Creator. The snowflake's perfectly engineered design, the sun tucking itself down on the horizon in Maui, and the cross in the core of the Whirlpool Galaxy didn't happen purposelessly and randomly. They are extraordinary demonstrations of a creative God's grandeur. His divine fingerprint is stamped across the universe just waiting to be uncovered.

Listen to the leaves blowing in an autumn wind, the song of a cardinal, or the sound of a babbling brook—his handiwork tailor-made for you. When you feel disconnected, walk outside, look in every direction, and whisper, "I hear you, Lord." Pay attention! Nothing is silent; everything proclaims God's glory. But it's on you to recognize the messages woven into the fabric of creation and allow them to draw you closer to the one who designed them.

Lord, help me hear your voice in the magnificence of creation.

# זָהָב—*Zah'hahv*

## "Gold"

The Word of the Lord is worth more than gold.
Psalm 19:10 NLV

Yesterday was about the Lord speaking and revealing himself through his creation. This is known as general revelation. However, if he only spoke to us through what we can see, hear, touch, feel, and taste, it would be impossible to grasp his love for us, his sovereign plans for us, and the fact that his Son died in our place. The Bible is God's special revelation and tells us things about the Creator we would never know if he didn't do something special to reveal them.

Praise the Lord for doing something special and unique. He gave us his written Word, and David told us it is "worth more than gold." David continued, saying it's worth "even more than much fine gold" and is "sweeter than honey, even honey straight from the comb" (v. 10). In the search for fulfillment, don't buy the lie that money and success will fill the emptiness. The truth found in the pages of Scripture reveals the nature of its Author, who will fulfill every need you could ever have. Embrace God's Word and watch your heart and mind be transformed, steering you straight into a saving relationship with the Lord of heaven.

Lord, speak to me through your written Word.

# מְלוּכָה—*M'lookhah*

## "Kingdom"

You [Timothy] have heard me [Paul] teach things that have been confirmed by many reliable witnesses. Now teach these truths to other trustworthy people who will be able to pass them on to others.

2 Timothy 2:2 NLT

Church folks often talk about adding to the kingdom when multiplication is the true biblical model. In 2 Timothy 2:2, Paul gave us a perfect template for kingdom multiplication. In this one little verse, we see the four generations of disciple making: Paul discipled Timothy. Then Timothy taught a group of people who then discipled others. You don't need a microscope to see the result is not addition; it is the multiplication of the kingdom of God.

Your role is twofold: (1) Be intentional about discipling others and (2) equip them to do the same thing. Passing on what you've learned about Jesus and the changes he ignited in your life is paramount. Find a couple of people in your church to meet with weekly and pour into them. Then arm them with the tools and confidence to mentor others. When you fan the flame of leadership in others, the reach of the gospel is exponentially broadened, and the kingdom multiplies.

Jesus, thank you for letting me be a link in the chain of transmitting your story.

SEPTEMBER 12

# יְשַׁנֵּא—*Y'shooneh*

## "To Change"

The hardness of his face is changed.
ECCLESIASTES 8:1 LEB

Jesus of Nazareth's thirty-three years of physical life, his death, and indeed, his resurrection made a greater impact on civilization than any other set of events in history. On the day of his death, Scripture records remarkable changes in the lives of three specific men.

First, a calloused Roman soldier who actively participated in the murder of the Savior of the world saw it all and, in the end, confessed, "Truly this man was God's Son!" (Mark 15:39). His hardened life was forever changed. Second, Joseph of Arimathea, a member of the Sanhedrin and a secret Christ follower, donated his unused tomb and prepared the Savior's body for burial (Matthew 27:57–60). His hardened life was also forever changed. Finally, a hardened criminal nailed on a cross next to Jesus asked the Savior to remember him. Jesus replied, "Today you will be with me in paradise" (Luke 23:43). His eternal life was most assuredly radically changed. He began as a bandit but died a believer, recognizing the divinity of the one stretched on a cross beside him.

No matter how far you believe you have wandered, when you encounter the Lord of lords and understand his sacrificial death, your hardened life will never be the same either.

Lord, I am forever yours. Save me, change me, and grow me.

# מְקוֹר חַיִּים—*M'kore Khahyeem*

## "Fountain of Life"

You are the Fountain of life; our light is from your light.
Psalm 36:9 TLB

Psalm 36 is a prayer of David that contrasts humanity's wickedness with the faithful love of the Lord. Verse 9 points us to Jesus as the source of all sources. He is the fountain of life, flowing with living water that refreshingly satisfies the soul, and he is the light that provides power to all other lights. He quenches every thirst and illuminates every dark path. Life can leave us bumped, bruised, empty, and lost, scrambling for fulfillment. We often grab the closest quick fix we can find, but quick fixes never deliver on their promises. Jesus, on the other hand, always delivers right on time, providing a well of grace, love, and mercy that never runs dry (John 4:14).

A thousand years after David declared, "Our light is from your light" (Psalm 36:9), Jesus proclaimed, "I am the Light of the world" (John 8:12). When you are facing a tough decision at a fork in the road or you feel like you're wandering around, lost in the dark, and unsure which way is left or right, Jesus is there with you to light the way forward.

Lord God, thank you for fountains and flashlights.

# עֵצָה—*Aytzah*

## "Purpose"

"My purpose is to finish my course and the ministry I received from the Lord Jesus, to testify to the gospel of God's grace."
ACTS 20:24 CSB

Raise your hand if you've ever looked in the mirror and asked, "What is my purpose?" Don't feel special. At some point, we could all raise our hands. Paul interrupted the waving with "Not me," boldly declaring, "My purpose is to finish my course and the ministry I received from the Lord Jesus—to testify to the gospel of God's grace."

You will discover your true purpose when you understand that it doesn't revolve around you but around God. Your purpose transcends you. And at the same time, it wholly involves you. If you earnestly examine yourself and consider the unique set of gifts, skills, and abilities God has freely given you, a beautiful picture will begin to emerge from the meaningful life he has designed for you. Maybe you're an encourager, problem solver, or leader. Whatever it is, leverage it to impact the world for Christ. Follow Jesus wherever he leads, and you'll end up in places you never thought you'd be while doing things you never thought you'd do with joy and fulfillment you never dreamed you'd have.

Jesus, lead me to where I can fulfill your desire for my life.

# זְאֵבֵי עֶרֶב—*Z'ayvay Ehrehv*

## "Evening Wolves"

Their horses are swifter than leopards, more fierce than the evening wolves.
HABAKKUK 1:8 RSV

In the prophetic book of Habakkuk, God frighteningly described the Chaldeans as menacing, violent, dreaded, fearsome, and cruel, with horses faster than leopards and fiercer than the evening wolves (Habakkuk 1:6–8). And Satan is the chief of all evening wolves. He is a thief who has come to steal, kill, and destroy God's plans for your life. The devil doesn't want you to reach, dream, or build. He's a murderer, deceiver, and liar. He wants to take you out to keep you from everything the Lord has for you. He has declared war on you, and he does his best work in the quiet darkness of night when you're alone and anxious and your mind is racing.

The battle is spiritual, so when the evening wolves come, give 'em this:

> Although we live in the flesh, we do not wage war according to the flesh, since the weapons of our warfare are not of the flesh, but are powerful through God for the demolition of strongholds. We demolish arguments and every proud thing that is raised up against the knowledge of God, and we take every thought captive to obey Christ. (2 Corinthians 10:3–5 CSB)

Lord, wreck any plans the Enemy has for me.

# קְבוּרָה מְסוּיָּדָא—*K'voorah M'sooyahdah*

## "Whitewashed Tomb"

"Woe to you, scribes and Pharisees, hypocrites! You are like whitewashed tombs, which appear beautiful on the outside, but inside are full of the bones of the dead and every kind of impurity."
MATTHEW 23:27 CSB

In preparation for Passover, the tombs along the roads to Jerusalem were smeared white to mark them. Why? Remember, ground burial did not begin in Jewish communities until the second century. Prior to this, tombs were usually hollowed out of rock formations in the landscape and could easily be stumbled on, causing the stumbler to become ritually unclean. People also felt whitewashing made the tombs appear beautiful. However, death, rot, and other nasty things lurked behind the surface.

Matthew 23 finds Jesus condemning the Jewish leadership for their continual, intentional desire to mask who they really were—total hypocrites. They looked neat, tidy, clean, and holy on the outside, but in actuality, they were as disgusting as a rotting corpse on the inside. You and I can undoubtedly fall into the trap of doing the very same thing. In our social media–driven world, it is incredibly easy to focus on outward appearances but neglect the condition of our hearts. Christ followers are called to be different. Jesus appeals for purity driven by internal heart transformation.

What can you do today to prioritize heart change over external image?

# בּוֹרֵא—*Boray*

## "Creator"

The LORD is an eternal God, the Creator of the whole earth.
ISAIAH 40:28 NET

When I think of God as the Creator, I am filled with awe at his immense power and authority. Who else could speak a word and, out of nothing, bring forth everything? Only a being that transcends time, space, and matter. Only the Creator! How could this truth not cause our knees to rattle and stir everything inside us to worship him? Yet humans "exchanged the truth of God for a lie, and worshiped and served the creature rather than the Creator" (Romans 1:25 AMP). Who does this? Who would trade the truth of Yahweh for the lies of the Adversary? The answer is those who've been deceived and bought the lie. Most deceptions are subtle and make us feel good about ourselves. They often rationalize our sin. Taken to its logical end, the deceptions turn people away from God to worship material possessions, status, people, self, or even culture.

Identify and recognize how culture's values can lead you away from God's truth. Ground yourself in the values conveyed by his Word, which is a firm foundation in a world of shifting values.

What modern-day idols have replaced God in your life, and how can you actively re-center your life around him?

# חֲגֻרִים מָתְנֵיכֶם—

# *Hahgooreem Maht'naykhem*

## "Gird Your Loins"

Stand firm therefore, having girded your loins with truth.
EPHESIANS 6:14 LSB

Elijah "girded up his loins and outran Ahab" (1 Kings 18:46). When God was preparing the Hebrew slaves to escape from Egypt, he told them to eat the Passover meal with their "loins girded" (Exodus 12:11). Huh? *Girding the loins* meant tucking all the loose fabric from the long robes they wore into their belts so they could move or fight unimpeded. In Ephesians 6, Paul encouraged individual believers to be prepared for spiritual warfare by putting on their full battle dress—head-to-toe offensive and defensive equipment, the whole armor of God. We fully gear up so we "will be able to resist in the evil day, and having done everything, to stand firm" (v. 13).

The first move toward standing firm is having our loins girded in truth. A Roman soldier's belt was critical because it held his clothes and his armor together. Paul likened this belt to truth, referring to God's Word and the Christian soldier's character, integrity, and faithfulness. Standing firm begins with being rock-solid and grounded in truth, which helps direct our decisions and shields us from the devil's deceit.

Lord, help me stand firm by first being "locked and loaded" in your truth.

# מָחָר—*Mahkhahr*

## "Tomorrow; a Time to Come"

"Let this serve as a sign among you, so that when your children ask in times to come, 'What do these stones mean to you,' then you'll say to them, 'Because the waters of the Jordan River were cut off.'"
JOSHUA 4:6–7 ISV

*Mahkhahr* can mean "tomorrow," but it can also refer to "a future time to come." As the Israelites were about to cross the Jordan into Canaan, the Lord stopped the river from flowing, allowing everyone to cross on dry ground. Afterward, they gathered twelve stones from the river and set them up as a memorial, honoring what God had done that day.

Just like the Israelites set up stones to remember this river crossing, it is essential to mark the big moments when God has showed up for you. When he answers a prayer, opens a door, closes a door, or walks with you through a rough time, take a minute to commit it to memory. These milestones will forever remind you of the Lord's faithfulness. They'll also give you opportunities to share God's faithfulness with others. Your daughter Rose may ask, "Why are those rosebushes planted in the shape of a cross in the backyard?" Your answer may very well be "Your father and I tried for ten years to get pregnant. Finally, we surrendered it to Jesus, and in six weeks, I was pregnant with you. We will never forget it."

Write down several God moments you'll never forget.

# מַחְשָׁבוֹת—*Mahkh'sh'vote*

## "Thoughts; Plans"

I know the thoughts that I think toward you, saith the LORD, thoughts of peace, and not of evil, to give you an expected end.
JEREMIAH 29:11 KJV

Jeremiah 29:11 was written in the early sixth century BC to Jewish exiles taken in chains to Babylon. They desperately needed encouragement. However, the truths in Jeremiah's words certainly travel beyond the time of exile to us. Contrary to the nasty things people sometimes say or do, God is always thinking about us, and his thoughts are always good because he is always abundantly good.

When fear, doubt, and anxiety creep in, remember that God is drawing you ever closer to himself, thinking, planning, and acting on your behalf. His plan for your life involves shalom (peace) and a hope-filled future—"an expected end." Even when it doesn't look like it, he is hard at work to sovereignly orchestrate events to lead you to a life packed with meaning, purpose, and passion. Although your daily walk is obviously a component of his thoughts and plans for you, his focus is infinitely more on your eternity. Ultimately, God's plan is about leading you into a redeeming, life-altering, and purpose-driven relationship with Jesus.

When you feel like you're in chains, how can you trust that God's plans are good?

# יָכִינוּ—*Yahkheenoo*

## "Prepared"

We are His workmanship, created in Christ Jesus for good works, which God prepared beforehand that we should walk in them.
Ephesians 2:10 NKJV

Before the apostle Paul talked about the "good works, which God prepared beforehand," he reminded us in Ephesians 2:8–9 that we deserve eternal death but are given the gift of eternal life by God's grace. We're not saved *by* good works; we're saved *for* good works. So what's the deal with the good works that God prepared for you? He has already teed up a million amazing things for you to jump into. It's like a path through an opportunity forest that he custom planted for you.

You just need to keep your antennae up and recognize the doorways God provides for you to display love, kindness, grace, and justice to those whose paths you cross. Maybe you need to listen compassionately to a friend struggling in her marriage, stand in the gap for someone being treated unjustly, or help a friend in need. You are God's workmanship—his masterpiece—tailor-made by Christ Jesus for the tasks he has for you. The opportunities he puts in your path are a privilege. Embrace them, knowing he has already laid the groundwork for success.

Lord, let me walk in every good thing you prepared for me.

# תִּשְׁפֹּט—*Teesh'pote*

## "To Judge"

"You will be judged in the same way that you judge others, and the amount you give to others will be given to you."
MATTHEW 7:2 NCV

Bill shouted, "Don't judge me!" Then he got *righteous*: "Don't you know Jesus said, 'Judge not, that you be not judged'?" (Matthew 7:1 NKJV). This is probably the most misinterpreted and taken-out-of-context verse in the Bible. People mistakenly believe it to be a blanket condemnation against making any moral judgments. But no! The verse must be balanced with Matthew 7:2. We need to *not* treat people the way we *don't* want to be treated. It's like the Golden Rule turned inside out. As difficult as it may sometimes be, we're called to examine our own junk before calling out the flaws in the other person. Take time to look in the mirror, repent, and own the places in your journey where you desperately need God's grace.

This humble approach to life will go a long way toward combating hypocrisy and will help cultivate a more forgiving spirit in your relationships. Don't allow yourself to excuse a certain sin in your life while condemning your friend for the same thing. Consistently live a life of empathy, self-examination, and grace in everything.

Father God, help me always be acutely self-aware.

# חִידוֹת—*Kheedote*

## "Hard Questions"

She came to test him with hard questions.
1 Kings 10:1 ERV

The Queen of Sheba asked Solomon the difficult questions in 1 Kings 10. After their Q and A, she concluded, "Praise the Lord your God!" (v. 9). You may wonder, *Are hard questions okay to ask? Is doubt evil? If I have a lot of questions, is my faith weak?* These are legitimate questions. However, I would argue that the answer to one question provides insight into the solution for all the others: Do you believe the Bible is inerrant and infallible?

When we face tough questions about faith, life, and eternity, Scripture stands strong because it is a fortress of truth. It is without error in everything it affirms and is reliable in every promise and command. Jesus said, "Heaven and earth will pass away, but my words will never pass away" (Matthew 24:35 CJB). Jesus' claim allows you to trust his words through any storm, doubt, or crisis of faith. Tough questions don't expose cracks; they invite you to dive deeper. So ask, search, explore, wrestle, and try to prove Scripture wrong. You will find that it can withstand the pressure because it is a bedrock of truth undaunted by time or critique.

Holy Spirit, please illuminate your Word for me.

# נָבְלָה—*Nahv'lah*

## "To Wither"

The land fades and withers, the world wilts and withers, the exalted of the land languish.
Isaiah 24:4 CJB

Isaiah 24–27 is pseudoapocalyptic, which means it looks at the end-of-time judgment that begins with the unraveling of the earth. "The world wilts and withers." Jesus touched on this theme the morning after he triumphantly entered Jerusalem on Palm Sunday. As he and his disciples walked, Jesus cursed a fig tree that bore all the indications it had produced fruit though it hadn't. The next day, they noticed that the fig tree had withered away and died. Jesus applied this object lesson to his current generation of Jews who looked green and full of life on the outside but were barren, withered, and dead on the inside. He condemned empty religion that lacked genuine substance and a relationship with the Lord.

Jesus' "live" parable with the fig tree teaches us the tremendous value God places on authenticity. Like this barren tree, hypocrisy often deceives others but never God. The fruit of authentic heart change is consistent, godly living that aligns with his Word. Take this week to identify areas where your walk and your talk don't match and make a conscious effort to live with integrity.

Lord, help me reflect Jesus in my words and my actions.

# רֹאשׁ הַשָּׁנָה—*Rosh Hahshahnah*

## "Head of the Year"

The only ones who may enter are those whose names are written in the Lamb's Book of Life.
REVELATION 21:27 CJB

*Rosh Hahshahnah* (Rosh Hashanah) is a celebration of God creating the universe. It is creation's birthday and is recognized as the Jewish New Year. God told Moses, "You shall observe a day of solemn rest, a memorial proclaimed with blast of trumpets, a holy convocation" (Leviticus 23:24 ESV). Therefore, its main feature is the one hundred shofar (ram's horn) blasts that occur during the holiday.

The rabbis teach that *Rosh Hahshahnah* is the day that God decides who will live and who will die the following year. On this day, God opens three books: one for the totally righteous, one for the totally wicked, and one for the average Joe who is somewhere in the middle. The average person's fate depends on how they do during the ten days between *Rosh Hahshahnah* and Yom Kippur.

Praise God that my inclusion or exclusion in the Lamb's Book of Life doesn't depend on my righteousness (for I am far from it). It is absolutely, completely dependent on Jesus' robe of righteousness, which he wrapped me in when I gave my life to him. Whose robe are you wrapped in today: yours or his?

Thank you, Lord, that salvation doesn't depend on me.

# עָנִי—*Ahnee*

## "Poor"

"Blessed are the poor in spirit, for theirs is the kingdom of heaven."
MATTHEW 5:3 NASB

Matthew 5–7 records a message Jesus delivered on a hillside overlooking the Sea of Galilee. In it, he revealed his perspective on the law—that it required love, compassion, faithful service, and sincere obedience to its spirit. This sermon called Israel back to the heart of the matter: the spirit of the law and where true righteousness comes from. Jesus called for an end to nit-picking, legalistic rules.

The sermon's first section, the Beatitudes, is like a job description for a Christ follower and describes how we should live. It begins in Matthew 5:3 with a declaration that those who acknowledge their inability to deliver anything of real value to God—those inwardly destitute, those whose every breath is solely dependent on God's mercy and grace—are blessed and highly favored. The kingdom belongs to them.

To the Jews of the day and most people today, this and the rest of the Beatitudes appear ridiculous. When the world celebrates pride and independence, Christians are called to rely on the Lord for everything. Are there areas in your life where you're putting faith in yourself rather than trusting in Jesus?

God, help me realize I want to be poor in spirit.

# אֵבוּס—*Ayvoos*

## "Feeding Trough"

"The donkey [knows] its master's feeding trough."
ISAIAH 1:3 ISV

In Isaiah, as God's spokesman, the prophet attacked the people of Israel for breaking their covenant with the Lord. In Isaiah 1:2, God said, "I've loved my children. I've taught them right from wrong. And now they're rotten and rebellious" (author's paraphrase). Then the Lord proclaimed they're also dumb as a rock: "The ox knows its owner, and the donkey its master's feeding trough, but Israel doesn't know, and my people don't understand" (v. 3).

Oxen are incredibly compliant creatures, and donkeys were considered the dumbest animals ever. So to say that donkeys and oxen were more intelligent than the people of Israel was an outright indictment of Israel's stupidity. These animals were more aware of the hand that nourished them than God's people were. Over several hundred years, Israel had reached the point where they didn't know God or acknowledge his sustaining hand in their lives.

Before you get high and mighty, ask yourself if you consistently see, acknowledge, and express thankfulness for God's presence and provision in your life. I'd like to challenge you today to track him. Jot down on a pad or in your phone every time you feel his presence or see him at work.

Father, let me be smarter than the ox and donkey.

# אֲבַטִּחִים—*Ahvahteekheem*

## "Watermelon"

"Remember the cucumbers, the watermelons, the leeks, the onions, and the garlic we had?"
NUMBERS 11:5 GNT

About two years after being liberated from slavery in Egypt, the Israelites left Sinai and headed for the desert of Paran. God had been daily raining manna from the sky so they could eat, and he also ensured they had enough water to drink. He was, without fail, delivering on his promise to be their God and take care of them.

And then, as frequently occurs, came the pity party. The Israelites essentially complained that they wanted steak, a loaded potato, and watermelon for dessert. They said, "In Egypt we used to eat all the fish we wanted, and it cost us nothing. Remember the cucumbers, the watermelons, the leeks, the onions, and the garlic we had?" (v. 5). Their whining revealed a profound lack of gratitude and an inclination toward complaining when "bread" was literally falling out of the sky. Just like them, our culture constantly minimizes the virtue of contentment and maximizes a never-enough mindset, which then results in missing God's blessings. Ask God to help you recognize his activity in your life and watch the whining *to* him morph into trusting and relying *on* him.

What can you do to cultivate a heart that trusts and is satisfied with God's provision?

# יַרְדֵּן נָהָר—*Yahr'dayn Nah'hahr*

## "Jordan River"

Jesus came from Nazareth in Galilee and was baptized by John in the Jordan.
MARK 1:9 ISV

John the Baptist's baptism was for repentance from sin, yet Jesus met him on the Jordan River to be baptized. Why? If Jesus was sinless, what was the point? Oh, I know. Maybe he had some little sin from when he was a kid that he needed to knock out. I think not. Frankly, John the Baptist wondered the same thing, and Jesus told him it would "fulfill all righteousness" (Matthew 3:15). What does that mean? Well, Jesus submitted to baptism primarily to align himself with the Father's will and to identify with sinful men and women like me and you. This set the act of baptism apart as something we could share with him. Finally, Jesus' baptism was a very public event that inaugurated his very public ministry and highlighted the importance of publicly professing our salvation.

How can you make your faith in Jesus more visible to the people around you without being obnoxious? More than anything, walk the talk. Let the change in your life be evident in how you act, speak, love, serve, and treat people. In simple terms, act like you believe what you say you believe.

Lord, let me share the gospel every day of my life, using words only when necessary.

# עֵגֶל־מַרְבֵּק—*Aygehl Mahr'bayk*

## "Fattened Calf"

"'Bring the fattened calf and kill it! Let us eat and celebrate.'"
LUKE 15:23 NET

The fattened calf held much cultural and religious importance in Jewish society during Jesus' time. It was the choicest food, usually reserved for special occasions, holidays, or certain sacrifices. Under the umbrella of hospitality, a fattened calf was often prepared for an honored guest or to mark an exceptionally joyous event.

In Luke 15, Jesus told a story about a son gone wild who squandered everything he had on "sex, drugs, and rock and roll." After reaching the pit of despair, he returned home fully expecting condemnation from his father. Instead, when his dad saw him coming, the dad jumped off the front porch and raced to his son, delivering love, grace, forgiveness, and the biggest bear hug ever. He effectively told everyone, "It's barbecue time. My lost son is found. Let's party!"

This parable reminds us of the heart of grace God freely showers us with. Regardless of how far we run or how nasty our mistakes are, grace welcomes us back with open arms and bear hugs. The father's reaction illustrates that repentance is always met with forgiveness. Remember, your value to God is never lessened by your failures; grace restores, renews, and redeems you.

Father, thank you for your relationship-restoring grace.

# רַב—*Rahv*

## "Enough"

Everyone ate until they were full, and the disciples filled twelve baskets with the leftovers.
LUKE 9:17 CEB

In Luke 9, Jesus essentially told his guys, "These people are *hangry*. Feed 'em." I can just hear Thomas whispering to John or Andrew, "Yeah, I seriously doubt it!" The task in front of the disciples was unrealistic and supremely daunting—feed five thousand men plus what must have been another five to seven thousand women and children with two measly fish and five loaves of bread. Well, what ensued? The Master Chef made it happen, and his staff served the massive crowd. In the most shocking of all outcomes, there wasn't *just enough* food, but there was *more than enough*. There were leftovers.

In our twenty-first-century world, we often act as if the gospel is Jesus plus this or that or Jesus minus this or that. Typically, "works" is a false add-on to the gospel, and "repentance" is the false subtraction. Both are lies from the pit. Jesus is infinitely more than *rahv* (rav). Paul wrote in Philippians, "My God will meet your every need out of his riches in the glory that is found in Christ Jesus" (4:19). To Ephesus, he wrote that Jesus can "do exceedingly abundantly above all that we ask or think" (Ephesians 3:20 NKJV).

Thank you, Lord, that your grace, love, and presence are more than enough for me.

# תְּוֹדִיעֵ—*Toh'deeyay*

"Show"

You will show me the path of life;
in Your presence is fullness of joy.
PSALM 16:11 AMP

Luke 24:13–35 tells the story of two disciples walking the road from Jerusalem to Emmaus on the first Easter morning—the day Jesus rose from the dead. Just like we would be, they were deep in a conversation about the events of the last three days. Then a stranger showed up and joined their walk. Though they didn't know it, this stranger was Jesus, and he was concealing his true identity. The two men were in the presence of the King, yet they were unaware. They explained to the "stranger" that they expected Jesus to regain Israel's independence from Rome, but instead he died, and his body was missing. For what must have been an incredible two or three hours, Jesus walked them through God's Word and showed them how it uniquely leads straight to him and him alone.

On reaching Emmaus, Jesus went in the house with them for dinner, and as he blessed the food, "their eyes were opened, and they recognized him" (v. 31 ESV). The joy and astonishment they experienced at that moment must have been overwhelming. He had indeed conquered death, was alive, and had been showing them his path for hours.

Is your current path leading you closer to or further away from the King?

# יְהוָה שָׁלוֹם—*Yahweh Shahlome*

## "The Lord Is Peace"

Keep putting into practice all you learned from me and saw me doing, and the God of peace will be with you.
Philippians 4:9 TLB

Gideon was a hero of the faith in the twelfth century BC, and his people cried out to the Lord because they were getting *whupped* by the Midianites. Gideon offered a sacrifice to the Lord, and the Lord basically said, "You can have peace! I have your back. You're not going to die." Gideon called this spot "the Lord is peace" (Judges 6:24 RSV).

In Philippians 4:9, God told the believers in Philippi that *Yahweh Shahlome* (Yahweh Shalom), the God of peace, had their backs as well. In the preceding verses, he told them not to be anxious, to always rejoice, to pray, and to show gratitude and that God would provide them with his peace (vv. 4–8). Just like Paul encouraged the believers in Philippi to follow his example, you and I should hunt down mature brothers and sisters who model Christlike behavior to learn from. Surrounding ourselves with people who embody godly influences will greatly contribute to the growth of our faith and our Christian walk.

Father God, use my brothers and sisters in Christ to teach me and lead me into faithful action for the sake of the gospel.

# אֹזֶן—*Ahz'n*

## "Ear"

If the ear says, "Because I am not an eye, I am not part of the body," it does not on that account cease to be part of the body.
1 Corinthians 12:16 EHV

King Solomon acknowledged that God crafted every body part with purpose when he wrote, "An ear that hears and an eye that sees—the Lord has made both of them" (Proverbs 20:12). For centuries, rabbis consistently used body parts to teach spiritual truths. I imagine Paul also learned this physiology-theology thing from his mentor, Rabbi Gamaliel.

Immediately after explaining spiritual gifts to the church at Corinth (1 Corinthians 12:1–11), Paul connected those gifts with unity in the body of Christ. He said the human body is made up of hundreds of different complementary parts, each one needing the others if the body is to function as God intended. We often mistakenly believe we are called to be good at everything, but Paul reminded us that we are like hands, feet, eyes, and ears; each believer is gifted and plays a unique role in the body of Christ. You might not be gifted to teach, but you serve faithfully, give generously, or encourage like Barnabas. Embrace and use your gifts for Jesus' sake, knowing that the body functions as God intends when we all do the same.

Lord, thank you for the amazing gifts you've given me.

OCTOBER 5

# מָלֵא—*Mahlay*

## "To Fill"

The priests could not enter into the house of the Lord, because the glory of the Lord had filled the Lord's house.
2 Chronicles 7:2 kjv

Have you ever felt overwhelmed by something unique or beautiful? The birth of a child? A sunset on a beach? A snowcapped mountaintop? At the dedication of Solomon's Temple, the sacrifices had been prepared, and when Solomon's prayer ended, "fire came down from heaven, and consumed" it all (v. 1). Imagine that moment. The Israelites had waited more than five hundred years for a house dedicated to Yahweh. Close your eyes and envision it: animals sacrificed and people singing, dancing, praising, rejoicing, and *bam*! The glory of the Lord took over and filled that place. It was so overwhelming, so powerful, and so completely all-encompassing that the priests couldn't even step inside.

Filling isn't just a volume thing; it's about transformation. When God fills us, he changes us internally, from the inside out. His Holy Spirit pours into every area of our lives—our thoughts, actions, and relationships—leaving no empty space for doubt or fear, just his overwhelming love and peace. Sometimes life gets bananas, and you can easily feel drained and empty. But God calls you to be filled with his Spirit and nothing else.

Lord, fill me up and overwhelm me with your presence.

# תּוֹלְדֹת—*Tole'dote*

## "Generations"

This is the book of the generations of Adam.
GENESIS 5:1 KJV

The genealogy of Adam in Genesis 5 begins with a quick look back, emphasizing that humans were created in God's image. Then it covers the ten generations from Adam to Noah. I'm sure Adam and his wife, Eve, told their kids all about the God they walked and talked with in the garden before that horrible day when they listened to the serpent and disobeyed him. Eve probably told Cain, Abel, Seth, and the other children bedtime stories about God's creative power, mercy toward them, and everything in between. Adam would chime in about free will, choices, and consequences and about being careful about whom you allow to speak into your life. Some listened, some didn't, and lineages changed.

When you surrender your life to Christ and live in obedience to his Word, you leave behind a legacy of faith for your family hundreds of years from now. Stories will be told not only about your faithfulness and, yes, your struggles but also about God's amazing grace in your life. Lineages change based on the choices we make. The eternal destinies of future generations can hang in the balance of a zig to Jesus or a zag to the serpent.

Lord, let your work in my life be an example to my family.

# נְזִיד—*N'zeed*

## "Stew"

Jacob gave Esau some bread and lentil stew.
Genesis 25:34 NLT

In Genesis 25, we read that Isaac and Rebekah struggled for years to have children, but the Lord eventually blessed her with twins. She felt the babies struggling in her womb, and the Lord told her that these two babies would father two nations that would be at odds with each other. Esau was born first, making him deserving of Isaac's birthright, and Jacob, grasping for Esau's heels, was born second. When the boys were teenagers, Esau came home famished from a day of hunting and traded his birthright to Jacob for a bowl of lentil stew. Big mistake! Putting his immediate physical needs above a lasting inheritance, Esau impulsively gave his birthright away for a pot of grits.

This is a mirror image of the temptation we face to satisfy our immediate desires—whether physical pleasure, wealth, or social status—at the expense of our spiritual well-being. Do everything you can to recognize circumstances where fleeting instant gratification tempts you to compromise your faith and values. Self-control is a virtue that, when nurtured alongside your relationship with Jesus, will help you resist the urge to make decisions that can have significantly detrimental long-term spiritual consequences.

Jesus, help me develop the habit of filtering my everyday choices through the lens of my spiritual inheritance in you.

# אָבַק—*Ahvayk*

## "To Wrestle"

A man came and wrestled with him until the dawn began to break.
GENESIS 32:24 NLT

Twenty years after deceiving his father, Jacob found himself grappling with a stranger. After hours of going at it, the man thumped Jacob, supernaturally dislocating his hip. Dawn broke, and the man said it was time for him to be on his way. Jacob objected, pleading for the man to bless him, to which the man asked Jacob for his name. "He replied, 'Jacob'" (v. 27). Jacob's rotten nature finally dawned on him, and he realized the rhythms of his life needed to change dramatically. His name was immediately changed to Israel, a word that points to struggle.

In this story, we tend to focus on the all-night wrestling match, but the point of the narrative is God changing Jacob into Israel. This name signified a new identity and an incredible new destiny as Israel went from being known as a con artist to being a man who struggled with God and humans and overcame. When you encounter the Lord, he offers you a new identity as his child. Accepting it means ditching past labels, names, and mistakes. He transforms your heart and mind, infusing your life with purpose and newness that shape your worldview and influence your decisions.

Lord, let me live out my new name as your child.

# לַעֲנוֹת—*Lah'ahnote*

## "To Answer"

Righteous people think carefully before they answer someone.
PROVERBS 15:28 EASY

Have you ever found yourself in a conversation about Jesus, and you're asked a question that completely befuddles you? Very early in my Christian walk, I thought I was supposed to immediately have a walking-Bible, encyclopedia-like answer for every question, and I arrogantly believed I did. But Solomon wrote, "Righteous people think carefully before they answer someone."

Witnessing is not a sprint. It's a marathon. Therefore, it is much better to carefully think through our words than to break the silence with nonsense. Don't allow yourself to be forced into an answer when you don't know. How about "That's a really good question. Let me think through it and let's have coffee on Friday to revisit it"? Humility and authenticity are Christlike qualities, so be humble and real. After all, sharing the gospel isn't about winning debates or proving you're C. S. Lewis. You can't coerce belief anyway. It's a leadership thing. No trickery. No coercion. As Christians, we should lead people to Jesus so they can conclude on their own that he is who he says he is. And remember, people don't argue with conclusions they come to on their own.

Father, let my conversations be saturated with grace and truth.

# סָלַח—*Sahlahkh*

## "To Pardon; to Spare"

Let them turn to the LORD, and he will have mercy on them, and to our God, for he will freely pardon.
ISAIAH 55:7 NIV

The verb *sahlahkh* or one of its derivatives appears in the Old Testament forty-six times and is never used for people forgiving people. God is the subject of the verb every time. He is the only one with the authority to forgive sin. Leviticus consistently records blood being shed for the atonement of sin and subsequently the Lord pardoning the sinner. It was always God who pardoned, never a priest or any other human.

Over the years, many have argued that Jesus never explicitly claimed to be God, but it takes a disingenuous approach to history and the Bible to make this accusation. When Jesus told the paralytic, "Son, your sins are forgiven" (Mark 2:5), it was a clear claim of deity. Why else would the Jewish scribes immediately say, "He's blaspheming! Who can forgive sins but God alone?" (v. 7). They and everyone who heard him preach understood he was declaring his divinity. Rest in the truth that when a repentant sinner turns to Jesus and asks to be pardoned, they are never turned down. The answer is always "Son or daughter, your sins are forgiven."

Jesus, thanks for forgiveness that knows no limits.

# חָכָם וְחָכְמָה—*Khahkahm V'khahkmah*

## "Wise and Wisdom"

Become wise by walking with the wise; hang out with fools and watch your life fall to pieces.
PROVERBS 13:20 MSG

*Khahkahm* translates as "wise" while *v'khahkmah* means "wisdom." The *khahkahm* constantly hunt for *v'khahkmah*. Wisdom isn't just head knowledge but a transformative power enabling us to make right decisions at right times. It is the appropriate use of knowledge and suggests maturity. This sounds good, but where do we begin? It all starts with the Lord. "Wisdom begins with fear and respect for the LORD. Knowledge of the Holy One leads to understanding" (Proverbs 9:10 ERV). He is not just *a* source but *the* source and fountainhead of wisdom, and knowing him opens the floodgates.

The people you spend time with profoundly influence (positively or negatively) your thoughts, actions, and habits. Surround yourself with godly people who inspire you to grow, make better choices, and pursue God-honoring goals. "Walking with the wise" means learning from the experiences and mistakes of others. When you're in a pickle, talk to the folks who have survived a similar struggle. They've been there and can offer you sound advice and counsel so you can avoid the rough waters they've already navigated.

Lord, give me the maturity to pursue wise counsel and the humility to listen.

OCTOBER 12

# אֱדוֹם—*Ehdome*

## "Edom"

This is the family tree of Esau, who is also called Edom.
GENESIS 36:1 MSG

Genesis 36 tracks more than a thousand years in the lineage of Isaac's firstborn son, Esau, the one who traded his birthright for some Campbell's soup. In Genesis 25, God revealed to Esau's mother,

> Two nations are in your womb,
> and two peoples from within you shall be divided;
> the one shall be stronger than the other,
> the older [Esau] shall serve the younger [Jacob]. (v. 23)

It appears a cosmic collision occurred when, fifty generations later, Herod the Great, a descendant of Esau, ruled Israel and Jesus, a descendant of Jacob, was born in a stable and laid in a manger in Bethlehem. Herod, one of the most powerful men on earth, made it his standard practice to take out any potential threats to his rule, including killing babies (Matthew 2:16–18). But God's sovereign plan trumped Herod's authority. Jesus' birth and ultimate triumph is another proof that God's purposes cannot be usurped by man.

You will face situations where opposition and overwhelming challenges appear 1,000 percent insurmountable. But the truths woven in Scripture from Abraham to Jesus' empty tomb remind you to trust God's unwavering authority over all earthly powers. God wins every time.

Place full confidence in God, knowing he will fulfill his plans for you despite any opposition.

# Mensch

## "Good Person"

Barnabas…, a Levite of the country of Cyprus, having land, sold it, and brought the money and laid it at the apostles' feet.
ACTS 4:36–37 NKJV

*Mensch* is a Yiddish word originating in the eighteenth century. It became popular in the mid-1900s. In our lingo, we would say a mensch is an all-around good dude—a person of hospitality, encouragement, generosity, selflessness, integrity, and kindness. Barnabas, Paul's partner early in his ministry, was certainly a mensch. His name even means "son of encouragement." He traveled with Paul on his first mission trip and helped him defend the gospel against the Judaizers, people who wanted gentile Christians to adopt Jewish customs. When the disciples in Jerusalem feared Paul, it was Barnabas who put their fears to rest.

If he went to our church, Barnabas would lead the guest services team. I would ensure that he served as a greeter every Sunday at one of the main entrances, always creating a warm, welcoming, and inviting atmosphere with words of encouragement rolling off his tongue to every visitor entering the church. Barnabas the mensch—always displaying a genuine smile, consistently listening to what people said, forever looking for ways to be of service to everyone (church family or not), never speaking an unkind word of anyone, and perpetually displaying an encouraging spirit—was the prototype witness for Christ.

Where are you on the mensch scale?

# אֶחָד—*Ekhahd*

## "One"

There is one body…one Spirit…one Lord, one faith, one baptism, one God.

Ephesians 4:4–6 NASB

The one-liner for Judaism is the Shema, a prayer that ends with "The Lord is one" (Deuteronomy 6:4). There is only one transcendent creator of the universe, and he is Yahweh. This truth weaves itself into Ephesians, Galatians, and 1 Corinthians. In Ephesians 4, unity is emphasized by the repetition of the word *one*: "One body…one Spirit…one Lord, one faith, one baptism, one God."

There is *ekhahd* (echad) body, the church, comprised of people from crazy diverse backgrounds, races, religions, socioeconomic classes, ethnicities, and nationalities. In God's economy, there is no Black church or White church—only *the* church. The proof of membership in the body is the indwelling of the same Holy Spirit within every believer. Christians are glued together by one Lord, Jesus Christ. We have one faith: the gospel. There is only one baptism, and it's an outward expression of salvation. Last, we have only one God: the merciful creator of all. The divisions that plague the church are unbiblical and man-made. Our battle cry is unity in the essentials, freedom in the nonessentials, and grace in and for everyone.

What changes can you make today to contribute to unity in your local church?

# יוֹם כִּפּוּר—*Yome Keepoor*

## "Day of Atonement"

Without the shedding of blood there is no forgiveness of sins.
HEBREWS 9:22 ESV

*Yome Keepoor* (Yom Kippur) is Judaism's holiest day. In biblical times, two goats were selected—one for a burnt offering and one for the ritual of Azazel. The high priest sprinkled the blood of the burnt offering on the mercy seat in the holy of holies to make atonement for himself, his family, and all Israel. The other goat was sent off into the wilderness to Azazel, a goatlike demon, as a sin offering to return the people's sins to where they came from.

The modern *Yome Keepoor* includes a twenty-five-hour fast and repeated prayers of repentance that appeal to God for forgiveness of our sins against him and ask others for forgiveness of our sins against them. According to Jewish thought, if our appeal is sincere, God will forgive despite the lack of animal sacrifices, which ended in AD 70. Yet God's Word never removes this requirement. Echoing Leviticus 17:11, which speaks of blood as necessary for atonement, Hebrews 9:22 says, "Without the shedding of blood, there is no forgiveness of sins." So how are we forgiven without a sacrifice? We're not—Jesus' blood eternally fulfilled the Old Testament sacrificial system, satisfying God's righteous demands once and for all. There is no longer a need for all the elaborate rituals.

Jesus, thank you that you are more than enough.

# עַל חֵטְא—*Ahl Khayt*

## "For the Sin"

If we confess our sins, he is faithful and just to forgive us our sins and to cleanse us from all unrighteousness.
1 John 1:9 ESV

The *Ahl Khayt* (Al Chet) is a prayer of confession recited ten times on Yom Kippur while beating the left side of one's chest (over the heart) in a tradition called hesped. The phrase "For the sin which we have committed before you by…" is repeated fifty-three times with fifty-three different sins. It is divided into three sections separated by the words "For all these, God of pardon, pardon us, forgive us, atone for us."

When we repent, believe, and accept Jesus Christ as our Savior, we are forgiven for past, present, and future sins. Why would John tell us to keep confessing our sins using a tense that indicates continual confession? Your salvation certainly isn't in jeopardy. You don't need to be pardoned twenty, thirty, or one hundred times. Once is sufficient. But when you sin, your fellowship with the Lord is at risk. By walking in disobedience, you are inching further and further away from him. By confessing to and being real with God, you refresh the relationship and restore intimacy. God wants deep, meaningful fellowship with you.

Own your junk and be real with the Lord today.

# מֶלֶךְ הַכָּבוֹד—*Mehlekh Ha'kahvode*

## "King of Glory"

We observed his glory, the glory as the one and only Son from the Father, full of grace and truth.
JOHN 1:14 CSB

David likely wrote Psalm 24 as he was escorting the ark of the covenant from Kiriath-jearim to Jerusalem and then to its placement in the tent he'd pitched for it (1 Chronicles 13–16). The presence of the King of Glory was entering Jerusalem triumphally. Twice David penned, "Lift up your heads, O gates!" (Psalm 24:7, 9 ESV). Twice he questioned, "Who is this King of glory?" (vv. 8, 10). And three times, the answer is the Lord: "The LORD, strong and mighty, the LORD, mighty in battle!" (v. 8), and "the LORD of hosts, he is the King of glory!" (v. 10).

John the Evangelist told us that the incarnate King of Glory "dwelt among us" (John 1:14). He went on to say that they saw his glory and that his glory was God's glory. Jesus' disciples saw beyond the flesh and blood of Jesus of Nazareth, an ordinary Galilean carpenter turned rabbi. They saw the indwelling King of Glory. As they walked with him for three and a half years, they saw the manifestation of God's divine presence, character, and power in him.

Who is Jesus to you? A first-century carpenter? Rabbi? Prophet? Good dude? Or is he the King of Glory?

# נָהַג—*Nah'hahgay*

## "Guide; Lead"

God is our God forever and ever. He will guide us until death.
Psalm 48:14 isv

Psalm 48:14 declares three simple yet ginormous promises: (1) Yahweh is eternally God. (2) If you are his, then he is your God. (3) God will lead and guide you not just for a season but for all the days of your life. He is committed to walking with you "from can to can't" in every stage no matter the ups, downs, twists, or turns.

Most of the time, we have no clue what's next, and life can feel like we're meandering through a pitch-black room. The powerful truths in this verse remind us that we are never alone or left without direction. God is acutely aware of the entire journey and promises to guide us all the way home, even when the Adversary hurls uncertainties along the path. If you are at a fork in the road, feeling confused, or if the future looks like a fog-covered mirror, remember that God is there beside you, holding your hand, leading you, and knowing the way ahead. Lean into his guidance, believing and trusting that he has a perfect plan.

In what areas of your life do you need to more deeply trust God's leadership and guidance?

# תָּמִים—*Tahmeem*

## “Perfect”

“‘It must be perfect to be accepted.’”
LEVITICUS 22:21 NKJV

Leviticus 22:21 describes the qualifications of a peace or freewill offering. For it to be acceptable to God, it must be *tahmeem*—perfect. Really? Yes, God is holy, and yes, his standard has always been perfection. And the bar is the same today. How can that be when we are so obviously messed up, flawed, and imperfect? The answer is Jesus! He sinlessly walked the dusty roads of Israel for thirty-three years and embodied the perfection we never could. When he died on the cross, he became the final and flawless sacrifice that fulfilled God’s righteous requirement of perfection.

Now we don’t have to “kill” ourselves to achieve something we never could anyway. Jesus’ righteousness is credited to us when we repent and place saving faith in him. He wraps us with his perfection, and when the Father looks at us, he sees the righteousness of his Son. Therefore, you can let go of the paralyzing stress of trying to be perfect. Your relationship with the Lord is founded on, grounded in, and relies solely on Jesus’ perfection, not yours. Because of this, you can confidently approach God’s throne with thanksgiving, knowing that through Christ, you have been made fully acceptable to a holy God.

Lord, let me rest in your perfect, sacrificial work on my behalf.

# כְּנָפֶ֫יךָ—*K'nahfeh*

## "Wings"

Hide me in the shadow of your wings.
PSALM 17:8 ESV

We all have seasons when we feel like a tornado spinning out of control. Work stinks, relationships are crashing, and we are just exhausted from all of it. David begged the Lord in Psalm 17 to "keep me as the apple of your eye" (v. 8). He fearfully and wonderfully created you, and you are incredibly precious to him. You, I, and every other believer are his beloved sons and daughters all at the same time. And, yes, he does love you more than you could ever imagine.

And then David prayed for protection in the shadow of God's wings. Picture a fierce bald eagle sitting atop a cliff, sheltering her eaglets and keeping them safe from anything that would harm them. In the same manner, God offers us a refuge where we can find safety and peace. So when life's challenges appear blinding, remember God always has his eye on you. He's always ready to shelter you from the storms of the world. All you have to do is crawl up in his "nest" and ask. Take a deep breath and let these truths saturate your spirit. You are treasured, extravagantly loved, and under the watchful care of your heavenly Father.

Father, thank you that I can always run to you for shelter.

# רְצוֹן יְהוָה—*R'tzone Yahweh*

## "The LORD's Will"

What does the LORD your God ask of you?
DEUTERONOMY 10:12 NIV

"What does the LORD your God ask of you?" Well, isn't that the question of the year? No. The millennium? No. All time? Yes! But Deuteronomy 10 is a perfect guide for discerning God's will for us. We often think of his will as a mysterious, complex, need-a-graduate-degree-to-understand, hard-to-reach plan, but God clearly lays it out here. First, he wants you to fear him (v. 12), to possess a gut-wrenching reverence and awe for who he is. Then, he calls you to "walk in obedience to him, to love him, [and] to serve the LORD your God with all your heart and with all your soul" (v. 12). Last, you are "to observe the LORD's commands and decrees" (v. 13). That is the syllabus for God's Will 101.

When you focus on Jesus-centric awe, love, obedience, and service in the day-to-day decisions, your life will organically begin to align with his will. Be faithful in the small stuff, live with integrity, and pray for his direction. He will guide you further into his unique plans for your life.

Lord, help me keep first things first: loving, serving, and obeying you with all my heart.

# סֻכּוֹת—*Sookote*

## "Booths"

"If anyone thirsts, let him come to me and drink."
JOHN 7:37 ESV

*Sookote* (Sukkot) is a seven-day harvest festival celebrated after Yom Kippur. It is a reminder of the wilderness journey the Israelites took from Egypt to the promised land. Its name comes from the temporary huts, "booths," built along their journey. Even today, many Jews erect a *sookah* (sukkah), meaning "booth," in their backyard, beautifully decorate it by hanging fruit and vegetables on its temporary walls, and live in it during the holiday.

In ancient times, on the first day of the harvest festival, Zechariah 14:8 was read: "On that day living waters shall flow out from Jerusalem." Every day except the last day, a priest stood outside the temple pouring water over a rock. This ritual commemorated God's provision of water in the wilderness (Exodus 17:1–7).

Yet when Jesus was teaching in the temple on the last day of the festival, on the day when no water was poured out, he invited people to come to him with these symbolic words: "If anyone thirsts, let him come to me and drink. Whoever believes in me, as the Scripture has said, 'Out of his heart will flow rivers of living water'" (John 7:37–38). He has been inviting the thirsty to come for two thousand years. Are you thirsty?

Jesus, thank you for providing your living water that satisfies like nothing else.

# לֵב עֶבֶד—*Lave Ehvehd*

## "Servant's Heart"

Not only has the LORD filled him with his Spirit, but he has given him wisdom and made him a skilled craftsman.
EXODUS 35:31–33 CEV

Have you ever seen a cheetah sprint across the African plains? While it's majestic, that cheetah is simply doing what God created it to do. Similarly, watching someone use the gifts God has given them to serve his people is a special thing to behold because they're doing what God created them to do. For instance, the Lord infused Bezalel with a servant's heart. Bezalel was not a priest, prophet, or king; he was an artisan, but when God filled him with his Spirit, it changed things. Now Bezalel's purpose was to use the unique skills God gave him to help build the tabernacle. Bezalel's story is a reminder that every gift is best used serving God and his people.

We often elevate gifts like preaching and teaching, but there is no hierarchy in God's eyes. When emanating from a servant's heart, all are equally valuable. God calls people with varied skills to build his kingdom—whether it's creating, organizing, leading, or helping behind the scenes. Like Bezalel, your skill set probably feels ordinary, but when God gets hold of it, it becomes extraordinary and can multiply the kingdom. He placed your unique gifts in you with great intention and purpose.

Lord, may I always use my gifts for your kingdom.

# אַבְרָהָם—*Ahv'rah'hahm*

## "Abraham"

"No longer shall you be named Abram,
but your name shall be Abraham."
GENESIS 17:5 NASB

*Ahv'rahm* (Abram) is introduced in Genesis 11:26 as the son of Terah, who was an idol worshiper (Joshua 24:2). His name, *Ahv'rahm*, means "exalted father," which points toward a royal or wealthy yet pagan family tree. From Genesis 11:26 to Genesis 17:4, which covers the first ninety-nine years of his life, he was called Abram. He was seventy-five when God first told him he would father children. And he was in his late seventies when Abram "believed in the LORD; and [God] credited it to him as righteousness" (15:6).

More than twenty years later, God reaffirmed his covenant with Abram, reiterated that Abram would be the "father of a multitude of nations" (17:4), and changed his name from *Ahv'rahm* to *Ahv'rah'hahm*, meaning "father of a multitude." Nearly two thousand years later, God's promises to Abraham found their full expression in Jesus of Nazareth. Through Christ, people from every ethnic background, religious tradition, race, creed, and national origin are beautifully grafted by faith alone into God's family (Galatians 3:7–9). This reminds us that "whatever God has promised gets stamped with the Yes of Jesus" (2 Corinthians 1:20–22 MSG).

Father, let me approach life boldly, knowing that Jesus completely fulfills your redemptive plan for humanity.

# פְּרִי—*P'ree*

## "Fruit; Result"

"I, the Lord, search the heart, I test the mind, even to give every man according to his ways, according to the fruit of his doings."
Jeremiah 17:10 NKJV

*P'ree* is used several times in the Old Testament to mean the product or result of some action or circumstance. On the heels of God stating that man's heart is jacked up and beyond human understanding, he declared that he alone can perfectly read the heart and mind and will "give every man according to his ways, according to the fruit of his doings."

When the precious blood of the Lamb saves us, the fruit of our doings will change. When we are born of the Spirit, there will be *p'ree* in keeping with the Spirit. God transforms hatred to love, sorrow to joy, chaos to peace, exasperation to patience, cruelty to kindness, depravity to goodness, faithlessness to faithfulness, ruthlessness to gentleness, and self-indulgence to self-control (Galatians 5:22–23). While you and I will never fully develop the fruit of the Spirit to the same degree as Jesus, with God's help, the fruit will manifest in our daily walk. Therefore, be intentional about asking him to grow you in these areas.

Lord, let me be more Christlike today than I was yesterday.

# אַחֲרִיתֵךְ—*Ahkhahreetaykh*

## "Your Future"

"There is hope for your future, declares the LORD."
JEREMIAH 31:17 ESV

I asked her, "What do you think happens when you die?" My mom's reply was "I don't care. I'll be dead." I remember thinking, *What a hopeless, futureless worldview*. But God's Word is full of hope, life-changing hope. Jeremiah 31 is about hope in a future restoration for God's people. In context, the prophet was writing about Israel, but this promise of a future quickly travels through time to all God's people for all time.

That promise is for you and me. In the April 6 devotion, I said that when the Lord saved me, he immediately removed my fear of death. He replaced that fear with an unambiguous hope in an eternal future with him. In the face of the uncertainties and challenges in our crazy world, Jesus fully expresses a hope-filled future that empowers us to overcome the struggles of life. When you submit to Jesus' lordship and trust in him alone, you can confidently and boldly face the future because you have a future secured by his death, burial, and resurrection. Rest in him as the anchor of your hope and the firm foundation of your future.

Jesus, I am forever grateful to you for securing my place in your kingdom.

OCTOBER 27

# אַיֶּכָּה—*Ahyehkah*

## "Where Are You?"

The LORD God called out to the man, asking him,
"Where are you?"
GENESIS 3:9 ISV

Close your eyes and imagine the most peaceful, quiet, serene place ever. That was Eden, where Adam and Eve lived—just them and God. It was also where Adam hid from God after eating from the one tree God made off-limits. The man and woman felt guilt and shame for the very first time. They disobeyed God's direct command and wrecked their relationship with their Creator.

Were God's first words to them "I can't believe this. You two can't be that stupid. What part of 'Don't eat it' did you not get"? No! He simply asked, "Where are you?" Do you really think God was putting out an all-points bulletin with the Eden PD because he couldn't find them? Again, no! This was not a geography question; it was a heart question. It was really a why question: "*Why* are you hiding?" Frankly, the inquiry was an invitation to come out into the open, face the truth, own it, repent, and begin the reconciliation and restoration process.

Where are you today? Are you hiding? Are you running away? God's voice doesn't roar with condemnation; it reverberates with love, inviting you back into his presence.

Lord, thank you for restoring my fellowship with you.

# שִׂמְחַת תּוֹרָה—*Seem'khaht Torah*

## "Joy in the Torah"

My soul longs for your salvation; I hope in your word.
Psalm 119:81 ESV

In synagogues around the world, the Torah, which includes Genesis through Deuteronomy, is read on a one-year cycle. *Seem'khaht Torah* (Simchat Torah) is a Jewish holiday that marks the end of one reading cycle and the beginning of a new one. As the Torah scrolls are paraded around the synagogue, Jews sing and dance and party, rejoicing that God loved his people enough to give them his Word.

About a thousand years after the psalmist penned the 176 verses about God's Word in Psalm 119, the apostle John began his gospel with the Word. The Word was in the beginning, was with God, and was God (John 1:1). At Jesus' birth, a new paradigm was born. God's means of communicating with humankind radically changed when his Son became incarnate. Christ is the ultimate revelation of God, wrapped in skin. He is the "exact imprint" of God's nature (Hebrews 1:3). The word translated as "imprint" is the word used for minting coins since each coin was a perfect representation of the original. Jesus is God! Rejoice today that the Word became flesh to rescue me and you. What better reason could you ever have to sing and dance and have *seem'khaht Mahsheeyakh* (joy in the Messiah)?

God, I celebrate that you loved us enough to become one of us.

# חַכֵּה—*Khahkay*

## "To Wait; to Persevere"

"At the time I have decided, my words will come true. You can trust what I say about the future. It may take a long time, but keep on waiting—it will happen!"
HABAKKUK 2:3 CEV

The prophet with the coolest name ever reminded us that God's promises rarely unfold instantly. They usually feel painfully slow, but Habakkuk still encouraged us to wait. This is not purely passive patience; it is persevering in faith, knowing beyond all doubt that when God promises, God delivers. Perseverance strengthens our resolve and matures our trust in the Lord.

Remember, joy came in the morning. After Jesus died on the cross and was buried, there were three agonizing days of silence before that first Easter morning. For his disciples, those days must have been torturously long and filled with doubt. But on the third day, Jesus ran triumphantly out of that tomb. What does his victory tell you? Your perseverance is not pointless. God uses hard times to prepare you, strengthen you, and grow your faith. When you hang tough even through the pain of silence, be reminded that joy always comes in the morning. Whatever you're waiting for, remember that God is in the background, moving the chess pieces around. His promises will come through.

How do you typically respond when you feel like God is taking too long?

# קֶבֶר—*Keev'ree*

## "Tomb"

Mary Magdalene and the other Mary went out to the tomb.
MATTHEW 28:1 TLB

When nearly all of Jesus' guys had tucked tails and run home, Mary Magdalene and the other Mary witnessed the Lord's horrifying murder, staying until the bitter end. Then they followed Joseph to the tomb so they would know where to find Jesus' body when they returned with burial spices. The culture of the day kept them from doing much for Jesus during the last week of his earthly life. After his arrest, they couldn't testify for him in any of his six trials since their testimony was deemed unreliable. What could they do? How could they help? They could stay with Jesus until he took his last breath and could stand ready to anoint his body with spices.

In a twist of divine irony and arguably because of their steadfastness, they were given the privilege of being the first to witness the empty tomb and the first to see the risen Christ. When you begin to feel like you bring very little to the table for Jesus, nip it! You're called to seize every kingdom-multiplying opportunity the Lord sovereignly places in front of you. Stop focusing on your can'ts and don'ts and start focusing on your cans and dos.

Jesus, I praise you for the honor of serving you.

# יָנוּם—*Yanoom*

## "Slumber"

He will not let you stumble; the one who watches over you will not slumber.
PSALM 121:3 NLT

My son Zach spent a summer building trails at Dinosaur National Park in western Colorado. He said the paths were steep, rocky, dangerous, and stumble inducing. Does that describe the way your life sometimes feels? In those seasons, doubt creeps in, and you may question whether you're negotiating the journey alone.

Psalm 121:3 provides a powerful yet comforting truth: You're never alone. God doesn't sleep, nap, or even take a break. His watchful eye is unwavering and fiercely protects you. Still, this promise doesn't mean you'll live free of life's ups and downs, challenges, or trials. Life is life and will still have its rocky moments, but God promises to be the great stabilizing force helping you keep it together. For those who place saving faith in him, he promises to strengthen our steps, keep us steady, and help us stay balanced when life gets unstable. His invitation is for you to find peace in the confidence of his faithful care. If you feel trapped in uncertainty, have a tough decision to make, or are just trying to get through the day without falling apart, take comfort in the knowledge that the Lord is always watching over you.

Lord, I praise you today for your divine insomnia.

# תִּרְצָח—*Teer'tzah*

## "Murder"

"You shall not murder."
Exodus 20:13 NKJV

Based primarily upon God's sovereign creation of humankind in his image, the sixth commandment uses just two Hebrew words—*Lo teer'tzah* (literally, "No murder"). Arguments can and have been made regarding the definition of *murder*. However, simply put, it is the unjust taking of a human life.

As Jesus commonly did, he centered his teaching on the spirit of the law rather than the technicalities. While murder is obviously a grave sin, Jesus' words in Matthew 5 teach us that God's concern far exceeds one's outward actions and looks at the condition of the heart. Jesus essentially said, "Grandpa taught you not to commit physical murder, and you better not. But I'm telling you not even to get angry at people, insult them, treat them with contempt, or call them idiots. If you do, you've really committed murder in your heart and violated the spirit of *Lo teer'tzah*."

Anger can fester like a boil, and at some point, it will burst and get really nasty. When that happens, anger ruins relationships and degrades people who are "fearfully and wonderfully made" (Psalm 139:14) in God's image. Looking beyond legalistic obedience, Jesus calls us to do everything possible to reconcile, forgive, and live a grace-filled life.

What unresolved anger do you need to surrender?

# מָן—*Mahn*

## "Manna"

"I am the bread of life. Your ancestors ate the manna in the wilderness, and they died.…I am the living bread that came down from heaven. If anyone eats from this bread he will live forever."
John 6:48–49, 51 NET

Six weeks removed from slavery in Egypt, the Israelites were kvetching (whining) about the lack of food. God has been in the providing business for a long time, so he rained down manna to save and sustain their lives. "It was like coriander seed, white, and the taste of it was like wafers made with honey" (Exodus 16:31 ESV). God delivered it right on time for forty years. It did not stop until they entered the promised land and tasted the sweetness of its produce (Joshua 5:12).

Fourteen hundred years later, God provided even sweeter sustenance—himself—in the person of Jesus Christ, the Bread of Life. While manna rained down to provide for the wilderness generation, Jesus is the manna from heaven who delivers every generation from certain death. He not only saves us but also nourishes us through our prayer life, Bible study, and corporate worship. What do you do daily to seek nourishment for your soul?

Jesus, your name is the sweetest ever. Thank you that I will never be hungry or thirsty again.

# יְהוָה צְבָאוֹת—*Yahweh Tz'vah-ote*

## "Lord of Hosts"

I can do all things through him who strengthens me.
Philippians 4:13 ISV

When David was a teenager, he dared go where no other man in Israel would go. He jumped in the ring with Goliath, a nine-foot-six Philistine champion who informed David that he would feed his flesh to the birds and beasts. But "David said to the Philistine, 'You come to me with a sword, a spear, and a javelin, but I come to you in the name of the Lord of hosts'" (1 Samuel 17:45 AMP).

It wouldn't have mattered if Goliath had been nineteen feet tall because David had the Lord of Hosts fighting for him. David could do all things through *Yahweh Tz'vah-ote* (Yahweh Tzva'ot), who gave him strength. Second Chronicles 20:15 records Jahaziel announcing to King Jehoshaphat, "Thus says the Lord to you, 'Do not be afraid…, for the battle is not yours but God's'" (ESV).

Whatever "giants" are breathing down your neck, rely on God's power rather than your own abilities. Face them confidently, knowing the Lord is on your side. Whether you encounter a personal struggle, a relationship issue, or a career obstacle, approach it with trust in him who gives you strength.

How does understanding that the battle is not yours but God's change the way you approach conflict?

# שְׁמוּעָה—*Sh'mooah*

## "News"

Mary Magdalene went to the disciples with the news:
"I have seen the Lord!"
John 20:18 NIV

At least six people were eyewitnesses to the empty tomb. Even though Jesus repeatedly told his disciples he would rise after three days, they all initially believed someone had taken their Lord's body. At this point, they really didn't know what to do, so they all went home except Mary Magdalene, the poster child for radical life change, the one whom Jesus cast seven demons out of. She stayed and wept when suddenly someone behind her asked, "Woman, why are you crying?" (v. 15).

She thought he was the yard guy there to cut the grass—that is, until he called her by name. It was Jesus! She was the first person to see him risen. He had chosen her, the woman who had lived in torment for so many years, to be his first witness. The flood of emotions must have been so overwhelming she probably felt paralyzed. But he instructed her to run and tell the guys that joy, indeed, does come in the morning. Mary had probably never run as fast as she did that first Easter morning. All the while, she was shouting the good news: "I have seen the Lord!"

Have you seen him?

# תִּצְלַח—*Teetz'lakh*

## "To Come Mightily"

The Spirit of the LORD came mightily upon David from that day forward.
1 SAMUEL 16:13 AMP

When Samuel came to anoint one of Jesse's eight sons as the next king, he found seven strapping young men and one runt named David. Surely the Lord wouldn't choose this David kid, would he? Yes, he would because our God is a master at selecting those of us who will be the most dependent on him. When Samuel anointed him, a mind-blowing thing happened: "The Spirit of the LORD came mightily upon David from that day forward."

This incredible event kick-started David's radical transformation from humble shepherd boy to Israel's greatest king. And it wasn't the anointing oil that did the trick; it was the indwelling and anointing of the Holy Spirit that equipped David for God's service. As a Christ follower, the same Spirit indwells you. He brings understanding to God's Word, convicts you when you mess up, fertilizes the fruit of the Spirit as you walk through life, and equips you to overcome hurdles and resist temptation. When you feel inadequate and scared to death about what lies in front of you, lean on the Holy Spirit for strength and encouragement.

How can you better allow the Holy Spirit to lead and empower you?

# שֹׁמֵר—*Sho'mayr*

## "Keeper"

Am I my brother's keeper?
GENESIS 4:9 KJV

When Cain committed the first murder and struck down his brother, Abel, God confronted him and asked, "Where is Abel your brother?" (v. 9 ESV). Cain's response was one of the most obnoxious and disrespectful things I have ever heard. First, he lied and basically said, "I have no idea, haven't seen him today." But then he condescendingly asked the Lord of heaven and earth, "Am I my brother's keeper?"

*Sho'mayr* is a rich Hebrew word packed with depth and nuance. It means "to keep watch over," "to guard," "to maintain from danger or injury," "to be responsible for," "to be attentive to," and "to be of service to." With that understanding of *sho'mayr*, the answer to Cain's repugnant question is "1,000 percent yes!" We are all responsible to watch out for those around us. In fact, the Christian walk is grounded in viewing others as higher than yourself (Philippians 2:3–4), loving God and loving others (1 John 4:21), displaying devotion to your brothers and sisters (Romans 12:10), serving them (Galatians 5:13), and sacrificing for them (1 John 3:16). Jesus definitively answered the "brother's keeper" question in John 13:34: "Love each other deeply and fully. Remember the ways that I have loved you, and demonstrate your love for others in those same ways" (VOICE).

How can you be your brother's keeper today?

# מֹץ—*Motz*

## "Chaff"

They are like worthless chaff, scattered by the wind.
PSALM 1:4 NLT

It's fitting that the longest book in the Bible begins by contrasting the path of godly people with that of the ungodly. The psalmist compared the righteous to "trees planted along the riverbank" (v. 3) while the wicked are paralleled with chaff (the husks that are separated from grain during winnowing), which the cool autumn breeze easily carries away. Chaff symbolizes a life lacking purpose, substance, and stability, a life not rooted in God and his Word. People who are like chaff live in a constant cycle of fear, anxiety, and vulnerability, continuously at risk of being swept away by the winds of circumstance and temptation. They tend to wander through life always wondering, *What's next?*

However, those who "delight in the law of the LORD" (v. 2) find meaning, direction, and steadiness in the leadership and guidance of God. They live fruitful lives grounded in obedience and faithfulness to the one who created them. This imagery of life-filled, lush trees versus lifeless chaff should challenge you to survey your walk transparently. Are you firmly rooted in the truths of God, or are you wandering around aimlessly? Are you investing in things that will easily blow away or things with eternal consequences?

Lord, keep me steady when the winds of deception blow strong.

# צַדִּיק—*Tz'deek*

## "To Justify"

"Judge Your servants,…justifying the righteous by giving him according to his righteousness."
2 Chronicles 6:23 NKJV

Only those determined to be righteous will be justified. Unless you are judged as righteous, you will not enter the gates of heaven. You might say, "That doesn't sound right. Paul even wrote, 'There is none righteous, no, not one' (Romans 3:10). If no one is righteous, how does anyone *get* righteous and *get* justified?" Great question. I'm glad you asked. Paul continued in Romans 4, "It shall be imputed to us who believe in Him" (v. 24). What's "it"? The righteousness of the Son of God. The righteousness of Christ is imputed, or credited, to our heavenly account, and we are judged righteous. The Father now looks at us, and rather than seeing our filthy rags (unrighteousness), he sees the beautiful, pure-white robe (righteousness) of his Son. Knowing that God sees us through the lens of Jesus' righteousness is a total game changer. Our reason for everything becomes gratitude for what he has done.

Jesus' defeat of sin, death, and the grave is your victory too. When you face struggles or feel beaten up, remember that you're not fighting alone. Jesus' righteousness empowers you to be an overcomer.

Thank you, Lord, that it's not up to me.

# חֹשֶׁךְ—*Hoshehkh*

## "Darkness"

The fool walks in darkness.
ECCLESIASTES 2:14 NASB

In Ecclesiastes, Solomon compared the wise to fools, writing that wise people walk in the light to see where they're going but that "the fool walks in darkness." Scripture describes fools as drunk babblers who revel in wickedness, calling it fun. And life without Jesus is like stumbling around in the dark and foolishly thinking, *Ain't this freedom fun!* John told us that "people loved the darkness rather than the Light" (John 3:19) because they didn't want their jacked-up behavior brought into the light.

In Ecclesiastes, Solomon noticed that the wise and the foolish face the same end: physical death (2:16). So why even bother with wisdom? Because Jesus changes how we live. Walking in the light helps keep us from tripping on obstacles and gives meaning, purpose, and direction to life. Walking in Jesus' light shifts our priorities, and we begin living for something greater than ourselves. So look in the mirror and ask, *Am I hanging out in the dark while thinking it's familiar, fun, and free?* And then consider stepping into the light even if it means addressing a few difficult truths about yourself. Remember, light removes darkness and brings clarity, hope, truth, and life.

Jesus, let me walk in your light even when it feels difficult.

# אֶרֶךְ אַפַּיִם—*Ehrehkh Ahpahyeem*

## "Slow to Anger"

"I knew that You are slow to anger and are filled with loving-kindness, always ready to change Your mind and not punish."
JONAH 4:2 NLV

Sometimes, church people behave like Christianity is an exclusive club they really don't want everybody to join. This was Jonah's attitude. God told him to preach to Nineveh, and Jonah answered, "Hmm, nah." He ran 180 degrees in the opposite way because he knew the Lord was "a kind and loving God Who shows pity," was "slow to anger," and was "filled with loving-kindness, always ready to change [his] mind and not punish" (v. 2). If Nineveh repented, he knew God would spare them, and he wasn't a fan of that outcome.

Jonah wasn't wrong: Yahweh is the consummate God of second, third, and fourth chances. He provides opportunity after opportunity for people to come back, even those we've determined don't deserve it. This is the essence of evangelism—sharing the good news of God's grace and mercy with everyone, not just the people we've deemed worthy. Don't ever assume person X won't listen to you or that person Y is unfit for God's overwhelming compassion and grace. Sharing Jesus is not about our decisions and determinations but about aligning with God's relentless determination to seek, find, rescue, and save the lost.

Father, thank you for unlimited chances.

# זֶרַע—*Zahreh*

## "Seed"

Sow your seed in the morning.
ECCLESIASTES 11:6 ISV

Ecclesiastes 11 tells us that we don't really have a clue regarding the moves God is constantly making in the background, so we should "sow [our] seed in the morning, and don't stop working until evening, since [we] don't know which of [our] endeavors will do well" (v. 6). We are called to be obedient to God's instruction, not to *be* God. Paul expanded on the analogy of farming in his first letter to Corinth: "I planted, Apollos watered, but God gave the growth" (1 Corinthians 3:6 ESV). The church in Corinth struggled with division because some were looking for credit rather than acknowledging God as the source of *all* the fruit.

As believers, we sometimes feel it is on us to save people, but Paul reminded us to stay in our lane and simply plant and water. God does the saving and growing. You're planting seeds when you share your faith, serve, and pray for others. But you have zero control over how, when, or even if the seeds will sprout and bloom. That's God's job. Relax, knowing that he, not you, transforms hearts and minds. Your role is to show up, love, plant, water, and leave the results to him.

Father, let me be a good and faithful farmer.

# חִצִּים—*Heetzeem*

## "Arrows"

As arrows are in the hand of a mighty man;
so are children of the youth.
PSALM 127:4 KJV

In this Psalm of Ascent, King Solomon told us that "children are a gift from the Lord" (v. 3 NLV). The word for "gift" in this verse can also be translated as "heritage" or "inheritance." Then, he compared children to arrows. This was way before the time of guns and missiles, so an arrow was the most potent weapon available for covering a distance. Solomon fully understood that arrows were an essential tool for protecting a nation.

And so are our children. They are the arrows we aim into the future. They'll inevitably fly off track and miss the target without being directed, shaped, and prepared. Remember, the day is coming when our kids will carry the gospel, authentic Christian faith, and biblical values forward. When you pour Jesus into them and model a life spent for his sake, you are preparing them to be ambassadors who will deliver God's love, truth, and saving grace into the messiness of life. Children with a biblical worldview are the most effective weapon for spiritual change in our arsenal. Every second you spend molding their spiritual life sets them up to make a lasting impact for Christ in a dark world.

Lord, give me the wherewithal to speak Jesus into the children in my life.

# תְּשׁוּקָתוֹ—*T'shookahtoe*

## "Desire; Want"

"If you do not do well [but ignore My instruction], sin crouches at your door; its desire is for you."
GENESIS 4:7 AMP

On the night of his arrest, Jesus' guys fell asleep twice when they should have been praying and keeping watch for him. How ironic is it that the same men who couldn't commit an hour for Jesus didn't struggle a bit staying awake all night fishing? Priorities matter. If you want to go to church, consistently read God's Word, and spend time in prayer, you'll do it. The reason you don't is because you don't want to. You say you do, but you don't. People act based on desire.

Have you ever said, "But I just don't have time for all that stuff," and then you binge-watched some lame show for twelve hours on Saturday? What you do reveals your priorities. If you're looking to grow your relationship with Jesus, you'll make time for him. If your Christian life is important, your calendar will reflect it. If attending church or being part of a small group matters, you'll figure out a way to get there. Maybe that means waking up a little earlier on Sundays—but only if you want to.

God, help me prioritize spending time with you and your children.

# אֵיפָה—*Ayfah*

## "Ephah"

"When will the new moon be over so that we may sell grain, and the Sabbath, so that we may offer wheat for sale? We will make the ephah smaller and the shekel heavier and practice deceit with false balances."

AMOS 8:5 NRSVUE

The folks Amos described couldn't wait for the holidays to end so they could get back to making some cash. The problem was that they were crooked; they were cheating people. They were cooking the numbers. They deceptively made the ephah (grain basket) smaller and the shekel (a weight for coins) heavier. They were ripping people off, particularly the poor.

This passage should make us consider whether we are always honest in our dealings. I don't imagine any of us deal with ephahs and shekels, but we do measure and trade time, money, and even promises. We cut corners, tell little white lies, or take advantage when we think no one's looking. But we're called to live with integrity and to be fair and just with everyone. Dealing with people honorably shouldn't be a matter of rule keeping; it should naturally flow from a heart and life that have been transformed by Jesus. So check your ephahs and shekels, remembering that living honestly honors God.

Lord, let me never cheapen your cross by being dishonest.

# אֹבוֹת—*Ohvote*

## "Wineskins"

"Indeed my belly is like wine that has no vent; it is ready to burst like new wineskins."
Job 32:19 NKJV

In Job, Elihu is a mystery. He shows up toward the end of the book, seemingly to prepare Job for God's revelation. Elihu's first words convey his extreme compulsion to say something. He was burning up in his gut, equating the feeling to fermenting wine that was about to burst open a wineskin.

As a believer, you will sometimes feel so moved by the Holy Spirit to share Jesus or simply a little nugget of truth from Scripture that staying silent seems impossible. This divine nudge isn't just an emotional thing; it's God stirring you in his perfect timing to communicate the truth of his love and hope to somebody in your world. So embrace it, love it, trust it, and do it. But when you do, remember Jesus' words: "Be wise as serpents and harmless as doves" (Matthew 10:16). Elihu waited patiently before opening his mouth to ensure his words were timely and appropriate. You need to follow Elihu's example and ask God to help you speak with love, grace, truth, and wisdom, ensuring that your words build up rather than tear down.

Father, help me discern the right time and way to share what you've placed inside me.

# יִרְאוּ—*Yeer'oo*

## "Awe"

By awesome deeds you answer us with righteousness…so that those who dwell at the ends of the earth are in awe at your signs.
Psalm 65:5, 8 ESV

Psalm 65 celebrates God's overwhelming goodness to his people, which often manifests itself in his supernatural signs, wonders, and help. This is the sphere in which God operates—always has and always will. And the birth, death, and resurrection of the Son of God are the most awe-inspiring signs in all of history.

On the first Good Friday ever, one of the members of the Roman "crucifixion detail," a crusty old centurion, carefully witnessed the day's events unfold. Two criminals hung nailed to their wooden crosses as Jesus, the Galilean rabbi, approached Golgotha. Jesus had submitted to a brutal and merciless beating and was ready to shoulder the agony of his own cross to fulfill the Father's will. All the while, the centurion watched. Several hours later, as Jesus hung on his cross, he said, "It is finished" (John 19:30), and died. The earth quaked, skies darkened, tombs were ripped open, and the temple veil tore. The centurion, after witnessing all this, was "filled with awe" (Matthew 27:54 AMP) and came to this heart-transforming, mind-renewing, life-changing conclusion: "Truly this was the Son of God!" (v. 54).

When was the last time you were filled with awe at God's awesomeness?

# קָדוֹשׁ יִשְׂרָאֵל—*K'doshe Yees'rah'ayl*

## "Holy One of Israel"

Let all the people of Jerusalem shout his praise with joy. For great and mighty is the Holy One of Israel, who lives among you.

Isaiah 12:6 TLB

The Holy One of Israel is one of the most beautiful names of God in the Old Testament. It emphasizes his uniqueness as the covenant God of Israel, who is faithful to his people. Holiness is often mistakenly spoken of as one of his attributes. However, *holy* is simply who he is in his essence, and all his attributes flow from his holiness. We are to be holy because he is holy (Leviticus 19:2).

All the people in Jerusalem, my family and I, and you and yours are called to scream his praises from the mountaintops and sing for joy with a grateful heart. Why? Because the presence of the living God is in our midst. We celebrate his proximity, love, holiness, and salvation. Isaiah reminds us of one of the most humbling yet greatest truths ever: The Holy One of Israel is present in our communities, homes, workplaces, and schools and passionately wants to be actively involved in our lives. Knowing this should encourage us to be strong and courageous when fear and uncertainty rear their ugly heads.

What changes can you make to better reflect God's holiness?

# אַרְבֶּה—*Ahr'beh*

## "Locusts"

"I will restore to you the years that the locust swarm devoured."
JOEL 2:25 ISV

Six or seven hundred years before Christ, a plague of locusts swarmed through Israel like warplanes and decimated the land. The resulting widespread famine and poverty were a wake-up call, summoning the people to turn from their wicked ways back to Yahweh. Like nearly every other prophet, Joel called for the nation to repent, fast, and hit their knees while begging God to have mercy on them. In covenant faithfulness, God said, "I will restore to you the years that the locust swarm devoured." He mercifully promised that if they came to him, not only would he stop all the destruction, but he'd also give them back what they lost.

The years stolen by the locusts' destruction would have seemed wasted and lost, but Yahweh is a God of restoration, reconciliation, redemption, and reboot. He makes all things new. It is simply who he is. While you may experience seasons of destruction caused by sin or circumstances, God is a promise keeper who fixes broken things. What seems lost or wasted gets restored into something a thousandfold greater. So praise him when you walk in the newness of life that his renewal ushers forth.

Lord, come into the desolate areas of my life and change me.

# לֵב—*Layv*

## "Mind"

"Give your servant an understanding mind to govern your people, so I can discern between good and evil. Otherwise, how will I be able to govern this great people of yours?"
1 Kings 3:9 isv

On February 8, I said the Hebrew word *layv* (lev) translates as "heart." It also sometimes translates as "mind" or "understanding" because the heart and mind are inextricably tied together. Today is about the mind.

American culture tends to place status, wealth, and power on the throne of life. Yet when God told Solomon, "Ask me for whatever you want and I'll give it to you" (v. 5), Solomon asked for wisdom and discernment. Depending on your worldview, Solomon's request could be shocking or convicting, or you may even think, *He had God's ear, could have requested anything, yet asked for discernment? Not me, baby. Gimme the Lamborghini.* Nonetheless, Solomon immediately recognized his lack and asked the Lord for discernment, acknowledging that his needs could only be filled with God's wisdom.

Are you tempted to focus your prayers on the stuff that you believe will make your life more comfortable? Solomon would respond, "Ask the Lord to give you a mind that aligns with his will, one that allows you to navigate life with humility, wisdom, and clarity." Riches fade—always! But God's wisdom never does.

How can you use God's wisdom for the sake of Christ?

# עֵדֻת—*Aydoot*

## "Testimony"

Put the Testimony, which I am about to give to you, into the ark.
Exodus 25:16 EHV

*Aydoot* is nearly always translated as "testimony," referring to the tablets containing the Ten Commandments. They exist as a perpetual testimony of God's covenant relationship with Israel. Moses placed them into "the Ark of the Testimony" (v. 22), which was kept in the holy of holies, where God's presence resided, in the tabernacle and later in the temple. Simply stated, God's people kept their testimony tucked safely inside God's house.

Today we refer to our personal stories of God's saving presence in our lives as our testimonies. We are God's temple, and God's Spirit resides in us (1 Corinthians 3:16). Your unique Jesus story lives in your heart as a perpetual testimony of God's covenant relationship with you. And that's another difference between then and now. Then, one man, once a year, ventured into God's presence and experienced his testimony, but now, your testimony of the change Jesus effected in your life calls to be proclaimed to everyone who will listen (Acts 1:8). Because he lives in you, when you forgive, help someone in need, or offer a shoulder to lean on, you're sharing your testimony.

Write your Jesus story with paper and pen and always keep a copy with you.

# בָּשָׂר—*Bahsahr*

## "Flesh"

God looked upon the earth, and indeed it was corrupt; for all flesh had corrupted their way on the earth.
Genesis 6:12 NKJV

The Hebrew word *bahsahr* typically refers to our physical bodies, mortality, or frailty. However, as far back as Noah, the word is linked with corruption: "All flesh had corrupted their way on the earth." As the truths of God were progressively revealed, Paul infused the word *flesh* with deeper and broader meaning. He wrote about the war between flesh and the Spirit: "The flesh desires what is contrary to the Spirit, and the Spirit what is contrary to the flesh. They are in conflict with each other" (Galatians 5:17 NIV).

The battle inside you between the flesh and the Spirit can feel like a fight for the heavyweight title of all time. You live with the never-ending tension between the sinful wants of your flesh and your new Spirit-filled life. Therefore, *don't* act like the battle isn't real but *do* resist those desires with everything you have. Ask the Holy Spirit to identify areas where your flesh tends to rise up, like anger or selfishness. Ask him to guide your thoughts and actions, helping you choose kindness over vengeance and patience over irritation.

Lord, I surrender my sinful desires and tendencies to you.

# שֹׁפְטִים—*Shofe'teem*

## "Judges"

The Lord raised up judges to rescue the Israelites
from their attackers.
Judges 2:16 NLT

The book of Judges illustrates Israel's heartbreaking cycle: They abandoned Yahweh, he hammered them by raising up an oppressor, the nation cried out for rescue, and God mercifully raised up a judge to deliver them. The entire book is one identical cycle after the next. Even dogs learn faster. The narratives highlight that God is long-suffering and merciful. Despite Israel's faithlessness, he remains true to his covenant. He doesn't kick them when they're down but delivers them via the judges. Over and over, "the people of Israel did what was evil in the sight of the Lord" (3:7 ESV), which indicates a huge propensity to forget that it was God who repeatedly saved them.

Before we judge too quickly, we may need to examine our own lives. We tend to do the very same thing. We wander off into rebellion, and God reels us back in, freeing us from the chains of our sin. And then we do it again. That dog analogy is making sense now, right? Are there recurring patterns of sin that need to be dealt with in your life? Repent today and lean on Jesus to crush those destructive cycles.

Jesus, thank you for rescuing me when I "outdumb" myself.

## NOVEMBER 23

# הַשְׁגָּחָה—*Hahsh'gahkhah*

## "Providence"

We make our own plans, but the Lord decides where we will go.
Proverbs 16:9 CEV

Are you a planner? I am. I love it when life feels like a thousand-piece puzzle because I enjoy solving problems, setting goals, making plans, and mapping out the next steps. Proverbs 16:9 reminds me that the Lord is okay with me crafting as many of my little plans as I want, but he decides which path I travel down. Solomon painted a majestic image here of God's providence—the governing power of the Lord that carefully watches over his creation and works out his plans for it.

Does that mean God usurps your free will? Of course not. He doesn't remove your ability to choose; he simply provides grace-filled oversight by weaving a tapestry of your autonomously free decisions into his grand plans and purposes. When your plans get completely messed up—and they will—you can trust that his ways and thoughts are bigger and better and more perfect than yours (Isaiah 55:8–9). He is constantly opening and closing doors and orchestrating events to lead you to what will bring him glory and bring you good. If you're at a fork in the road, surrender your plans to Jesus today, trusting in his wisdom and perfect timing.

Lord, I surrender my feet to you. Guide them.

# נָבִיא—*Nahvee*

## "Prophet"

If what a prophet says in the name of the Lord does not happen, it is not the Lord's message.
Deuteronomy 18:22 NCV

According to Deuteronomy, the test of a prophet is twofold: First, his message must line up with God and his Word, and second, his predictions must come to fruition. About seven hundred years before Jesus, God raised up a bold prophet named Isaiah who spoke God's Word to a people who stubbornly didn't want to hear it. Depending on who you ask, Isaiah contains twenty to forty prophecies regarding the person and work of Christ. From the virgin birth (Isaiah 7:14) to Jesus' lineage through Jesse (Isaiah 11:1) to the Holy Week prophecies in Isaiah 53 and everything in between, every prophecy came true. You can trust that God's Word is wholly reliable. Knowing that so many prophecies about Jesus were undeniably fulfilled is a clear display of God's sovereignty, which can provide a huge boost for your faith. Let them remind you that he always tees things up for your best.

In every situation, we should be cautious about who we listen to (Deuteronomy 18:14–22). The prophetic fulfillment in Jesus' life serves as a yardstick of truth in a confused world of competing truth claims. Measure everything against the veracity and consistency of the Bible.

How can you ensure you're following authentic teachings rather than being misled?

# קָצִיר—*K'tzeer*

## "Harvest"

Ruth stayed close to Boaz's female servants and gathered grain until the barley and the wheat harvests were finished. And she lived with her mother-in-law.

Ruth 2:23 HCSB

The harvest season in the story of Ruth the Moabite woman is far more than a simple basis for the narrative; it is a deeply spiritual representation of God's faithful provision. After a tough season of tragedy, Ruth and her mother-in-law, Naomi, found their needs fulfilled along with sparks of hope in the fields of Boaz. In Ruth, harvests depict physical provision and spiritual abundance. God calls you to glean hope and restoration from his goodness and faithfulness like Ruth gathered barley and grain from the land. Yahweh is a God of provision who ensures his people are always taken care of.

Seasons of harvest mirror our obedient labor for the Lord, which is never in vain or fruitless. Paul wrote, "We must not get tired of doing good. We will receive our harvest of eternal life at the right time" (Galatians 6:9 ERV). Your role is to provide the labor, but the Lord is the harvester, so remain yoked to him. Ruth found life-altering favor and provision on Boaz's farm, and you and I experience life-giving grace and abundance in Jesus.

Thank you, God, for tirelessly working in the background on my behalf.

# חַיִל—*Khayeel*

## "Valor"

Joshua chose thirty thousand mighty men of valor and sent them away by night.
JOSHUA 8:3 NKJV

At Ai, Joshua tasted defeat for the first time and needed to get right with God. Rather than throwing in the towel, he and his men got up and got ready to move ahead. They chose courage over fear, decisiveness over uncertainty, and action over tentativeness. When God ordered Joshua to attack Ai again, the Lord powerfully spoke in the past tense: "I have handed over to you the king of Ai, his people, city, and land" (v. 1 CSB).

Valor doesn't mean fearlessness; it is about taking faithful steps based on God's character even when there is significant risk. Joshua wasn't sure how the rematch would go, but he trusted that the God of heaven was with him and his men. He displayed valor by obeying and leading his soldiers in confident faith. When you face a setback or even a defeat, trust the Lord, learn from it, and keep moving. And remember, valor is not something you muster on your own; it's the strength Jesus gives you to keep pressing ahead, especially when it's tough. Whatever hurdle is in front of you, ask the God of angel armies for the courage to face it.

Lord, give me your strength to persevere in all things.

# מְשָׁחֲךָ—*M'shah'khahkhah*

## "Anointed"

Samuel took a flask of olive oil, poured it on Saul's head, kissed him, and said, "The LORD has anointed you to be ruler of his people Israel."

1 SAMUEL 10:1 GW

The anointing of Saul as the first king was a giant fulcrum in Israel's history. It wasn't ceremony for ceremony's sake but a declaration from heaven's throne that the Lord handpicked Saul and set him apart for the task of leading and shepherding the people of God.

Saul didn't fill out an online job application to be the king of Israel; in fact, when the call came, he was minding his own business looking for his dad's lost donkeys. This is often God's way of doing things. He chooses the most unlikely people and equips them to accomplish his purposes in mighty ways. While few of us are called to be kings, every Christian is anointed by the Holy Spirit to do ministry. You are gifted and equipped.

> You are the ones chosen by God, chosen for the high calling of priestly work, chosen to be a holy people, God's instruments to do his work and speak out for him, to tell others of the night-and-day difference he made for you—from nothing to something, from rejected to accepted. (1 Peter 2:9–10 MSG)

Have you embraced the purpose for which God has anointed you?

God, fill me with your Spirit so I can lead others into your presence.

# נַעֲמָן—*Nah'ahmahn*

## "Naaman"

Naaman went down and bathed in the Jordan seven times, just as the man of God had said. His skin was restored like that of a young boy, and he became clean.
2 KINGS 5:14 CEB

Naaman was a gentile Syrian commander during Joram's reign as king of Israel. Despite Naaman's military prowess, he suffered from leprosy, a disease believed to be the consequence of sin and one that resulted in separation from people and community. Naaman heard about a prophet in Samaria who could cure him, so he sought healing. God led him into an encounter with Elisha, who told Naaman to wash himself in the Jordan seven times. Naaman did, and he was cleansed both physically and spiritually.

But Naaman's cleansing wasn't only about healing. It exposed the truth that Yahweh is the God of *all* nations. This truth vividly points to the nature of the gospel. It is not limited to one type of person. The saving blood of Christ is offered to and heals everyone who repents, believes, and cries out to be saved, transcending all man-made boundaries. What limits have you placed around God's grace? He wishes that all would know him. Be bold and share him with everyone.

Lord, thank you that no one is excluded from your offer of salvation.

# הִתְנַדְּבוּ—*Heet'nahd'voo*

## "Generosity"

The people rejoiced because they had given willingly, for with a whole heart they had offered freely to the LORD.
1 CHRONICLES 29:9 ESV

First Chronicles 29 details David's campaign to build the temple. Verses 6–9 paint an image of the heart of giving and joyful generosity. David sought building resources, and the leaders gave not begrudgingly or out of some weird arm-twisting obligation but with overwhelming enthusiasm. Their generosity was a natural response to a God who was incredibly good to them. He was doing something, and they wanted to be part of it. How could they not be generous? They understood that everything was his anyway.

This snapshot in time reminds us that generosity emanates from a heart in tune with God's will. The Israelites' willingness to sacrifice wasn't just about the money; it was an act of worship and indicated trust in Yahweh Jireh (the LORD who provides). When you give to your local church, which, by the way, is where your tithe should go, you are fulfilling an essential component of worship. Time, talents, or dollars—God wants joyful willingness more than a big check. When you give joyfully, you reflect your love for him and trust in his stewardship.

Father, thank you for blessing me so I can bless others.

# שְׁמְרִים—*Shome'reem*

## "Watchmen"

I have posted watchmen on your walls, Jerusalem; they will never be silent day or night.
Isaiah 62:6 NIV

The scribbled notes in the margins of my Aunt Sarah's Bible told me she had prayed for my salvation every day for nearly twenty years before I was saved. Aunt Sarah and Isaiah both remind us to "pray without ceasing" (1 Thessalonians 5:17 ESV)—to never stop, no matter how long it takes. Likewise, when the watchmen grabbed their weapons and stood guard, they never slept and always kept a keen eye out for Jerusalem's enemies. They were like spiritual lookouts, praying day and night for the fulfillment of God's plans. As a Christ follower, you're invited to be a watchman, boldly approaching God's throne through prayer.

Jesus perfectly modeled this for us as he prayed with perseverance even in the most trying circumstances, trusting his Father completely. His death tore the veil (Matthew 27:51), providing us with a hotline straight to the God of heaven. We can know that he hears us when we cry out to him. So what concerns are burdening your heart today? Is it a prodigal child? A sick parent? A failing marriage? Unrest in your country? Your prayers matter, so don't stop. Jesus said, "Ask, and it will be given to you" (7:7). Trust him.

Jesus, thank you for the Aunt Sarahs of the world.

# בֵּית יְהוָֹה—*Bayt Yahweh*

## "House of the LORD"

The glory of the LORD filled the house of the LORD.
1 KINGS 8:11 NKJV

Seven years after King Solomon and his 180,000-person workforce began construction on the temple, it was finally complete. The priests carefully brought the ark of the covenant containing the stone tablets of testimony and placed it in the Most Holy Place inside the temple.

> When the priests came out of the Holy Place, a cloud filled the house of the LORD, so that the priests could not stand to minister because of the cloud, for the glory of the LORD filled the house of the LORD. (vv. 10–11 ESV)

What an awesome sight this must have been. H. D. M. Spence pled, "The God who filled the Temple must also hallow the church."[11] King Solomon prayed for God's presence to dwell in the temple (vv. 27–30). Because of Jesus' sacrificial death and triumphant resurrection, God's presence is no longer restricted to a physical building but lives within Christ followers through the Holy Spirit. Just as the temple was a place where God's glory was displayed, your Christian life should reflect his presence through your faith, words, actions, service, and character.

Lord, thank you for your manifest presence in my life.

11 H. D. M. Spence-Jones, ed., *1 Kings*, The Pulpit Commentary (Funk & Wagnalls, 1909), 163.

# דָּבָר—*Dahvahr*

## "Word; Promise"

Not one promise out of all the good promises that the LORD your God promised you has failed. All of them have come true for you.

JOSHUA 23:14 EHV

The Hebrew word *dahvahr* does not translate exclusively as "promise." However, when it comes from God, the *dahvahr* always carries the weight of a promise or a commitment that we can "take to the bank."

Joshua's farewell address reminded Israel that the Lord does not make empty promises. If he says he'll provide for, protect, and lead you, he will. Even if it's not according to your schedule, he will not fail you—ever. Joshua emphasized that every promise came to fruition. Your takeaway is that you do not have to live wondering if God will keep his word. He will—always. Joshua challenged his people to remember all the times God had been faithful and true to his promises. We should too! When the trials and struggles of life rear their ugly heads, remember how God has kept his promises in the past. Allow those experiences to build your faith for the future. Because he has done it over and over in the past, he'll do it again.

Write down the times when God kept his word to you. Keep writing them down until he calls you home.

# אֶבֶן יִשְׂרָאֵל—*Ehvehn Yees'rah'ayl*

## "The Rock of Israel"

"He aims his bow well. His arms are made strong. He gets his power from the Mighty God of Jacob. He gets his strength from the Shepherd, the Rock of Israel."
Genesis 49:24 ICB

Years ago, my family was standing on the bank of Jenny Lake in Wyoming and looking across at the majestic Teton Range. It was one of the most awe-inspiring things my eyes have ever seen. I was overwhelmed by its strength. In that moment I couldn't help but think of my Lord—the Rock of Israel. Genesis 49:22–26 records Jacob's profound blessing over his son Joseph. It was the Rock who aimed Jacob's bow, the Rock who gave strength to his arms, the Rock who empowered him. The image of God as a rock evokes a sense of all-encompassing reliability.

Peter, though in chains, declared to the religious leaders, "This Jesus is the stone you builders rejected; he has become the cornerstone!" (Acts 4:11 CEB). What an incredible turn of events! The resurrected Christ—once rejected, scorned, and crucified—is the stone that holds everything in the universe together. Where do you find strength? Purpose? Meaning? Passion? When you feel rejected, where do you turn?

Lord Jesus, I declare my strength is in you. You are my Rock.

DECEMBER 4

# רָצָא—*Rahtzah*

## "To Accept; to Receive Favorably"

"I have come into your presence as one would come into the presence of God, and you have received me favorably."
GENESIS 33:10 NCB

"Come as you are" looks great on church T-shirts, but the proof has to be in the pudding. People often walk into church with real struggles, doubts, and rough pasts. But instead of finding a warm welcome, they're met with judgment and a cold stare. It's easy to say we're welcoming, but walking that talk means loving on folks in the middle of their mess, which is precisely what Christ does.

Jesus accepts you, flaws and junk included. However, he doesn't save you so you can remain the same. You can't meet the risen Christ without being transformed. We are called to "accept one another, then, just as Christ accepted [us], in order to bring praise to God" (Romans 15:7 NIV). Churches should be Holy Spirit hospitals where people can bring all their burdens, doubts, and illnesses without fearing scorn and rejection. The Lord chose the church to be the institution where broken people can be favorably received and experience the life-changing presence of Jesus. When we do that, we become a beautiful reflection of him and bring honor, praise, and glory to God.

Lord Jesus, let me love the sick but not their disease.

# בוֹ בָּחַר—*Voe Bahkhar*

## "To Call Him; to Choose Him"

"The LORD your God has chosen him and his sons from all your tribes, to stand to serve in the name of the LORD always."
DEUTERONOMY 18:5 NASB

God's will is a done deal. Yet we see God calling and using individuals for his specific purposes all over the Bible. The Levites were called to "stand to serve in the name of the LORD," and just like them, God has a unique calling for you.

Paul handed us a timeless life principle: "Let every one lead the life which the Lord has assigned to him, and in which God has called him" (1 Corinthians 7:17 RSV). Regardless of background, we're all called to be a light in the darkness, and it probably looks very different for each one of us. I may be primarily called to write devotionals, pastor a church, and share Jesus on film sets. You might be called to be his hands and feet in your community or to influence kids for Christ on a soccer or baseball field. Whatever it is and wherever he has placed you, he does not call the equipped; he equips the called.

God, lead me to where you want me to be and to whom you want me to serve. Let me follow you.

# נִקְדֵּימוֹן—*Neek'daymone*

## "Nicodemus"

There was a man from the Pharisees named Nicodemus, a ruler of the Jews.
JOHN 3:1 HCSB

Nicodemus was an influential Jewish leader, Pharisee, and member of the Sanhedrin. Among the four gospel writers, only John mentions him. I trust that John included his story because *believe* is the keyword and major theme in his gospel (20:30–31). And I believe Nicodemus eventually placed saving faith in Jesus.

The image the apostle John painted of Nicodemus is one of a learned Jewish leader investigating the truth claims made by a Jewish carpenter from Nowheresville, Israel. Nicodemus came to Jesus in the privacy of evening and questioned him. It was not an undercover interrogation on behalf of the Sanhedrin. By honestly questioning, he exemplified the pursuit of truth. Are you or any of your friends or family searching for truth? Jesus said, "This is why I was born and came into the world: to tell people the truth. And everyone who belongs to the truth listens to me" (18:37 NCV). Searching for the truth, Nicodemus met the Truth and listened to him. In the white noise of life, listen for God's voice, hear his words, and align your life with his truth.

Lord, thank you for Nicodemus' example of searching for truth and finding Jesus, the Truth.

# מְקַדֵּשׁ—*M'kahdaysh*

## "To Sanctify"

""""I am the Lord who sets apart and sanctifies Israel.""""
Ezekiel 37:28 AMP

When the Lord saves you, you are justified. As you pray, fast, worship, and dig into God's Word, you become more and more sanctified. Justification happens at the precise moment when you are saved and God pardons you. But sanctification is a growth process that extends through the rest of your life. Once you give your life to Jesus, God wants you to grow spiritually. Paul wrote, "This is the will of God, that you be sanctified" (1 Thessalonians 4:3).

The first thing on your agenda is to recognize that your spiritual growth requires intentionality—a conscious effort to align your behaviors, thoughts, and attitudes with God's will as it is revealed in the pages of the Bible. Decide to live with moral purity, character, integrity, and godliness. And make choices that nurture spiritual maturity. Join a small group to systematically study God's Word with a community of believers. Pray every day. Kindness matters, so be kind and compassionate. Consistently attend a local, Bible-teaching church. Serve somewhere for the sake of Christ. This lifestyle creates the perfect environment for God to work on your heart, transforming you more and more into the likeness of his Son.

Jesus, I'm yours. Pour into me and grow me.

# צָבָא—*Tzahvah*

## "Warfare"

The Philistines gathered their armies together for warfare, to fight with Israel.
1 Samuel 28:1 KJV

First Samuel 28 records the Philistines mobilizing their military forces to attack Israel. The Philistines gathered their troops, drew up their battle plans, and locked and loaded their weapons in preparation for a large-scale, physical confrontation. Centuries later, Paul wrote about another type of war: "We are not fighting against flesh-and-blood enemies, but against evil rulers and authorities of the unseen world…and against evil spirits in the heavenly places" (Ephesians 6:12 NLT). This is a reminder that behind every physical challenge lies a more profound spiritual battle. Just as God's people constantly faced the Philistines, we also have an enemy that hates our guts and relentlessly fires spiritual bullets at us. These battles often manifest as temptations, doubts, fears, and discouragements that look to derail our faith.

When engaging in spiritual battle, first acknowledge both that it is real and who the real enemy is. Your struggle isn't just against circumstances or people but against the unseen evil that opposes everything God stands for. Second, equip yourself with God's armor (vv. 13–17). Third, rely on God's strength to victoriously deliver you through the war. And finally, spiritual warfare requires watchfulness, so abide deeply in prayer, stay alert, and be discerning.

Lord Jesus, strengthen and equip me for the battle ahead.

# גֶּשֶׁם—*Gehshehm*

## "Rain"

"As the rain and the snow come down from heaven, and do not return to it without watering the earth…so is my word that goes out from my mouth."
Isaiah 55:10–11 NIV

God does nothing without purpose, and rain is no different. It nourishes the soil, bringing with it life and growth. Isaiah told us that the Word of God works the same way. When God speaks, he doesn't say dry words in an empty vacuum. Like rain, his Word is alive and active, watering our minds, changing our hearts, and nourishing our souls. All this results in spiritual growth.

Jesus is the ultimate Word to us, making salvation available to all men and women across time. Just as rain doesn't stop until it does its job, Jesus accomplished his mission of bringing hope and redemption to the world and declared, "It is finished" (John 19:30). God's Word never returns void or empty. He says it "will accomplish what I desire and achieve the purpose for which I sent it" (Isaiah 55:11). When you open the pages of your Bible, God is feeding and watering you with purpose. Sometimes you won't even realize it, but he plants little seeds of faith and grows you in ways you may not see for years.

Father, I trust that your Word will grow me like a springtime shower.

# מְצָרֵף—*M'tzahrayf*

## "Refiner"

"He will sit as a refiner and purifier."
MALACHI 3:3 ESV

Malachi 3:2–3 paints a vivid image of Jesus' return not just as our loving Savior but as a refiner who cleanses and purifies. The fire of a refiner isn't used to burn up and destroy. It purifies gold, silver, and bronze by getting rid of the little impurities that decrease each metal's value and hinder its usefulness. Jesus intends to purify our hearts by removing anything that doesn't align with his holiness. To submit to this process, we need to consistently give ourselves checkups. Are there areas in your life keeping you from being who Jesus wants you to be? Are you clinging to bitterness, shackled in addiction, or simply wandering away from truth? This is not about piling guilt and shame on you; it's about recognizing that Jesus has your back and wants only the best for you.

When the refining process gets uncomfortable (code for "Change isn't always easy"), remember that refiners remain intimately close to the fire while meticulously watching the metal until it's shaped precisely how they intend it to be. In the very same way, Jesus is with you in every fire, trial, and challenge (Daniel 3:25; Matthew 28:20) to fashion you into the godly man or woman he wants you to be.

Lord, refine and cleanse me from anything that separates me from you.

# גַּמְלִיאֵל—*Gahm'leeyayl*

## "Gamaliel"

"Stay away from these men and leave them alone."
ACTS 5:38 HCSB

Oddly enough, Gamaliel still remains a highly respected rabbi among Jews. A learned doctor of the law and a member of the Sanhedrin, he was honored with the weightier title of rabban. *Rabban* means "our teacher." Paul studied under and was a disciple of Gamaliel.

In Acts 5, the Sanhedrin imprisoned Peter and several apostles for preaching about the risen Christ and told them to keep their mouths shut. In response to the gag order, the apostles declared, "We must obey God rather than men" (v. 29). Gamaliel advised his fellow leaders to handle these Jesus followers with caution. "Leave them alone," he urged (v. 38). He went on to say that if this Jesus stuff was man-made, it would wander off into the sunset on its own. He warned, however, "If God is behind it, you cannot stop it anyway" (v. 39 CEV). These words serve as a powerful reminder that God is unstoppable. Whatever originates with him cannot be thwarted. Trust that his purposes will prevail even in your roughest seasons of life. Align your plans with his will, have faith in his timing, and rest assured that his intentions for you are always good.

Father, help me always obey you rather than men.

# לְנִשְׁבְּרֵי־לֵב—*L'neesh'bray Layv*

## "Brokenhearted"

He has sent me to heal the brokenhearted.
ISAIAH 61:1 CSB

Isaiah's prophetic voice shouts to us in Isaiah 61 about the Messiah, the one sent to bring the best news ever to the poor. Jesus didn't show up for the perfect and put-together; he came to "heal the brokenhearted, to proclaim liberty to the captives and freedom to the prisoners" (v. 1) and for all of us burdened by pain, disappointment, or loss. The brokenhearted aren't ignored or rejected but are the very heart of God's mission.

Redemption, healing, and restoration are at the core of the gospel. Rather than ignoring your brokenness, Jesus dives headfirst into the mess with you, ready to stitch and bandage your cuts and bruises. If your heart aches, Jesus came for you. Held captive by grief? He came for you. Imprisoned by addiction? He came with hope and comfort to heal your every wound and hurt. When he ran out of the grave alive, the wages of sin were crushed. Through the power of his resurrection, he delivers wholeness, transforming your brokenness into something beautiful and breathtaking. Leave all your hurt at the foot of his cross and let the one who came for you comfort you with his mercy and grace.

Lord, thank you for putting my shattered pieces back together.

# קְדִימוּיוֹת—*K'deemoo'yote*

## "Priorities"

"My house lies in ruins, says the LORD of Heaven's Armies, while all of you are busy building your own fine houses."
HAGGAI 1:9 NLT

Did your parents ever tell you, "You better get your priorities in line"? People have allowed their priorities to get out of whack forever. For example, when the people of Israel had returned from seventy years of captivity in Babylon, they focused on their comfort—fancy homes, luxury cars, prestigious yachts, busy schedules, and self-centered aspirations—instead of rebuilding the temple. Me, me, me! Meanwhile, on Mount Moriah, God's house was still in ruins. Because their priorities were way out of line, they found themselves paralyzingly frustrated. Nothing worked right, and nothing went their way. Money dried up along with their agriculture, and satisfaction with life was gone.

The battle cry from Haggai was "When God is relegated to second or third place, everything goes haywire." It's not that building houses or owning cars and boats are inherently evil, because God wants us to enjoy life. But when *our* desires jump to the front of the line, we're off course and feel empty. Think about it: Do you ever get so caught up in your own pursuits that God moves down the pecking order? Remember Jesus' words: "Seek first the kingdom of God" (Matthew 6:33 ESV).

Are you keeping first things first?

# מַרְעִישׁ—*Mahr'eesh*

## "Shake"

"'I will shake up sky and earth, ocean and fields. And I'll shake down all the godless nations. They'll bring bushels of wealth and I will fill this Temple with splendor.'"
Haggai 2:6–7 MSG

While Haggai's words encouraged Israel to rebuild the temple, they also looked forward to the Lord's final shaking of the heavens and earth when his kingdom was fully established. His intervention into history brings full expression to the word *mahr'eesh*, which he will do when he reboots things, prepping the world for his eternal purpose.

Haggai said that this new temple will outshine even Solomon's (v. 9) and that "bushels of wealth" will flow into it from everywhere. True glory will not come from the buckets of money but from the Lord's presence with his people. Therefore, don't fret when you witness the world shaking. Know that God's at work, tearing down what needs to go and preparing history's stage for something better. Out with the old and in with the new. The new heaven and new earth, where peace and righteousness dwell, are right around the corner. Your role is threefold: Cling to God's promises, remain faithful to Jesus, and share your hope in Christ with everyone you meet.

Jesus, strengthen my faith as I look toward the amazing things you have in store.

# שַׁעַר—*Shah'ahr*

## "Gate"

This is the gate of the LORD; the righteous will enter through it.
PSALM 118:20 HCSB

The Hebrew word *shah'ahr* usually refers to any enclosure's entrance, but it can also be symbolic. It carries both meanings in Psalm 118. "The gate of the LORD" refers to the temple gate as well as the salvific path into the very presence of Yahweh.

In Matthew 6, Jesus described what a righteous life looks like and encouraged us to embrace God's righteousness. In chapter 7, he capped off his lengthy message with this:

> Enter through the narrow gate. For wide is the gate and broad is the road that leads to destruction, and many enter through it. But small is the gate and narrow the road that leads to life, and only a few find it. (vv. 13–14 NIV)

The entire sermon was a discourse juxtaposing the Pharisees' external, hypocritical righteousness—the wide gate that leads to death and destruction—with internal, Jesus-infused righteousness—the narrow gate that leads to eternal life. "Narrow" doesn't mean it's difficult and complicated. It means that there is only one way, and that way is through placing saving trust in Jesus.

Lord, I praise you today not because there's *only one* way but because there is even *any* way at all.

# נֵצֶר—*Naytzehr*

## "Branch"

A branch from his roots shall bear fruit.
Isaiah 11:1 ESV

Do you ever feel stuck, stagnant, and unproductive? Just blah? Like a dead tree stump? The prophet Isaiah gave us legit hope: "There shall come forth a shoot from the stump of Jesse, and a branch from his roots shall bear fruit. And the Spirit of the Lord shall rest upon him" (vv. 1–2). This messianic promise came during one of Judah's most tumultuous times—one marked by horrific political and social injustices and terrifying threats from Assyria. Into that chaos, God assured his people that a new branch would come from Jesse's family tree. From what appeared to be a worthless, dead stump, the Lord would bring new life and hope through a woodworker from Nazareth named Jesus. The Spirit of the Lord was with him, bringing wisdom, understanding, counsel, comfort, strength, grace, and light into a dark, bleak world.

If you're feeling like a lifeless stump—dry, brittle, and hollowed out—find hope in the Branch. He still creates new life from dead things. Allow him to plant himself in your heart and fertilize you with his Spirit. And then get ready for the harvest of fruit he will bear in your life.

Jesus, I ask you today to breathe your Spirit into the dead areas of my life.

DECEMBER 17

# יְהוָה רֹעִי—*Yahweh Ro'ee*

## "The LORD Is My Shepherd"

"I am the good shepherd, who is willing to die for the sheep."
JOHN 10:11 GNT

"O say can you see…" I bet you can finish these lyrics to "The Star-Spangled Banner" without even thinking about them. I bet you can mindlessly finish this line too: "The LORD is my shepherd…" (Psalm 23:1). Psalm 23:1 is one of the most recognized Old Testament verses. Shepherding is one of the oldest occupations known to humanity. Shepherds guarded their animals as if they were their children. They often protected the flock by sleeping between them and any potential danger, willing to sacrifice their own safety for the sheep. God as a shepherd is a perfect metaphor. He is our protector, defender, and bodyguard who searches for us when we stray.

The New Testament continues this metaphorical name, attributing the title of Good Shepherd to Jesus. Because I would probably wander off into darkness without him, I need his tender, loving protection every day, and I'm sure you do too. Knowing that he safeguarded my life and the lives of millions of other sheep by sacrificing his life gives me meaning and purpose.

How does knowing the Good Shepherd, who gave up his life for yours, impact your meaning and purpose?

# אַרְיֵה—*Ar'yay*

## "Lion"

"Stop weeping! Look, the Lion of the tribe of Judah, the heir to David's throne, has won the victory. He is worthy to open the scroll and its seven seals."
REVELATION 5:5 NLT

When Jacob blessed his son Judah, he prophetically compared him to a lion (Genesis 49:8–10). The lion, the fiercest and most powerful animal in ancient Israel, symbolizes strength, victory, and the Messiah. However, Satan is also depicted as "a roaring lion looking" (1 Peter 5:8 CJB) to devour you and your family.

In John's visions, the scroll in Revelation 5, when opened, set into motion the events of the last days. John began to weep "because no one was found worthy to open the scroll" (Revelation 5:4 NLT). But wait! There is one who is worthy, one who has the purity and authority, and one who has the appropriate lineage—"the Lion of the tribe of Judah, the heir to David's throne." Jesus is the one who holds the future in his hands, not the Deceiver. This gives me hope that despite life's challenges, Jesus will overcome and fulfill God's plan. He is the one in control, and I can live victoriously because he has already won the war over evil and death.

Jesus, thank you for looking after me with the fierce, protective love of a lion.

## DECEMBER 19

# צִיּוֹן—*Tzee'own*

## "Zion"

The Lord has chosen Zion; he has desired it for his dwelling place: "This is my resting place forever; here I will dwell, for I have desired it."
Psalm 132:13–14 ESV

While the Hebrew word *tzee'own* typically refers to Jerusalem or Mount Zion, it often represents more than simply a GPS location on a map. It is majestically symbolic of God's presence with his people. Consider the creator of everything that will ever exist—the one with endless options—saying, "This is where I want to hang out." He is not some faraway God removed from his creation; he is personal.

Through Jesus the Messiah, Zion takes on an even deeper meaning. God lovingly chose *tzee'own*, just as he lovingly chooses us as believers to become his dwelling place. His Holy Spirit rests on us and in us, fulfilling the eternal promise of his presence. His words to Joshua travel through history to us: "I will be with you. I will not leave you or forsake you" (Joshua 1:5). When doubt and fear begin to whisper lies into your ear, remember this: God will never ever abandon his dwelling place. When you invite him in through faith, he always says yes by grace, permanently making you a living Zion.

Lord, thank you for not walking away when things get messy.

# סַעַר־גָּדוֹל—*Sah'ahr Gahdole*

## "Violent Tempest; Great Storm"

The Lord hurled a great wind toward the sea, and there was a violent tempest on the sea so that the ship was about to break up.
Jonah 1:4 AMP

God told Jonah to go to Nineveh and call them out for their wicked ways. Laughably, Jonah's response was to jump on a ship and head for "Tarshish to escape from the presence of the Lord" (v. 3). The story reminds us that God's love is bigger than our hide-and-seek games. He'll often intervene when we wander off. Jonah did board the ship, but God hurled a *sah'ahr gahdole*—a big, violent, raging storm—against it. It wasn't intended to punish Jonah; it was designed to reel him back to obedience.

The tempest symbolizes how God sometimes allows chaos and turmoil in our lives to seize our attention and get us back on course, aligned with his will. The storms nearly always feel overwhelming, but they are actually the winds of grace, usually protecting us from greater unseen dangers. Of course, not all life's storms are caused by disobedience. However, when you find yourself in a mess, it's worth asking, *Is God trying to get my attention?* His intervention is always meant to correct, never to destroy.

God, thank you for calling me back when I stray.

# כֹּהֲנִים—*Kohahneem*

## "Priests"

"You priests turned aside from the way, and by your teaching you caused many to stumble."
MALACHI 2:8 ISV

As a pastor, Malachi 2 scares me. Okay, I said it. Every Sunday morning, I sneak into a little room in our church and pray, *Lord, don't let me say something dumb or heretical that pushes someone away from you. Give me your words, not mine. Let me preach truth—the whole gospel.* After all, false teaching is a big deal. In Malachi 2:8, God chastised Israel's priests for leading people down the wrong road. When they should have been guiding people in truth, their jacked-up teaching caused many to stumble. It spit in God's face and broke the very covenant they were meant to uphold.

If you are ever entrusted with teaching or leading anyone, this warning is also for you. Causing people to stumble may come from bad intentions, but it can also originate from carelessness, laziness in study, or personal bias about God's Word. Either way, it confuses, misleads, and harms the faith of others. What you teach or share with others about Jesus either draws them closer to him or pushes them further away. Test your words against Scripture. Be careful with God's truth. Pray for his wisdom.

Jesus, keep me grounded in your Word and focused on pointing people to you.

# שָׂטָן—*Sahtahn*

## "Satan"

The Lord said to Satan, "Have you considered my servant Job?"
Job 1:8 esv

*If God is good, bad things wouldn't happen. If God is all-powerful, he would stop them from happening. Therefore, God either can't stop it or doesn't care.* Lie, lie, and lie. Job's story reminds us that nothing happens outside of God's control. Job 1:7–12 is one of the strangest conversations in Scripture: a back-and-forth between God and Satan. Satan wants to take Job out, but he can only do what God allows. This fact may be tough to swallow, but Satan's attacks don't sneak up on God. God uses them for his glory and our growth as Christians. Satan wanted to crush Job, but God took the darts Satan threw and deepened Job's faith.

God didn't create robots. He created human beings and gave us each a free will, and he wants us to choose him over evil. Bad things do happen. Pain does infiltrate our lives, but God sees you and is with you in the middle of the pain, hurt, and heartache. Because Satan is pride incarnate, he will always think he's winning, but he's on a leash and doesn't even realize it. God always has the final say, period. Trust him. He has your back.

Lord, help me trust that you are always in control.

# חֲנֻכָּה—*Khahnookah*

## "Dedication"

"I am the light of the world."
JOHN 8:12 ESV

In 168 BC, the Syrian Greeks (Seleucids) tried to force on Israel the Greek culture along with their pagan beliefs, practices, and sacrifices. A small band of poorly armed warriors, led by Judah the Maccabee, rebelled and defeated the Seleucids. Then the Jews took back the temple. *Khahnookah* (Hanukkah) commemorates its rededication, which occurred in 164 BC. As the second-century BC Jews went to light the menorah (a seven-branched candelabra), they realized that all the oil had been defiled except a container with a one-day supply. Miraculously, the menorah burned for eight days. Today, *Khahnookah* (also known as the Festival of Lights) is celebrated for eight nights.

One of the major themes in the gospel of John is light. John 8 finds Jesus in conversation with Jewish leadership on the Festival of Sukkot, when giant torches were lit in the temple to commemorate the pillar of fire that led the Jews through the wilderness in Exodus. In John 8:12, Jesus proclaimed, "I am the light of the world. Whoever follows me will not walk in darkness, but will have the light of life." Jesus became the light of God in human form. He was the personification of shekinah—the very presence of God.

Follow Jesus and allow him to illuminate your life. You will never be in the dark again.

# נַהֲפוֹךְ—*Nah'hahfoke*

## "Reversal"

The day on which the enemies of the Jews hoped to obtain power over them, the situation was reversed so that the Jews would gain power over those who hated them.

Esther 9:1 EHV

Have you ever felt like everybody and every circumstance were working against you? I know I have, and it stinks. In Queen Esther's time, the Jews faced a royal decree that was set to wipe them off the planet. Their enemies were sure nothing stood in the way. In their minds, exterminating the Jews would be a cakewalk. But the God of intervention jumped in the middle of it. On the day set for their demise, the opposite happened. The Jews overcame those looking to obliterate them. There was a divine reversal of fortune—God's providential hand turned despair into triumph.

There is no pickle you can find yourself in that is beyond the Lord's control. When the strong arm of injustice and oppression seems overwhelming, God is moving in the background. With the snap of a finger, he can transform the most frightening situation into a highlight reel of his justice and mercy. If you feel hopeless, pray; if you're facing unfairness, pray; if you're suffering persecution, pray. God specializes in flipping the script and righting wrongs in his ways and his timing.

God, thank you for toppling unjust powers.

# סִימָן טוֹב—*Seemahn Tove*

## "Good Tidings"

The angel said unto them, Fear not: for, behold, I bring you good tidings of great joy, which shall be to all people.
LUKE 2:10 KJV

*Seemahnn tove oo'mahzehl tove* (good tidings and good luck) is a phrase commonly used in Jewish celebrations like weddings, bar mitzvahs, or the birth of a child. Other than reading the Christmas story every year, you've probably never used the word *tidings* in your life. Me neither. It means "news" or "information."

Around 4 BC, the most significant birth of all time occurred when the Virgin Mary gave birth to Jesus the Messiah—the most joyful of all celebrations. That very night an angel appeared to several shepherds tending their flocks and brought them good tidings that would impact humanity forever: "Unto you is born this day in the city of David a Savior, which is Christ the Lord" (v. 11). The angel announced the good tidings for everyone. Let this force you to think beyond yourself and embrace the truth that the gospel message is for all people. Be intentional about sharing the hope of Christ with your friends and family. Tell them how the good news of Jesus transformed your life.

Father, thank you for your Son, Jesus, the best tidings ever.

# רַחוּם—*Rahkhoom*

## “Mercy”

The Lord passed before him, and proclaimed, “The Lord, the Lord, a God merciful and gracious, slow to anger, and abounding in steadfast love and faithfulness.”
Exodus 34:6 RSV

When God came down in a cloud to meet with Moses, God gave Moses—and us—a clear indication of who he is. He didn’t whisper it; he “proclaimed” his character—merciful, gracious, patient, loving, and faithful. And God didn’t screech, “By the way, I’m all-knowing, all-powerful, and omnipresent,” even though he is. Instead, he focused on the attributes that convey his care and concern for his people. He is merciful and gracious, always standing ready to forgive when we mess up, and he’s patient because we mess up a lot. The heavens and earth can’t contain his love and faithfulness—they flood creation.

Is this your view of God? Or has life corrupted you into believing that he’s a mean, old god sitting up in the sky just waiting for the chance to punish you? Commit to memory the way God described himself to Moses in Exodus 34:6. He is precisely the same today. Remember, the very last thing he wants to do is punish you. He wants to lavish you with forgiveness and have a relationship with you that never ends.

Lord, forgive me for my wrong view of who you are.

DECEMBER 27

# יֹאשִׁיָּהוּ—*Yosheeyahoo*

## "Josiah"

The people did not turn away from the LORD God of their ancestors for the rest of Josiah's rule as king.
2 CHRONICLES 34:33 CEV

During Josiah's reign as Judah's king, the high priest Hilkiah found "*The Book of God's Law*" (v. 15). This was probably Deuteronomy, but it could have been the entire Pentateuch (first five books of the Old Testament). After hearing God's Word, Josiah was deeply convicted and repented, but he didn't stop there. He led all Judah in reform. He obliterated all the idols, stopped the accompanying pagan worship practices, and called the people to renew their covenant with Yahweh. These Spirit-led actions displayed the heart of a godly leader who inspired his people to remove the spiritual distractions in their lives and seek the Lord. He understood that true worship meant eliminating everything that competed for the people's brain space, time, and devotion.

Look for the blind spots in your life. Have you allowed wealth, ambition, social status, or just everyday distractions to draw you away from God and his Word? Devotion to Jesus demands that you surrender whatever it is and turn your heart back to him. Let Josiah remind you that your faithfulness to Jesus is a lifelong commitment, not a one-time event.

Father God, expose the areas in my life where I've allowed idols to creep in.

# תִּגְנֹב—*Teeg'nove*

## "Stole"

"Tell the people that Jesus' followers came during the night and stole the body."
MATTHEW 28:13 ICB

After Jesus broke the chains of death and walked triumphantly out of his tomb, the guards told the chief priests that he was missing. They and the elders were petrified of losing their power, control, and authority. As any good crook would do, they bribed the soldiers guarding the tomb to spread a fake news story. "Tell the people that Jesus' followers came during the night and stole the body," they said. Their response isn't surprising: People will go to great lengths to deny the truth, sometimes spreading lies to create confusion. Despite the Jews' painstaking effort to conceal Jesus' resurrection, the reality of his victory over death could not be contained. The good news spread like wildfire because the Holy Spirit's power is unaffected by human plans.

You will undoubtedly encounter attempts to undermine and dismiss the message of the gospel. Haters are gonna hate. Skepticism and hostility toward biblical faith are not new phenomena. Yet the resurrection-induced transformation of billions of lives is undeniable. As a Christ follower, you are called to speak 100 percent truth delivered with 100 percent compassion—no more, no less. So don't be discouraged by opposition. It means you're doing something right.

Lord, thank you for the truth of your resurrection.

# אִישׁוֹן—*Ee'shone*

## "Apple"

"God protected them in the howling wilderness as though they were the apple of his eye."
DEUTERONOMY 32:10 TLB

In Deuteronomy 32:10, Moses painted a vivid image of just how much Yahweh loves his people. God didn't simply abandon them to their directionless wanderings in the barren Judean wilderness; no, he embraced, guided, and protected them. He affectionately called Israel "the apple of his eye." The word *ee'shone*, also translated as "pupil," truly conveys the next-level love and concern that God has for his people. He even cares for the tiny, little pupils of our eyes.

Consider the barren wilderness as a brutal season in your life, a time when you feel lost, isolated, and ready to give up. This is the moment when God dials up the love-fueled watchfulness. His eyes never come off you or any of his other children, who are all apples of his eye. He shields you from harm and illuminates your path back to him. Today, reflect on the feeling of being this incredibly cherished by the creator of the universe. Amazingly, it's not because of your merit but because of his covenantal love. In moments of doubt, embrace the truth that you are invaluable to him.

Father, thank you for never taking your eyes off me.

# שִׁיר—*Sheer*

## "Song"

Sing a new song to the Lord, for he has done wonderful deeds.
Psalm 98:1 NLT

Psalm 98 opens up with an invitation that should stir our hearts: "Sing a new song to the Lord, for he has done wonderful deeds." *Sheer* is much more than simply music. It speaks to something radically personal, a unique and creative response to God's "wonderful deeds" in the past, his miraculous acts right now, and the unknown mighty works he will do in the future.

When lyrics are married to a melody, we are lifted up, are connected to him, and become grounded in the truths found in his Word. But new songs of worship aren't just the blending of lyrics and music; they are an outburst of our gratitude for his presence. God relentlessly works on our behalf, unseen in the background, and our song is an organic response to his faithfulness. When we see his steadfast love break through heaven and into our lives in visible ways, these are times to start singing new songs again. What does that look like for you? It may be renewed vigor in your prayer life or sharing his goodness with someone who doesn't know him.

Lord, please don't ever stop putting new songs in my heart.

# סְלִיחָה—*S'leekhah*

## "Forgiveness"

With you there is forgiveness.
Psalm 130:4 CJB

Psalm 130 is a Psalm of Ascent beginning with the psalmist pleading for the Lord's attentive and merciful ear. He immediately stated the obvious: "Lord, if you punished people for all their sins, no one would be left" (v. 3 NCV). If we got what we deserved, we'd all be flicked off the planet by God's pinky finger. So thank goodness for the word *but* in the Bible. Listen closely, and you can almost hear the sigh of resplendent relief in the psalmist's voice as he joyfully shouted, "But with you there is forgiveness" (v. 4 CJB). Other than simple compassion, we are given the reason for God's forgiveness: "So that [he] will be feared" (v. 4).

Fear in this context equates to a reaction of obedience. A healthy fear of the Lord has an uncanny way of turning sinners into saints. One of the chief ways God's forgiveness does this is by relieving you from carrying the heavy weight of the past. Embracing his forgiveness supernaturally allows you to shed that burden, knowing that he will never drag your past back up. Focusing on this new freedom rather than the punishment empowers obedience and enables growth.

Don't let the new year come and go without fully embracing the Lord's forgiveness.

# Acknowledgments

The acknowledgments section of a book is all about thank-yous. Considering that obvious truth, the biggest thank-you clearly falls in Jesus' lap for saving me on January 17, 2001. I still wake up every day and can't believe I'm saved.

A huge thanks also to my wife, Susan, who received daily text messages for the last several months that went something like this: *Devo #1 emailed. Please advise whether it's any good*; *Devo #2 emailed, thoughts?*; *Devo #3 emailed, does it stink?* And on and on.

Thank you also to Heather Orenstein for painstakingly reviewing many of these devotions and offering her heartfelt suggestions.

A huge thanks to Stephen Kendrick for his friendship, wisdom, inspiration, and guidance along the way.

The Lord providentially placed Susan and me on a film set in January 2023 with Suzanne Niles, the director of Relationship Development for BroadStreet Publishing. Thank you, Suzanne, for listening to the Lord's nudge and connecting the dots.

# Word Index

*Strong's Exhaustive Concordance of the Bible* typically lists the root form of Hebrew words, not every inflected or derived form of the word. The root listed is usually the masculine singular for nouns and the third person masculine singular perfect for verbs.

When using *Strong's*, you're usually not looking up the exact form of the word found in the verse (especially if it's conjugated, plural, feminine, etc.). You're being pointed to the base or root word, which can help you understand all related meanings and forms.

For example:

- חַיִּים (*chayim*)—the plural word for "life"—is listed under Strong's number 2416, which is חַי (*chai*), the singular root.
- וַיִּכְתֹּב (*vayikhtov*)—"and he wrote"—would point you to Strong's number 3789, which is כָּתַב (*katav*), the root verb for "to write."

Please also note that not every Hebrew word has a Strong's number. If one does not exist for a specific word, that column is left blank in the following table.

# Hebrew

| Phonetic Transliteration (Common Spelling) | Hebrew | Meaning | Strong's Number | Date Word Appears |
|---|---|---|---|---|
| *Ahbah* (Abba) | אַבָּא | "Father" | 1 | August 18 |
| *Ahdone Olahm* (Adon Olam) | אֲדוֹן עוֹלָם | "Lord of the World" | 113, 5769 | August 17 |
| *Ahf* | אַף | "Anger" | 639 | May 2 |
| *Ahfahr* | עָפָר | "Dust" | 6083 | March 6 |
| *Ahfahr Hah'ahrehtz* | עֲפַר הָאָרֶץ | "Superabundant" | 6083, 776 | July 13 |
| *Ah'hoov* | אָהוּב | "Beloved" | 157 | May 12 |
| *Ahkaydah* (Akedah) | עֲקֵדָה | "Binding of Isaac" | 6123 | January 3 |
| *Ahkhahreetaykh* | אַחֲרִיתֵךְ | "Your Future" | 319 | October 26 |
| *Ahkhee* | אָחִי | "Brother" | 251 | May 30 |
| *Ahkove* | עָקֹב | "Deceitful; Crooked" | 6121 | April 28 |
| *Ahl Khayt* (Al Chet) | עַל חֵטְא | "For the Sin" | 5921, 2403 | October 16 |
| *Ahmahn* | אָמַן | "Believe; Trust" | 539 | September 7 |
| *Ahmeedah* (Amidah) | עֲמִידָה | "Standing" | 5975 | February 17 |
| *Ahnah* | עָנָה | "To Respond" | 6030 | May 11 |
| *Ahnahn* | עָנָן | "Cloud" | 6051 | June 2 |
| *Ahnahvah* | עֲנָוָה | "Humility" | 6038 | March 3 |
| *Ahnahveem* | עֲנָוִים | "The Meek" | 6035 | June 24 |
| *Ahnee* | עָנִי | "Poor" | 6041 | September 26 |
| *Ahr'beh* | אַרְבֶּה | "Locusts" | 697 | November 18 |

| *Ahvahkaysh* | אֲבַקֵּשׁ | "I Will Search" | 1245 | August 21 |
|---|---|---|---|---|
| *Ahvahteekheem* | אֲבַטִּחִים | "Watermelon" | 20 | September 28 |
| *Ahvayk* | אָבֵק | "To Wrestle" | 79 | October 8 |
| *Ahv'rah'hahm* | אַבְרָהָם | "Abraham" | 85 | October 24 |
| *Ahyeen Tahkhaht Ahyeen* | עַיִן תַּחַת עַיִן | "Eye for an Eye" | 5869, 8478, 5869 | March 15 |
| *Ahyeen Tovah/ Ahyeen Rah'ah* | עַיִן טוֹבָה/עַיִן רָעַע | "Good Eye/Evil Eye" | 5869, 2896, 5869, 7489 | August 16 |
| *Ahyehkah* | אַיֶּכָּה | "Where Are You?" | 346 | October 27 |
| *Ahz'n* | אָזְן | "Ear" | 241 | October 4 |
| *Ahz'voo* | עָזְבוּ | "Abandoned" | 5800 | March 17 |
| *Ar'yay* | אַרְיֵה | "Lion" | 738 | December 18 |
| *Ayd* | עֵד | "Witness" | 5707 | May 6 |
| *Aydoot* | עֵדֻת | "Testimony" | 5715 | November 20 |
| *Ayfah* | אֵיפָה | "Ephah" | 374 | November 14 |
| *Aygehl Mahr'bayk* | עֵגֶל־מַרְבֵּק | "Fattened Calf" | 5695, 4770 | September 30 |
| *Ayl Kahnah* (El Qanna) | אֵל קַנָּא | "A Jealous God" | 410, 7067 | September 3 |
| *Ayl Olahm* (El Olam) | אֵל עוֹלָם | "Everlasting God" | 410, 5769 | June 3 |
| *Ayl Rah-ee* (El Roi) | אֵל רֳאִי | "The God Who Sees" | 410, 7210 | April 3 |
| *Ayl Shahdai* (El Shaddai) | אֵל שַׁדַּי | "God Almighty" | 410, 7706 | May 3 |
| *Aysheht Khahyeel* (Eshet Hayil) | אֵשֶׁת חַיִל | "Woman of Valor" | 802, 2428 | April 8 |
| *Ayt Mo'ayd* | עֵת מוֹעֵד | "Appointed Time" | 6256, 4150 | June 13 |

| *Aytzah* | עֵצָה | "Purpose" | 6098 | September 14 |
|---|---|---|---|---|
| *Aytz Hahdah'aht Tov Vahrah* | עֵץ הַדַּעַת טוֹב וָרָע | "Tree of the Knowledge of Good and Evil" | 6086, 1847, 2896, 7451 | February 27 |
| *Aytz Khahyeem* | עֵץ חַיִּים | "Tree of Life" | 6086, 2416 | February 28 |
| *Ayvoos* | אֵבוּס | "Feeding Trough" | 18 | September 27 |
| *Bahkhahr* | בָּחַר | "To Choose; Chosen" | 977 | July 9 |
| *Bahrah* | בָּרָא | "Create" | 1254 | August 10 |
| *Bahr Ehnahsh* (Bar Enosh) | בַּר אֱנָשׁ | "Son of Man" | 1247, 606 | March 12 |
| *Bahr Meetz'vah* (Bar Mitzvah) | בַּר מִצְוָה | "Son of the Commandment" | 1121, 4687 | February 2 |
| *Bahsahr* | בָּשָׂר | "Flesh" | 1320 | November 21 |
| *Bayt Yahweh* | בֵּית יְהֹוָה | "House of the LORD" | 1004, 3068 | December 1 |
| *Beekooray* | בִּכּוּרֵי | "Firstfruit" | 1061 | June 27 |
| *B'kahd'sho* | בְּקָדְשׁוֹ | "His Sanctuary" | 6944 | August 3 |
| *Bokehr* | בֹּקֶר | "Morning" | 1242 | May 13 |
| *Bokhayn* | בֹּחֵן | "To Test" | 974 | August 23 |
| *Boray* | בּוֹרֵא | "Creator" | 1254 | September 17 |
| *B'reet* (B'rit) | בְּרִית | "Covenant" | 1285 | February 3 |
| *B'reet Meelah* (Brit Milah) | בְּרִית מִילָה | "Covenant of Circumcision" | 1285, 4135 | January 9 |
| *Chahzahk Veh'ehmahtz* | חֲזַק וֶאֱמָץ | "Strong and Courageous" | 2388, 553 | January 20 |
| *Chai* | חַי | "Life" | 2416 | February 14 |
| *D'ahgah* | דְּאָגָה | "Anxiety; Worry" | 1674 | July 5 |
| *Dahvahk* (Davak) | דָּבַק | "Cling" | 1692 | April 11 |
| *Dahvahr* | דָּבָר | "Word; Promise" | 1697 | December 2 |

| | | | | |
|---|---|---|---|---|
| *Dahyahn Hah'ehmeht* (Dayan Ha'emet) | דַּיָּן הָאֱמֶת | "The Righteous Judge" | 1777, 571 | August 12 |
| *Dahyaynoo* (Dayeinu) | דַּיֵּנוּ | "It Would Have Been Sufficient" | | April 17 |
| *Dehrehkh* | דֶּרֶךְ | "The Way" | 1870 | September 4 |
| *Dehshehn* | דֶּשֶׁן | "Fullness" | 1880 | July 10 |
| *Doomeeyah* | דּוּמִיָּה | "Silence" | 1747 | July 12 |
| *D'vahr* (Davar) | דָּבָר | "Word" | 1697 | March 26 |
| *Eemah* | אִמָּה | "Mother" | 517 | May 5 |
| *Eemahnoo Ayl* | עִמָּנוּ אֵל | "Immanuel" | 5973, 410 | April 14 |
| *Eeshah* (Ishah) | אִשָּׁה | "Woman" | 802 | May 27 |
| *Ee'shone* | אִישׁוֹן | "Apple" | 380 | December 29 |
| *Eet* | עֵת | "Time" | 6256 | July 19 |
| *Eev'reem* | עִוְרִים | "The Blind" | 5787 | August 22 |
| *Ehdome* | אֱדוֹם | "Edom" | 123 | October 12 |
| *Eh'h'yeh* (Ehyeh) | אֶהְיֶה | "I Am" | 1961 | August 28 |
| *Ehlahah Ee-lah'yah* | אֱלָהָא עִלָּיָא | "Most High God" | 426, 5943 | May 16 |
| *Ehloheem* (Elohim) | אֱלֹהִים | "God" | 430 | March 8 |
| *Ehloheem Khahyeem* (Elohim Chayim) | אֱלֹהִים חַיִּים | "The Living God" | 430, 2416 | March 14 |
| *Ehmeht* (Emet) | אֱמֶת | "Truth" | 571 | February 7 |
| *Ehrehkh Ahpahyeem* | אֶרֶךְ אַפַּיִם | "Slow to Anger" | 750, 639 | November 10 |
| *Ehsh'kahkh* | אֶשְׁכַּח | "Forget" | 7911 | July 30 |
| *Ehvehn Yees'rah'ayl* | אֶבֶן יִשְׂרָאֵל | "The Rock of Israel" | 68, 3478 | December 3 |

| | | | | |
|---|---|---|---|---|
| *Ekhahd* (Echad) | אֶחָד | "One" | 259 | October 14 |
| *Gahleel* (Galil) | גָּלִיל | "Galilee" | 1551 | April 7 |
| *Gahm'leeyayl* | גַּמְלִיאֵל | "Gamaliel" | 1583 | December 11 |
| *Gaht Shehmehn* | גַּת שֶׁמֶן | "Gethsemane; Olive; Oil Press" | 1660, 8081 | March 18 |
| *Gay* | גַיא | "Valley" | 1516 | June 26 |
| *Gehfehn* (Gefen) | גֶּפֶן | "Vine" | 1612 | March 24 |
| *Gehshehm* | גֶּשֶׁם | "Rain" | 1653 | December 9 |
| *Go'ayl* (Goel) | גֹּאֵל | "Redeemer" | 1350 | February 6 |
| *G'own* | גְּאוֹן | "Pride" | 1347 | June 30 |
| *Goyeem* (Goyim) | גּוֹיִם | "Gentiles" | 1471 | March 1 |
| *Hahdome Rahg'lay* | הֲדֹם רַגְלַי | "Footstool" | 1916, 7272 | July 22 |
| *Hahgooreem Maht'naykhem* | חֲגֻרִים מָתְנֵיכֶם | "Gird Your Loins" | 2296, 4975 | September 18 |
| *Hahlahkhah* (Halaka) | הֲלָכָה | "The Path or Way of Life" | 1980 | September 1 |
| *Hahl'loo* | הַלְלוּ | "Praise" | 1984 | January 16 |
| *Hah'reeshone Yeeyeh Ahkhahrone* | הָרִאשׁוֹן יִהְיֶה אַחֲרוֹן | "The First Will Be Last" | 7223, 1961, 317 | March 31 |
| *Hahr M'geedoe* (Har Megiddo) | הַר מְגִדּוֹ | "Armageddon" | 2022, 4023 | March 30 |
| *Hahshaym* (Hashem) | הַשֵּׁם | "The Name" | 8034 | March 20 |
| *Hahsh'gahkhah* | הַשְׁגָּחָה | "Providence" | | November 23 |
| *Hahv'deel* (Havdil) | הַבְדִּיל | "Separate" | 914 | March 11 |
| *Haykhahl* | הֵיכָל | "Temple" | 1964 | July 24 |
| *Heef'raytee* | הִפְרֵתִי | "To Be Fruitful" | 6500 | June 8 |

| *Heenahm* | חִנָּם | "For Nothing" | 2600 | June 4 |
|---|---|---|---|---|
| *Heen'nee Sh'lahkhaynee* | הִנְנִי שְׁלָחֵנִי | "Here I Am. Send Me!" | 2009, 7971 | August 25 |
| *Heesh'lakh'tah* | הִשְׁלַכְתָּ | "You Have Cast" | 7993 | May 18 |
| *Heet'nahd'voo* | הִתְנַדְּבוּ | "Generosity" | 5068 | November 29 |
| *Heetzeem* | חִצִּים | "Arrows" | 2671 | November 12 |
| *Heh'akh* | הֶאָח | "Aha" | 1889 | June 16 |
| *Hehspehd* (Hesped) | הֶסְפֵּד | "Traditional Beating of the Chest" | 5594 | January 2 |
| *Hone* | הוֹן | "Wealth" | 1952 | February 29 |
| *Hoshehkh* | חֹשֶׁךְ | "Darkness" | 2822 | November 9 |
| *Hoy* | הוֹי | "Woe" | 1945 | July 3 |
| *Kahdosh* (Kadosh) | קָדוֹשׁ | "Holy" | 6918 | January 25 |
| *Kahl* | כָּל | "All" | 3605 | March 25 |
| *Kahrah* | קָרָא | "To Call" | 7121 | April 27 |
| *Kahshroot* (Kashrut) | כַּשְׁרוּת | "Dietary Laws" | | January 19 |
| *Kahtone'tee* | קָטֹנְתִּי | "Am Not Worthy" | | August 31 |
| *Kapporehth* | כַּפֹּרֶת | "Mercy Seat" | 3727 | January 17 |
| *Kayfah* (Kefa) | כֵּפָא | "Rock; Stone" | | April 1 |
| *K'deemoo'yote* | קְדִימוּיוֹת | "Priorities" | | December 13 |
| *K'doshe Yees'rah'ayl* | קְדוֹשׁ יִשְׂרָאֵל | "Holy One of Israel" | 6918, 3478 | November 17 |
| *Keedoosh* (Kiddush) | קִדּוּשׁ | "Sanctification" | 6942 | February 19 |
| *Keenah* | קִנְאָה | "Envy" | 7068 | July 14 |
| *Keepah* (Kippah) | כִּפָּה | "Head Covering" | | January 11 |
| *Keesay* | כִּסֵּא | "Throne" | 3678 | June 7 |

| *Keesay Shehl Ayleeyahoo* | כִּסֵּא שֶׁל אֵלִיָּהוּ | "Chair of Elijah" | 3678, 452 | February 16 |
|---|---|---|---|---|
| *Keev'ree* | קִבְרִ | "Tomb" | 6913 | October 30 |
| *Kehrehm* | כֶּרֶם | "Vineyard" | 3754 | June 19 |
| *Kehtzehf* | קֶצֶף | "Wrath" | 7110 | April 10 |
| *Kehvehs* | כֶּבֶשׂ | "Lamb" | 3532 | March 10 |
| *Khahdahsh* | חָדָשׁ | "New" | 2319 | July 8 |
| *Khahkahm V'khahkmah* | חָכָם וְחָכְמָה | "Wise and Wisdom" | 2450, 2451 | October 11 |
| *Khahkay* | חַכֵּה | "To Wait; to Persevere" | 2442 | October 29 |
| *Khahmaytz* (Chametz) | חָמֵץ | "Leavened" | 2557 | January 24 |
| *Khahnookah* (Hanukkah) | חֲנֻכָּה | "Dedication" | 2598 | December 23 |
| *Khahrehv* | חֶרֶב | "Sword" | 2719 | June 14 |
| *Khahrosh* | חֲרֹשׁ | "To Plow" | 2790 | August 29 |
| *Khahshahvah* | חִשָּׁבָ | "Planned; Meant; Devised" | 2803 | May 26 |
| *Khahtah* (Chata) | חָטָא | "Sin" | 2398 | February 22 |
| *Khahzone* | חָזוֹן | "Vision" | 2377 | July 26 |
| *Khatahv'tee* | כָתַבְתִּי | "Inscribe" | 3789 | July 20 |
| *Khayeel* | חַיִל | "Valor" | 2428 | November 26 |
| *Khayn* | חֵן | "Favor; Grace" | 2580 | June 28 |
| *Kheedote* | חִידוֹת | "Hard Questions" | 2420 | September 23 |
| *Khehsehd* (Hesed) | חֶסֶד | "Steadfast Love; Loving-Kindness" | 2617 | January 6 |
| *Khomah* | חוֹמָה | "Wall" | 2346 | April 26 |

| *Khoopah* (Chuppah) | חֻפָּה | "Canopy" | 2646 | June 1 |
|---|---|---|---|---|
| *Khoteh Gekhahleem* | חֹתֶה גֶחָלִים | "Heap Burning Coals" | 2846, 1513 | March 13 |
| *K'nahfeh* | כְּנָפֶי | "Wings" | 3671 | October 20 |
| *Koce Hahg'oolah* | כּוֹס הַגְּאֻלָּה | "Cup of Redemption" | 3563, 1353 | April 18 |
| *Kohahneem* | כֹּהֲנִים | "Priests" | 3548 | December 21 |
| *Koom* (Kum) | קוּם | "Arise" | 6965 | March 29 |
| *K'ree'yah* (Keriah) | קְרִיעָה | "Tearing" | 7167 | April 21 |
| *K'toobah* (Ketubah) | כְּתֻבָּה | "Marriage Covenant" | | January 10 |
| *K'tzeer* | קְצִיר | "Harvest" | 7105 | November 25 |
| *K'voorah M'sooyahdah* | קְבוּרָה מְסוּיָּדָא | "Whitewashed Tomb" | | September 16 |
| *Lah'ahnote* | לַעֲנוֹת | "To Answer" | 6030 | October 9 |
| *Lahg bah-Omehr* (Lag b'Omer) | לַג בָּעֹמֶר | "Thirty-Three of the Omer" | | May 15 |
| *Lahlehkheht* | לָלֶכֶת | "To Go" | 1980 | May 22 |
| *Lahvahsh* | לָבַשׁ | "To Clothe" | 3847 | May 4 |
| *Lave Ehvehd* | לֵב עֶבֶד | "Servant's Heart" | 3820, 5650 | October 23 |
| *Laykh Ahkharai* | לֵךְ אַ חֲרָי | "Follow Me" | 3212, 310 | April 9 |
| *Laytz* | לֵץ | "Scoffer" | 3887 | August 24 |
| *Layv* (Lev) | לֵב | "Heart" | 3820 | February 8 |
| *Layv* (Lev) | לֵב | "Mind" | 3820 | November 19 |
| *L'neesh'bray Layv* | לְנִשְׁבְּרֵי־לֵב | "Brokenhearted" | 7665, 3820 | December 12 |
| *Mah'ahs* | מָאַס | "Reject" | 3988 | May 25 |

| *Mah'ahsayr* | מַעֲשֵׂר | "Tithe" | 4643 | March 2 |
|---|---|---|---|---|
| *Mah'ahsay Yahdai* | מַעֲשֵׂה יָדַי | "Handiwork" | 4639, 3027 | September 9 |
| *Mahf'tayakh* | מַפְתֵּחַ | "Key" | 4668 | April 12 |
| *Mahkhahr* | מָחָר | "Tomorrow; a Time to Come" | 4279 | September 19 |
| *Mahkh'sh'vote* | מַחְשְׁבוֹת | "Thoughts; Plans" | 4284 | September 20 |
| *Mahl'akh* (Malak) | מַלְאָךְ | "Angel" | 4397 | March 28 |
| *Mahlay* | מָלֵא | "To Fill" | 4390 | October 5 |
| *Mahn* | מָן | "Manna" | 4478 | November 2 |
| *Mahraht* | מָרַת | "Bitterness" | 4784 | May 23 |
| *Mahr'eesh* | מַרְעִישׁ | "Shake" | 7493 | December 14 |
| *Mahsheeyakh* | מָשִׁיחַ | "Messiah; Anointed" | 4899 | August 1 |
| *Mahtay Mosheh* | מַטֵּה מֹשֶׁה | "Moses' Staff" | 4294, 4872 | April 22 |
| *Mah Tovoo* (Mah Tovu) | מַה טֹּבוּ | "How Good; How Lovely" | 4100, 2896 | May 9 |
| *Mahtzah* | מַצָּה | "Unleavened Bread" | 4682 | February 15 |
| *Mahveht* | מָוֶת | "Death" | 4194 | April 6 |
| *Mayeem Khahyeem* (Mayim Chayim) | מַיִם חַיִּים | "Living Water" | 4325, 2416 | January 4 |
| *Meedah* | מִדָּה | "Measure" | 4060 | August 20 |
| *Meed'bahr* | מִדְבָּר | "Wilderness" | 4057 | August 4 |
| *Meeg'dahl Oze* | מִגְדַּל־עֹז | "Strong Tower" | 4026, 5797 | July 16 |
| *Meek'vay Yees'rah'ayl* | מִקְוֵה יִשְׂרָאֵל | "The Hope of Israel" | 4723, 3478 | June 17 |
| *Meek'veh* (Mikvah) | מִקְוֶה | "Ritual Bath; a Gathering [of Water]" | 4723 | January 30 |

| *Meel'khahmah* | מִלְחָמָה | "Battle" | 4421 | August 7 |
|---|---|---|---|---|
| *Meen'yahn* (Minyan) | מִנְיָן | "Number" | 4487 | February 20 |
| *Meesh'nah* (Mishnah) | מִשְׁנָה | "Repeated Study" | 4932 | February 25 |
| *Meesh'paht* | מִשְׁפָּט | "Justice" | 4941 | June 12 |
| *Meetz'vah* (Mitzvah) | מִצְוָה | "Commandment" | 4687 | May 17 |
| *Meez'bay'akh* | מִזְבֵּחַ | "Altar" | 4196 | March 27 |
| *Mehlekh* (Melek) | מֶלֶךְ | "King" | 4428 | May 1 |
| *Mehlekh Ha'kahvode* | מֶלֶךְ הַכָּבוֹד | "King of Glory" | 4428, 3519 | October 17 |
| *M'hahdahr* | מְהַדָּר | "To Honor" | 1921 | August 8 |
| *M'kahdaysh* | מְקַדֵּשׁ | "To Sanctify" | 6942 | December 7 |
| *M'kore Khahyeem* | מְקוֹר חַיִּים | "Fountain of Life" | 4726, 2416 | September 13 |
| *M'lookhah* | מְלוּכָה | "Kingdom" | 4410 | September 11 |
| *Moahveeyah* | מוֹאֲבִיָּה | "Moabite Woman" | 4124 | January 21 |
| *Modeh Ahnee* (Modeh Ani) | מוֹדֶה אֲנִי | "I Gratefully Thank" | 3034, 589 | February 9 |
| *Mosheh* (Moshe) | מֹשֶׁה | "Moses" | 4872 | April 4 |
| *Motz* | מֹץ | "Chaff" | 4671 | November 7 |
| *Moze'nahyeem* | מֹאזְנַיִם | "Balances" | 3976 | April 25 |
| *M'shah'khahkhah* | מְשָׁחֲךָ | "Anointed" | 4886 | November 27 |
| *M'tzahdah* (Masada) | מְצָדָה | "Stronghold" | 4686 | April 20 |
| *M'tzahrayf* | מְצָרֵף | "Refiner" | 6884 | December 10 |
| *M'tzoolah* | מְצוּלָה | "Deep; Depth" | 4688 | August 26 |

| *M'zoozah* (Mezuzah) | מְזוּזָה | "Doorpost" | 4201 | January 28 |
|---|---|---|---|---|
| *Nah'ahmahn* | נַעֲמָן | "Naaman" | 5283 | November 28 |
| *Nah'hahfoke* | נַהֲפוֹךְ | "Reversal" | 2015 | December 24 |
| *Nah'hahgay* | נַהֲגֵ | "Guide; Lead" | 5090 | October 18 |
| *Nahkhahlaht* | נַחֲלַת | "Inheritance" | 5159 | July 31 |
| *Nahkhahmoo* | נַחֲמוּ | "Comfort" | 5162 | June 25 |
| *Nahkhahsh* | נָחָשׁ | "Serpent" | 5175 | August 5 |
| *Nahsah* (Nasa) | נָסַע | "Journey" | 5265 | May 24 |
| *Nahvee* | נָבִיא | "Prophet" | 5030 | November 24 |
| *Nahv'lah* | נֶבְלָה | "To Wither" | 5034 | September 24 |
| *Nahzeer* (Nazir) | נָזִיר | "Nazarite" | 5139 | February 11 |
| *Naytzehr* | נֵצֶר | "Branch" | 5342 | December 16 |
| *Neek'daymone* | נִקְדֵּימוֹן | "Nicodemus" | | December 6 |
| *N'oom* | נְאֻם | "Utterance; Declaration" | 5002 | June 5 |
| *N'tahtee* | נְתַתִּי | "Given" | 5414 | April 24 |
| *N'zeed* | נְזִיד | "Stew" | 5138 | October 7 |
| *Ohvayd* | עֹבֵד | "Work" | 5647 | May 20 |
| *Ohvote* | אֹבוֹת | "Wineskins" | 178 | November 15 |
| *Olahm Hahbah* (Olam Haba) | עוֹלָם הַבָּא | "The World to Come" | 5769, 935 | February 10 |
| *Ore* | אוֹר | "Light" | 216 | May 10 |
| *Pahnai* | פָּנֶי | "Face" | 6440 | June 10 |
| *Pahrokheht* (Parochet) | פָּרֹכֶת | "Veil" | 6532 | January 23 |
| *Pahroosh* (Parush) | פָּרוּשׁ | "Pharisee" | | January 26 |
| *Peh* | פֶּה | "Mouth" | 6310 | April 30 |

| | | | | |
|---|---|---|---|---|
| *Pehsahkh* (Pesach) | פֶּסַח | "Passover" | 6453 | April 16 |
| *Pehtahkh* | פֶּתַח | "Door" | 6607 | May 8 |
| *Pooreem* (Purim) | פּוּרִים | "Lots" | 6332 | March 23 |
| *P'ree* | פְּרִי | "Fruit; Result" | 6529 | October 25 |
| *Rah-ah* | רָעָה | "To Feed" | 7462 | August 19 |
| *Rahkhoom* | רַחוּם | "Mercy" | 7349 | December 26 |
| *Rahtzah* | רָצָא | "To Accept; to Receive Favorably" | 7521 | December 4 |
| *Rahv* (Rav) | רַב | "Enough" | 7227 | October 1 |
| *Rahv* (Rav) | רָב | "Rabbi" | 7227 | March 9 |
| *Rahvah* | רָבָה | "To Multiply" | 7235 | April 29 |
| *Ray'ay* | רֵעַ | "Friend" | 7453 | June 18 |
| *Rehgehl* | רֶגֶל | "Feet" | 7272 | March 7 |
| *Rooahkh hah-Kodehsh* (Ruach ha-Kodesh) | רוּחַ הַקֹּדֶשׁ | "The Holy Spirit" | 7307, 6944 | January 31 |
| *Rosh Hahshahnah* (Rosh Hashanah) | רֹאשׁ הַשָּׁנָה | "Head of the Year" | 7218, 8141 | September 25 |
| *R'tzone Yahweh* | רְצוֹן יְהוָה | "The LORD's Will" | 7522, 3068 | October 21 |
| *Sah'ahr Gahdole* | סַעַר־גָּדוֹל | "Violent Tempest; Great Storm" | 5591, 1419 | December 20 |
| *Sahlahkh* | סָלַח | "To Pardon; to Spare" | 5545 | October 10 |
| *Sahnay* | שָׂנֵא | "To Hate; to Set Against" | 8130 | June 29 |
| *Sahtahn* | שָׂטָן | "Satan" | 7854 | December 22 |
| *Saydehr* (Seder) | סֵדֶר | "Order" | | April 19 |
| *Saytehr* | סֵתֶר | "Secret" | 5643 | September 6 |

| *Seemahn Tove* | סִימָן טוֹב | "Good Tidings" | | December 25 |
|---|---|---|---|---|
| *Seem'khah* (Simcha) | שִׂמְחָה | "Joy" | 8057 | February 23 |
| *Seem'khaht Torah* (Simchat Torah) | שִׂמְחַת תּוֹרָה | "Joy in the Torah" | 8055, 8451 | October 28 |
| *S'fahtah* | שְׂפָתַי | "Lips" | 8193 | August 9 |
| *S'goolah* | סְגֻלָּה | "Special Treasure" | 5459 | July 28 |
| *Shah'ahloo* | שַׁאֲלוּ | "To Ask" | 7592 | June 21 |
| *Shah'ahr* | שַׁעַר | "Gate" | 8179 | December 15 |
| *Shahbaht* (Shabbat) | שַׁבָּת | "Sabbath" | 7676 | January 8 |
| *Shahkh* | שַׁח | "To Be Humbled" | 7743 | May 28 |
| *Shahlehg* | שָׁלֶג | "Snow" | 7950 | April 2 |
| *Shahlome* (Shalom) | שָׁלוֹם | "Peace; Welfare" | 7965 | February 5 |
| *Shahmoah Teesh'm'oo* | שָׁמוֹעַ תִּשְׁמְעוּ | "Obey!" | 8085 | July 27 |
| *Shahreht* | שָׁרֵת | "To Serve" | 8334 | May 19 |
| *Shahv* | שָׁוְא | "In Vain" | 7723 | August 6 |
| *Shahvah* | שָׁבָה | "Restore" | 7725 | July 25 |
| *Shahvoo'ote* (Shavuot) | שָׁבוּעוֹת | "Feast of Weeks; Pentecost" | 7620 | June 15 |
| *Sh'ayreet* | שְׁאֵרִית | "Remnant" | 7611 | July 29 |
| *Sheer* | שִׁיר | "Song" | 7892 | December 30 |
| *Sheev'ah* (Shiva) | שִׁבְעָה | "Seven" | 7651 | February 1 |
| *Sh'kheenah* (Shekinah) | שְׁכִינָה | "Divine Presence" | 7931 | January 22 |
| *Sh'mah* (Shema) | שְׁמַע | "Hear" | 8085 | January 27 |
| *Sh'meetah* | שְׁמִטָּה | "Release" | 8059 | April 5 |

| | | | | |
|---|---|---|---|---|
| *Sh'mooah* | שְׁמוּעָה | "News" | 8052 | November 4 |
| *Shofahr* (Shofar) | שׁוֹפָר | "Trumpet" | 7782 | February 18 |
| *Shofe'teem* | שֹׁפְטִים | "Judges" | 8199 | November 22 |
| *Sho'mayr* | שֹׁמֵר | "Keeper" | 8104 | November 6 |
| *Shome'reem* | שֹׁמְרִים | "Watchmen" | 8104 | November 30 |
| *Shome'rone* | שֹׁמְרוֹן | "Samaria" | 8111 | March 16 |
| *Shoov* (Shuv) | שׁוּב | "Repent" | 7725 | January 13 |
| *S'leekhah* | סְלִיחָה | "Forgiveness" | 5547 | December 31 |
| *Sookote* (Sukkot) | סֻכּוֹת | "Booths" | 5521 | October 22 |
| *Tahleet* (Tallit) | טַלִּית | "Prayer Shawl; Cloak; Sheet" | | February 4 |
| *Tahlmeed* (Talmid) | תַּלְמִיד | "Disciple; Pupil" | 3925 | January 5 |
| *Tahlmood* (Talmud) | תַּלְמוּד | "Learning" | 3925 | February 26 |
| *Tahmay* | טָמֵא | "Unclean" | 2931 | February 21 |
| *Tahmeem* | תָּמִים | "Perfect" | 8549 | October 19 |
| *Takh'reekheem* | תַּכְרִכִים | "Shroud" | | September 2 |
| *T'aynah* | תְּאֵנָה | "Fig" | 8384 | August 14 |
| *Teeg'nove* | תִּגְנֹב | "Stole" | 1589 | December 28 |
| *Teer'tzah* | תִּרְצָח | "Murder" | 7523 | November 1 |
| *Teesh'ah-b'Ahv* (Tishah-b'Av) | תִּשְׁעָה בְּאָב | "9th of Av" | 8672 (9th) | August 13 |
| *Teesh'pote* | תִּשְׁפֹּט | "To Judge" | 8199 | September 22 |
| *Teetz'lakh* | תִּצְלַח | "To Come Mightily" | 6743 | November 5 |
| *T'feelah* (Tefillah) | תְּפִלָּה | "Prayer" | 8605 | February 24 |
| *T'feeleen* (Tefillin) | תְּפִלִּין | "Phylacteries" | | January 18 |
| *T'mooraht* | תְּמוּרַת | "Substitute" | 8545 | July 11 |

| *Toh'deeyay* | תּוֹדִיעַ | "Show" | 3045 | October 2 |
|---|---|---|---|---|
| *Tole'dote* | תּוֹלְדֹת | "Generations" | 8435 | October 6 |
| *Too b'Ahv* (Tu b'Av) | טו בְּאָב | "15th of Av" | | April 13 |
| *Too Beesh'vaht* (Tu Bishvat) | טו בִּשְׁבָט | "15th of Shevat" | | January 29 |
| *Toon Noorah* | תַּוּן נוּרָא | "Fiery Furnace" | 8574, 5135 | April 23 |
| Torah | תּוֹרָה | "Law" | 8451 | January 15 |
| *Tove* | טוֹב | "Better" | 2896 | June 20 |
| *T'shookahtoe* | תְּשׁוּקָתוֹ | "Desire; Want" | 8669 | November 13 |
| *Tzahrahaht* | צָרַעַת | "Leprosy" | 6883 | March 22 |
| *Tzahvah* | צָבָא | "Warfare" | 6635 | December 8 |
| *Tz'dahkah* | צְדָקָה | "Righteousness" | 6666 | September 8 |
| *Tz'deek* | צְדִיק | "To Justify" | 6662 | November 8 |
| *Tzee'own* | צִיּוֹן | "Zion" | 6726 | December 19 |
| *Tzeetzeet* (Tzitzit) | צִיצִת | "Fringe; Tassel" | 6734 | January 1 |
| *Tzehlehm* | צֶלֶם | "Image" | 6754 | July 15 |
| *Tzone Shah'ahr* | צֹאן שַׁעַר | "Sheep Gate" | 6629, 8179 | August 15 |
| *Tzoom* (Tsum) | צוּם | "Fast" | 6685 | February 12 |
| *Vahmehr'khahv* | בַמֶּרְחָב | "Set Me Free" | 4800 | July 4 |
| *Vehgehd* | בֶּגֶד | "Garment" | 899 | August 27 |
| *Voe Bahkhar* | בוֹ בָּחַר | "To Call Him; to Choose Him" | 977 | December 5 |
| *Yahd* | יָד | "Hand" | 3027 | May 14 |
| *Yahkheenoo* | יָכִינוּ | "Prepared" | 3559 | September 21 |
| *Yahmeen* (Yamin) | יָמִין | "Right" | 3225 | March 5 |
| *Yahnee'oo* | יָנִיעוּ | "Wag" | 5128 | July 23 |
| *Yahr'dayn Nah'hahr* | יַרְדֵּן נָהָר | "Jordan River" | 3383, 5104 | September 29 |

| | | | | |
|---|---|---|---|---|
| *Yahweh Ehloheem* (Yahweh Elohim) | יְהוָֹה אֱלֹהִים | "LORD God" | 3068, 430 | April 15 |
| *Yahweh Neesee* | יְהוָֹה נִסִּי | "The LORD Is My Banner" | 3068, 5251 | August 2 |
| *Yahweh Ro'ee* | יְהוָֹה רֹעִי | "The LORD Is My Shepherd" | 3068, 7462 | December 17 |
| *Yahweh Rofeh* | יְהוָֹה רֹפְאֶ | "The LORD Who Heals" | 3068, 7495 | July 2 |
| *Yahweh Shahlome* (Yahweh Shalom) | יְהוָֹה שָׁלוֹם | "The LORD Is Peace" | 3068, 7965 | October 3 |
| *Yahweh Tz'vah-ote* (Yahweh Tzva'ot) | יְהוָֹה צְבָאוֹת | "LORD of Hosts" | 3068, 6635 | November 3 |
| *Yahweh Yeereh* (Yahweh Jireh) | יְהוָֹה יִרְאֶה | "The LORD Will Provide; the LORD Will See to It" | 3068, 7200 | August 11 |
| *Yahyeen* | יַיִן | "Wine" | 3196 | May 31 |
| *Yanoom* | יָנוּם | "Slumber" | 5123 | October 31 |
| *Yayd'oo* | יֵדְעוּ | "To Know" | 3045 | June 23 |
| *Yay'khahlayk* | יֵחָלֵק | "To Divide" | 2505 | June 22 |
| *Yeelode* | יִלּוֹד | "To Be Born" | 3209 | July 7 |
| *Yeer'oo* | יִירְאוּ | "Awe" | 3372 | November 16 |
| *Yees'bah* | יִשְׂבָּע | "Satisfied; Content" | 7646 | June 6 |
| *Yees'geh* | יִשְׂגֶּה | "Grow" | 7685 | July 21 |
| *Yeesh'bote* | יִשְׁבֹּת | "To Cease; to Rest" | 7673 | July 18 |
| *Yeesh'tahkhoo* | יִשְׁתַּחוּ | "Worship" | 7812 | July 6 |
| *Yeev'neh* | יִבְנֶה | "Build" | 1129 | September 5 |
| *Y'hoshooah* (Yeshua) | יְהוֹשֻׁעַ | "Jesus" | 3091 | January 12 |
| YHWH | יהוה | "The LORD; Yahweh" | 3068 | January 7 |
| *Yohkh'loo* | יֹאכְלוּ | "Devour; Eat" | 398 | June 9 |

| | | | | |
|---|---|---|---|---|
| *Yome* (Yom) | יוֹם | "Day" | 3117 | May 21 |
| *Yome Keepoor* (Yom Kippur) | יוֹם כִּפּוּר | "Day of Atonement" | 3117, 3725 | October 15 |
| *Yosheeyahoo* | יֹאשִׁיָּהוּ | "Josiah" | 2977 | December 27 |
| *Y'shooneh* | יְשַׁנֶּא | "To Change" | 8138 | September 12 |
| *Y'tomeem V'ahl'mahnote* | יְתוֹמִים וְאַלְמָנוֹת | "Orphans and Widows" | 3490, 490 | June 11 |
| *Y'vahrekh* | יְבָרֵךְ | "To Bless" | 1288 | February 13 |
| *Zah'hahv* | זָהָב | "Gold" | 2091 | September 10 |
| *Zahreh* | זַרְעֲ | "Seed" | 2233 | November 11 |
| *Z'ayvay Ehrehv* | זְאֵבֵי עֶרֶב | "Evening Wolves" | 2061, 6153 | September 15 |
| *Zehrah Khahr'dahl* | זֶרַע חַרְדָּל | "Mustard Seed" | 2233 (seed) | March 4 |
| *Z'kahr* | זְכָּר | "Remember" | 2142 | March 21 |
| *Z'roh-ohteh* | זְרֹעוֹתֶי | "Arms" | 2220 | May 29 |

# Yiddish

| Yiddish | Meaning | Date Word Appears |
|---|---|---|
| Chutzpah | "Gall; Nerve" | January 14 |
| Kvetch | "Relentless Whining" | July 1 |
| Mensch | "Good Person" | October 13 |
| *Meshuggeneh* | "Foolish Person; Foolish Behavior" | May 7 |
| Schmooze | "To Chat Casually" | July 17 |
| Tsuris | "Troubles" | March 19 |
| Yenta | "Gossipmonger" | August 30 |

# About the Author

Ed was raised in a devout Jewish home in South Georgia, immersed in the traditions, holidays, customs, and rituals of his family's faith. His father was a West Point graduate, and his mother's family narrowly escaped Nazi Germany in the late 1930s.

For much of his life, Ed dismissed the Bible as nothing more than a book of fairy tales—useful for moral guidance, perhaps, but hardly true. At thirty-five, he decided it was only fair to read the book he had so easily rejected. Disproving it, he assumed, would be simple enough. But God had other plans. On January 2, 2000, he opened to Genesis 1:1 and spent the next year voraciously engulfed, verse by verse, in God's Word. On January 17, 2001, he surrendered his life to Christ.

Ed spent three decades in the business world before becoming a pastor, author, and speaker. He currently serves as a lead pastor in Georgia and is the director of the Christian Film Foundation. He also founded M2540—a nonprofit ministry to the homeless—and cofounded Set Shepherds, which provides chaplains on film sets. Married to Susan since 1988, he is the father of two sons and the proud grandfather of four.

He holds a BA from the University of Georgia and a master of theological studies (with high distinction) from Liberty University. You can connect with him at edgrifenhagen.com or on social media @edgrifenhagen.